WE TOOK TO THE WOODS

Pond-in-the-River

Photo by Fred Adam

WE TOOK
TO
THE WOODS

LOUISE DICKINSON RICH

Introduction by Robert Kimber
Afterword by Alice Arlen

Down East

ISBN-10: 0-89272-736-5
ISBN-13: 978-0-89272-736-0

Down East
BOOKS·MAGAZINE·ONLINE
w w w . d o w n e a s t . c o m
Distributed to the trade by National Book Network

Library of Congress Control Number: 2007922080

To my boys

Ralph
Gerrish
Rufus
Kyak
Tom

This book is dedicated

ACKNOWLEDGMENTS

My many thanks to Susan Renwick Driver, of Summit, N.J., for the loan of her old map of the Rangeley district; to Fred Adams, of Brattleboro, Vt., for the photographs he contributed; and to my sister Alice Dickinson, of Newton, Mass., for her help and advice.

L. D. R.

CONTENTS

ILLUSTRATIONS

Introduction

We Took to the Woods is Louise Dickinson Rich's signature book. First published in 1942, it drew rave reviews and became an instant best seller, propelling its author into national prominence and bringing her what she desperately wanted and needed at that point in her life: a substantial boost to the family finances and the prospect of future steady income as an established professional writer. And a professional writer she remained for the rest of her days, turning out over the years a formidable number of short stories and books. She served her apprentice years from 1937 to 1942, publishing several short stories in magazines as varied as *Outdoor Life*, *Saturday Evening Post*, *Good Housekeeping*, and *Woman's Home Companion*. After the great success of *We Took to the Woods*, she continued to write short stories but gradually gave more and more of her attention to books, producing twenty-three titles in the next thirty years of her life. The mark of the professional is the ability to turn out a good job of work, no matter what the assignment. Rich wrote non-fiction books for young adults on topics ranging from the Vikings to the fur trade, the Kennebec River, and China clippers. She wrote four novels for young readers, two of them adventure tales featuring Bill Gordon, young Maine Guide, and drawing, in clearly recognizable detail, on the world of *We Took to the Woods*. She wrote books that libraries categorize as "Maine—History," "Maine—Description and Travel," books like *State O' Maine* and *The Coast of Maine: An Informal History and Guide*. Louise Dickinson Rich was a pro. No question about that.

But competent as she was in whatever genre she put her hand to, her forte was the personal, essayistic, semi-autobiographical book that incorporated landscape description, natural history, neighbors, folkways, anecdote, portraits: *The Peninsula*, *Happy the Land*, *My Neck of the Woods*, and, of course, *We Took to the Woods*. Of her twenty-four book titles I find in the University of Maine System catalog, only these last three, along with *Coast of Maine*, are still in print; and if you ask readers reasonably familiar with Maine literature to name books by Louise Dickinson Rich, some of them may mention *Happy the Land*, maybe *The Peninsula*, maybe *My Neck of the Woods*, but most will probably name *We Took to the Woods* and stop right there.

So what is it about this book? Why did it soar to popularity in 1942–'43, and, more interesting yet, why are people still checking it out of libraries today? Why will you still find it on the bookshelves of just about any woods camp in Maine? Why, sixty-plus years after its initial publication, is it still selling a thousand copies a year?

I might as well say right now that a few of the answers I will propose to those questions will be personal ones. I like Louise Dickinson Rich because I see eye to eye with her on a lot of matters and because the world she writes about in *We Took to the Woods* in particular, the forest and hill and lake country of western Maine, holds the same kind of place in my personal history as it did in hers.

But first to the important matter of writing itself because the clarity and accessibility of Rich's prose are surely factors accounting in some part for the success of her book. Edmund Wilson once called lucidity, force, and ease the three hallmarks of good prose. Rich delivers on all three, line by line, paragraph by paragraph, and in overall design. Take this short paragraph on the first page of *We Took to the Woods*:

> There is nothing that I so greatly admire as purposefulness. I have an enormous respect for people who know exactly what they are doing and where they are going. Such people are compact and integrated. They have clear edges. They give an impression of invulnerability and balance, and I wish I were one of them.

Rich states a theme, amplifies on it, then ends the paragraph with a funny, punchy, mildly self-deprecating twist. Maybe Rich didn't think she was purposeful, but this short paragraph is. It knows every inch of the way what it is doing and where it is going; and, consequently, we as readers also know what we are doing and where we're going.

This same simplicity and clarity characterize the design of the whole book. Each chapter title is a question that some urban-dwelling visitor ignorant of woods ways actually did ask or might have asked. The chapter itself then provides the answer to the question, an organizational pattern that is simplicity itself and, given the questions posed, often results in lists. Because, for instance, the Rich household earned its keep with a variety of jobs, the chapter titled "But How Do You Make a Living?" proceeds to list and expound upon those various jobs. The question "But You Don't Live Here All the Year 'Round?" naturally calls for a chronological list focused on winter and preparations for it: laying in clothing and food supplies, deer hunting, working up the firewood, the complications of Christmas shopping when the post office where the Mail Order gifts come in is some twenty often impassable miles away in Andover.

This question-and-answer structure also leads just as naturally to "yarning," that easy-going, apparently rambling mode of storytelling that often follows on a question and leads off the response with "That reminds me of the time when . . ." Sentences of that kind abound in *We Took to the Woods*: "Let me tell you about the best trip we ever made to B pond." Or: "Take the matter of smelting, for example." Or: "This is the way it happened." Because the Riches made some of their living with a "taxi and transport service" that ferried itinerant woodsmen, canoeists, and all manner of dunnage over the five-mile Carry Road between Lower Richardson Lake and Umbagog Lake, this particular occupation provides an opportunity to digress about the four automobiles the Riches owned, how those cars were acquired, their particular eccentricities, and Ralph Rich's emotional attachment to anything with an internal-combustion engine in it. And that digression leads in turn to a car story that starts with this line: "The most unlucky day we ever had started out all right."

The book progresses in this yarning mode, one story and one digression seeming to randomly generate the next. But behind the scenes, Rich always knows what she is doing and where she is going, with the result for her readers that they follow her prose as easily as they would follow a well marked forest trail.

But writing does not live by form alone, and we all know that the world's classic bores, too, are much given to "yarning." If a good storyteller says, "That reminds me of the time…" we'll be all ears; if a bad one uses those same words, we'll all be looking for the door. Content matters; voice and timing and pace matter. Intangible things like animation and attitude matter. So what are the elements that fell together in just the right combination to create the special appeal of *We Took to the Woods*?

It's impossible to underestimate the deep and lasting imprint the Rapid River and Rich's Forest Lodge home there left on her work and her life. I don't know whether every life has a place in it where all the pieces necessary to sheer, unmitigated, overflowing happiness are present, but surely for Rich that place was her home on the Rapid River, the place against which she would measure all other places she had known before it and against which she would measure all others she would ever know after it. As she wrote in her introduction to *Only Parent*, published in 1953, when she and her children were living in her hometown of Bridgewater, Massachusetts:

> "If only he hadn't known the Popo Agie!" I read that the other day in "The Way West," a very good book by A. B. Guthrie, and it struck a responsive chord in my heart. The mountain man of the book would have been able to settle down in his later years, if only he hadn't in his youth lived for a time on the wild and beautiful river, the Popo Agie. If only we hadn't known the Rapid River! Then perhaps we, too, would have been able to accept and enjoy the conventional life of our day and age, the life of

commuters' trains, and Country Club memberships, of rumpus rooms in the basement, and a quiet and desperate struggle to acquire for me a mink coat that would compare favorably with those of my Bridge Club associates. But we had known the Rapid River, and everything else thereafter was second best.

The Rapid River was also, of course, where Louise Dickinson met Ralph Rich quite by chance and was instantly smitten by him. To say Louise was "smitten" by Ralph is not to use the word lightly. She was as if poleaxed by love, whacked hard between the eyes. "I became obsessed with the idea," she wrote, "that if I didn't see more—a lot more—of this Ralph Rich, I'd quietly go into a decline and die."

If, as Freud has told us, love and work are the two things we most need to live happy, productive lives, then Rich had them in spades at Rapid River. She had Ralph; not long after, she had her infant son, Rufus; she had Gerrish, "the hired help," about whom she wrote one of her most loving portraits in *Happy the Land*. She had Kyak the dog, Tom the cat. She had her neighbors Larry and Al Parsons two miles up the Carry Road at Middle Dam.

Along with all this human and animal love, both given and received, she had her love of this place that had taken hold of her and would never let her go. Scattered throughout the pages of *We Took to the Woods* are innumerable passages that reflect the deep attachment that devotees of the Maine woods feel year round, summer and winter, spring and fall. Here, for instance, is how things look when Louise and Gerrish go smelting where the Rapid River comes into Pond-in-the-River.

We stand on bare gray rock and look out over an open stretch of fretted gray water to the dirty white line of the ice pack. All the delicate and subtle coloring that is a part of the winter landscape—the faded gold of dead grass heads, the fine red lines of the stems of low bushes, the orange of a fungus on a stump, the lavender of distance—has been drained away by the dusk that lies on the surface of the Pond and the darkness that lurks in the enfolding hills. There is nothing at all to be seen but gray—a hundred different tones of gray, from not-quite-white to almost-black. It's dreary and desolate and lonely, and I love it.

Or this passage describing what it is like to stand on the Pond-in-the-River dam when the river drivers open the gates and let the pulpwood gathered in the boom go sluicing on downstream:

It's lovely on the dam on a bright spring morning, with the wind blowing down across the boom and filling the air with the sharp smell of resin, so strong and fresh that you can taste it. The planks tremble under your feet, and the roar of the river and the thumping of the wood fill the ears. The river is deep blue and crisping white, and the cut ends of the pulp are like raw gold in the sun. All the senses come alive, even that rare sense that tells you, half a dozen times between birth and death—if you are lucky—that right now, right in this spot, you have fallen into the pattern of the universe.

It's passages like these that explain the presence of this book on all those woods camp bookshelves and its enduring appeal for anyone ever bitten by the Maine woods bug, passages that evoke an admiring, "Yes, by gorry. She got that just right" from me and just about anyone else who has lived in a woods camp and seen the year roll around on a Maine pond or river.

Mainers and, by extension, New Englanders in general could enjoy the pleasant shock of recognition here. This is a book certain to win Yankee interest and feed Yankee patriotism: "This is our country," all good Yankees could say as they turned these pages, "God's country, and these are the good people that inhabit it"

But if *We Took to the Woods* offered nothing more than well written local color, it would not have found the national audience it did. What accounts for the special appeal it had on first publication?

In 1942, the United States was a country just emerging from the Great Depression and just plunging into World War II. It was also a country considerably more rural than it is today. Louise joined Ralph at Forest Lodge in the late fall of 1933 and completed the manuscript of *We Took to the Woods* in February of 1942, so the book is a chronicle of how one couple scratched together a living and made a life for themselves in one of the toughest places to make a living in these United States and during one of the bleakest economic periods in the country's history. Not only did they succeed at scraping by and making do, they also had a lot of fun doing it. Their story was one of adversity overcome, a story that people all over America—and rural people in particular— could relate to.

Louise's feeling for, and her ability to connect with, her country cousins in Montana or Minnesota is nowhere more evident than in her addiction to the Sears, Roebuck and Montgomery Ward catalogs, those great mail-order emporia that served the needs of country people not just during the Depression but on into the postwar decades as well. In the chapter titled "Isn't Housekeeping Difficult?" the sample order blank in the back of the Sears catalog sets Louise to imagining the life and circumstances of this fictional Mrs. John T. Jones of Tipton, Iowa:

> She hadn't been married very long, I think, and she didn't have very much money to spend . . . She had only thirty dollars . . . I know that, because the order came to $29.42. That's just about as close as you can come to a specified sum . . .
>
> This is what she bought. Four yards of rose-printed chintz, a dusty rose chenille bedspread, and a pair of dusty rose curtains. You see? She was fixing up a bedroom . . . None of the articles is the best grade—that I remembered from my own perusals of the catalog. But they're the best she could afford. She wanted her house to be nice . . .
>
> Then she bought three pairs of flag-red ankle socks— that's how I know she must be young, and therefore newly married—and a green suit, Cat. No. 55H7186, which cost $15.59. I remembered Cat. No. 55H7186. It's a nice suit, very young and dashing. She hesitated a long time before she spent that much money on a suit . . .
>
> . . . Oh, I know Mrs. John T. Jones of Tipton, Iowa. Perhaps she is just someone dreamed up in the advertising department of Sears' Chicago office! But she's me, too, and a million other women like me, scattered from here to the Rio Grande, who do their shopping through the magic of the Mail Order.

Hauling water in buckets to do the laundry, laying in the winter's firewood, struggling to build up thin, acidic forest soil with truckload after truckload of manure so that it will eventually produce a few carrots and cabbages—these are struggles common to country dwellers everywhere, and it is easy to see why Rich's often comic renderings of these mundane day-to-day battles with recalcitrant people, critters, and things would win her a large rural readership.

But books do not become bestsellers by appealing to country folks alone, and the chapter titles—all those questions the city and suburban visitors would be most likely to ask—make it clear that Rich was writing with her urban audience in mind. The strategy behind those questions is as ingenious as it is simple. The imagined interlocutor has already answered each of the questions in his own mind. "Isn't Housekeeping Difficult?" Of course it is! You don't have electricity; you don't have running water; you don't have a gas or electric cookstove. Housekeeping must be a living hell for you.

Louise's answer, of course, is "No. Housekeeping in the woods is—for me—not at all difficult." And why not? Because: "Here I can be a rotten housekeeper, and it doesn't make much difference."

After this disarming introduction to the subject, Louise then settles down to tell us about housekeeping in the woods, and what we learn from her detailed analysis is that housekeeping is difficult anywhere but that the difficulties she faces in the woods are just different from those faced by housekeepers on Fifth Avenue or in Westchester County. She may have to cook in a kitchen populated with a cat, a dog, a husband patching a tire tube in the middle of the floor, a son playing with his toy truck, a kitchen cluttered with guns, fly rods, wet socks threatening to fall into the soup from a drying rack over the stove, and engine parts taking up half of the kitchen table. But, as compensation, she doesn't have to polish silver or worry about breaking any of the crystal glassware Aunt May gave her as a wedding present. Life, in short, is just as easy—or difficult—in the woods as it is anywhere else. It's just different. And in Louise's telling, it's a lot more fun.

A book about farm or ranch or backwoods living that is going to appeal to an urban audience has to both fulfill the dreams city dwellers may have about living an idyllic country life in the country yet not paint so glowing a picture that all credibility is lost. The reaction of one early reviewer, Clifton Fadiman writing in the *New Yorker* in November 1942, illustrates just how skillful Rich was in striking that balance: "*We Took to the Woods*," Fadiman wrote, "[is] a book which will arouse in readers sharp envy of, and warm admiration for, Mrs. Rich, together with a fierce determination to go and do likewise. The fierce determination will last about six hours. The charm of this loosely composed, informal record is unimposing but genuine."

The topics Louise deals with have universal appeal because everyone, whether urban or rural, has to deal with them: making a living, taking care of the kids, doing the cooking, but the backwoods context makes these familiar enterprises just exotic enough to add spice to what is mundane and everyday fare.

And then there are the enterprises and the people that are exotic indeed for urban readers but about which and whom the city dweller will be cherishing all sorts of myths that Louise herself once cherished but now proceeds to debunk. Take the river drive and river drivers, for example: "I knew all about the thrill and perils of white-water driving—the big jam, the narrow escapes, the cat-footed agility of the drivers on the huge, plunging logs. I knew just what a river driver would look like. He should be big and bold and dark, with plaid shirt, well-cut riding breeches, caulked boots, and a mouthful of picturesque curses and ribald songs."

Everything about this picture, her readers learn, is wrong. Huge, plunging logs are no more. The wood the river drivers drive is four-foot pulpwood that is too short to produce even a small log jam, much less a big one. Nor is a river driver a river driver in local parlance; he is a river hog, and his appearance matches that title. He is not big and bold (he may be dark); he tends instead to be a short, scrawny, scruffy figure dressed from the waist up in wool longjohns and from the waist down in well-worn suit pants cut off just below the knee. Less glamorous these men could not be.

But much as their appearance may fail to live up to the Paul-Bunyan image, their substance far surpasses all expectations. They are skillful, hard-working, unpretentious, generous, good-hearted. Tony, a particularly rough looking customer, turned out in fact to be as good a friend to four-year-old Rufus as the boy ever had. Tony would give Rufus rides on his horse, take him for walks in the woods, bring him presents of partridge feathers and hand-carved toys. But when an F.B.I. agent turned up in the logging camp one day, Tony didn't go back into camp for his supper that evening. He stayed out in the woods, waiting until the middle of the night to return, pack up his kit, and shave off his beard. Early the next morning, he was at Louise's kitchen door to say good-bye. "He didn't know where he was going, he told me cheerfully. He was just going." As for personal histories, she concluded, it was perhaps best not to inquire but just to take each man as he came.

The qualities Louise admired in the woodsmen and in her neighbors were the ones she displayed herself, and if there is any one feature of *We Took to the Woods* that accounts for its enduring success, it is the voice and persona of its author. Louise Dickinson Rich, as she presents herself in these pages, is well-nigh impossible to dislike.

In the chapter "Don't You Get Awfully Out of Touch?" she confesses that she felt raging jealousy toward Ralph's first wife and did her best to forestall a visit from this cosmopolitan woman, against whom she felt she would probably measure up badly. "I didn't have any clothes. I didn't have any conversation. I hadn't been anywhere or done anything interesting. She'd been everywhere. She'd have lots of interesting experiences to talk about. She'd have trunks full of gorgeous clothes. She'd be witty and fascinating."

As things turned out, it was impossible for Ralph to contact his wife in time to cancel the visit, which—against all Louise's fears—turned out just fine because, she writes, "as soon as I met Terp, I liked her."

In the matter of cultivation and culture, Louise again confesses to her weaknesses. "I'm very sorry to say—and I mean this; I am truly sorry, because I know I miss a lot—that I don't appreciate good music. I don't understand it and it doesn't speak to me at all. I wish it did…"

Theater, too, she says, is a "blind spot of mine."

She makes these confessions not to pander to the know-nothing crowd but simply to state the case as she sees it: This is who I am. Take me or leave me on those terms. And if she lacks the ear and the mind for good music, she surely makes up for that in her devotion to the written word. "I never can get over the power of some combinations of words to stir the heart."

All right, so she's no fan of Bach or Beethoven, but words are her métier, and there's nothing about living in the back-woods that prevents her from reading to her heart's content. So is she "out of touch"? Not at all. She has what she needs to sustain her.

When it comes to the question of human contacts, city dwellers may be inclined to pity the lack of "your sort of people" in the neighborhood. "As a matter of fact," Louise responds, "I don't know exactly what is meant by 'your sort of people.' There are plenty of people around here that we would be highly complimented to be classed with. Perhaps they didn't come from Boston, and perhaps they aren't college graduates. So what? They have qualities—generosity and honesty and humor—that we would be happy to feel we shared."

Generosity, honesty, humor, physical courage, a willingness to roll up one's sleeves and work hard—these are the qualities Louise valued in others and, to the extent that she felt she had them, in herself. These are human qualities that are admirable at any time and in anyone, but I suspect they had a special appeal in those bleak, early months of World War II. On the one hand, *We Took to the Woods* provided an almost idyllic respite from the war and its worries; yet on the other, it struck a strong and hopeful chord in the face of that catastrophic event because it embodied the determination to prevail that the coming years would demand. Not least of all, Louise herself emerges from these pages as a kind of backwoods Rosie the Riveter: a spunky, down-to-earth, no-nonsense, let's-get-the-job-done woman. Hers was a voice Americans wanted and needed to hear.

Rosie the Riveter and Louise the Writer had a lot in common. One of the things I've always liked best about Rich is her journeyman view of her métier, her respect for her reader, and her hard-headed assessment of her own place in the annals of literature. "I've read a lot of first-rate writing, and I have some critical sense," she writes, "so I know where I stand. I'll never be first-rate. I'll improve with practice, I trust, but I haven't got what it takes to reach the top."

A confession like that may seem self-deprecating to the extreme, an undermining of one's own sense of self, destructive to the confidence and motivation a writer needs to sit down every day to the daunting task of filling blank pages with words worth reading. But think about it for a minute. How many names belong under the heading "First-Rate"? Tolstoy, Shakespeare, Dante, Goethe, Homer, Proust? The giants come easily to mind. And who, then, belongs on the list of the second-rate, running a very close second behind the giants? George Eliot, Balzac, Melville, Jane Austen? The list of the second-raters is huge and formidable. Up against that kind of competition, third-rate looks pretty good. Fourth- and fifth-rate aren't exactly slouches either. One could do worse than be a third-rate professional writer.

"Third-rate" is, of course, not a precise term. It means simply way short of what Louise termed "the top." Reaching "the top" calls for special gifts of imagination and sensibility that are granted to relatively few. Louise Dickinson Rich did not have those gifts, and she was honest enough and modest enough in her self-appraisal to know that. You'll look in vain in her work for those breakthroughs in consciousness, those assemblings of life's seemingly infinite, incomprehensible complexities into elegant, comprehensible patterns that set the work of the first-rate writers apart.

But what you will find are the qualities she admired in her Yankee neighbors: hard work, honesty, persistence in the face of adversity, the ability to make do with the resources on hand, lack of pretension, the clarity of vision to call a spade a spade.

Because Rich had no illusions about herself and her work, she avoided that common writerly failing of taking herself and her career too seriously, which is not to say, however, that she didn't take her work seriously. "Everything I write, no matter how lousy it turns out to be, is the very best I am capable of at the time. My writing may be third-rate, but at least it's honest. You can't be even a third-rate writer without taking your work seriously."

And then she adds the acid test for the serious professional: "I believe that any writer who sells enough to eat off the proceeds is writing the very best he can all the time. When he stops, he stops eating."

I'm not familiar with every detail of Rich's biography in the years after *We Took to the Woods*, but I don't believe she ever went hungry, and her list of published books indicates that she kept sitting down in front of that typewriter day after day, year after year. That this book you hold in your hands right now, gentle reader, is the eighteenth printing (since its current publisher took it over in 1982) of a book that first appeared sixty-three years ago and is likely to go into many more printings in the decades to come is proof enough that being a third-rate professional writer is no mean trick and pretty darn good indeed. All honor to Louise Dickinson Rich, say I.

Robert Kimber,
Temple, Maine

I

"Why Don't You Write a Book?"

DURING MOST OF MY ADOLESCENCE—SPECIFICALLY, BETWEEN the time when I gave up wanting to be a brakeman on a freight train and the time when I definitely decided to become an English teacher—I said, when asked what I was going to do with my life, that I was going to live alone in a cabin in the Maine woods and write. It seemed to me that this was a romantic notion, and I was insufferably smug over my own originality. Of course, I found out later that everybody is at one time or another going to do something of the sort. It's part of being young. The only difference in my case is that, grown to womanhood, I seem to be living in a cabin in the Maine woods, and I seem to be writing.

There is nothing that I so greatly admire as purposefulness. I have an enormous respect for people who know exactly what they are doing and where they are going. Such people are compact and integrated. They have clear edges. They give an impression of invulnerability and balance, and I wish that I were one of them.

I wish that I could say that, from the moment I first

thought about this kind of a life to the moment almost two decades later when I finally began living it, I had been working single-mindedly toward it. But it wouldn't be true. Actually I'd forgotten all about it long before. I did a lot of things—graduated from college, taught school, worked in an institution for the feeble-minded, went to Europe—but none of it was in preparation for an end. At the time it seemed end enough in itself.

I was shocked, therefore, to receive not long ago and within the same week, letters from two old friends saying virtually the same thing, although the writers are strangers to each other. What they said, in effect, was this: "Isn't it wonderful that you're at last doing what you always said you wanted to do! It proves that anything is possible, if one wants it enough to work for it."

My two friends, I thank you for your high opinion of my character, and I hate to have to disabuse you of it. It is wonderful—far more wonderful than you know—that I am doing what I once, without really believing it, said I was going to do. But if it proves anything, it is only that some people are fools for luck. Let me admit that not only is my living in the woods and writing an accident on both counts, but that until I received your letters I had been so busy coping with the situation that I hadn't even realized that I was living my old dream. It's a very queer feeling to wake up and find that the dream has sneaked up on you and become the reality.

There are differences, of course. My idea was a little log cabin in a sort of spacious park. There is nothing park-like about this northwestern-most corner of Maine. Here, between two ranges of mountains, the Boundary Mountains and the Blue Mountains, lies a high, wild valley, the basin that holds the Rangeley Lakes. The country is criss-crossed with ridges, dotted with swamps and logans, and covered with dense forest. There are very few people living here, and no roads down into what we call The Outside. There are a few narrow trails, but travel through the woods is so difficult, with the swamps and blowdowns and underbrush, that the lakes have remained what they were to the Indians, the main thoroughfare.

I like to think of the lakes coming down from the north of us like a gigantic staircase to the sea. Kennebago to Rangeley to Cupsuptic, down they drop, level to level, through short, snarling rivers; Mooselukmeguntic to the Richardsons to Pond-in-the-River, and through Rapid River to Umbagog, whence they empty into the Androscoggin and begin the long south-easterly curve back to the ocean. I like to say their names, and I wish I could make you see them—long, lovely, lonely stretches of water, shut in by dark hills. The trees come down to the shore, the black growth of fir and pine and spruce streaked with the lighter green of maple and birch. There is nothing at all on the hills but forest, and nobody lives there but deer and bear and wildcats. The people keep close to the lakes, building their dwellings in narrow clearings they have made by pushing the trees a little way back from the water.

Our own clearing is on the Rapid River, just below Pond-in-the-River Dam; and because Rapid River is not navigable, being the swiftest river east of the Rockies—it drops a hundred and eighty-five feet in three miles, with no falls, which is some kind of a record—we amazingly live on a road. It doesn't go anywhere. It's really a carry between two lakes, so it is sensibly called the Carry Road.

It starts at Middle Dam, on the Lower Richardson, and roughly follows the course of the river five miles to Sunday Cove, on Umbagog.

Middle Dam is quite a community. There is the dam itself, a part of the system for water control on the Androscoggin, with the dam-keeper and his family, Renny and Alice Miller and their three children, in year-round residence. Then in summer the hotel is open. We only call it a hotel; it's really a fishing camp. In winter it is closed, but there is a caretaker, Larry Parsons, who stays in with his wife, Al, and a hired man or two. So the permanent population of Middle Dam hovers at around nine, and that is comparative congestion. We get our mail and supplies through Middle, and it is the point of departure for The Outside, so its importance is all out of proportion to its population.

Sunday Cove, the other end of the carry, is something else again. The rutted, grass-grown road dips down a last steep hill and ends in the lake. There is an abandoned lumber camp rotting down on the shore, and a pair of loons living in the Cove, and that's all there is to it.

And halfway along, between road and river, is Forest Lodge, the sole address on the Carry Road, and our home.

When I said we lived in a cabin in the woods, I was speaking loosely. Forest Lodge is in the woods all right; there is nothing north or south of us but trees for so many miles that sometimes it scares me to think about it. But actually it consists of one cabin, one shack, one large house in the worst cracker-box style, and an assortment of lean-to's, woodsheds, work-shops, and what are euphemistically known as out-houses. These latter are necessary because we have no plumbing, and therefore no bathroom.

Above: The Summer House—porch lookout over Rapid River.

Below: The Winter House—note curious Kyak.

We get our water from the river and from a spring up back in the woods. We do our bathing in wash-tubs in front of the kitchen stove, and for other uses of the bathroom, we resort to the out-houses. This is no great hardship in summer, but in winter, with the snow knee deep, the wind howling like a maniac up the river, and the thermometer crawling down to ten below zero, it is a supreme test of fortitude to leave the warmth of the fire and go plunging out into the cold, no matter how great the necessity. We like to think, however, that it builds character.

The cabin, hereafter to be referred to as the Winter House, was the original Forest Lodge, built for a fishing camp. It is a low building with a porch and an ell, set on a knoll with a view up the river to the Pond-in-the-River. From the outside, it's not a bad little house, but everything that could possibly be wrong with it inside is wrong. The ceilings are too high and the windows are too small, although Ralph, my husband, ripped out the old ones and doubled the window space the first year we were here. The living-room, where we spend much of the time in winter, is on the north side, toward the woods, while the bedrooms, which we use only at night, are on the sunny, open side toward the river. The reason for this irritates me. In the country, the living quarters are always on the road side of a house, so that the inhabitants can keep tabs on the passers-by. In winter there are normally about three passers-by in seven months, here, but still the old rule holds. Apparently it's preferable to sit forever in sunless gloom than to lose one opportunity to speculate about someone's identity, starting point, destination, family connections, and probably discreditable purpose. We can't do anything about the arrangement, because the chimney

is in the living-room, and that's where we have to have
the stove.

That chimney is another wrong thing. It rises out of a
fire-place—which is too shallow to draw properly—and instead of being in the wall, it is set out into the room about
four feet. This splits the room into two parts, making the
attractive and comfortable arrangement of furniture impossible. In winter the fire-place itself is of no use whatsoever, as anyone who has lived in the country in winter
knows. A fire-place is pretty, and on chilly fall evenings,
will keep you warm enough; but what you need in winter
is a stove. So we have a stove. We boarded up our pretty
fire-place, punched a hole in the side of the chimney, and
set up an air-circulating wood heater. It isn't very attractive, and it takes up a lot of room, and set cheek by jowl
with the fire-place, it looks silly. But it keeps us warm.

The only advantage of that half-witted chimney arrangement that has appeared to date is that the otherwise waste
space behind it can be used as a woodbox. Ralph, known
in these parts as "an ingenious cuss," cut a hole in the house,
fitted it with a beveled door like an ice-chest door, and now
we can put the wood in from outdoors. This doesn't sound
like much of a triumph, but it is, nevertheless. Nothing
will cool a house off quicker than opening and closing the
front door forty times, while arm-loads of wood are brought
in; and nothing will enrage and discourage the housewife
more surely than the pecks of dirt and snow inevitably
tracked onto her clean-swept floor. This little wood-box
door, therefore, contributes largely to the peace and comfort of the Rich menage.

Why don't we just burn the Winter House down and
forget about it? Because it's the only house that can be

heated in really cold weather. Ralph has insulated it properly and finished the inside with really beautiful hand-rubbed pine paneling, and in spite of all I have said against it, it's not half bad, actually. It hasn't any kitchen, either, which is a point in its favor, odd as that may sound. We use the kitchen ell of the Big House all the year round, so the cooking odors that always collect in small country houses in the winter, no matter how often they are aired, never get into the Winter House.

About the last of May, or as soon as it is warm enough, we move down into the Big House, and the Winter House becomes the guest house for the summer. The Big House was built at a later date for a summer camp, and that is all it is good for in its present state. It is big and airy and the walls are too thin for warmth and it sprawls all over the place. I like it because it is on a high bluff over the river, with a view and sun-light and space to spread out in; because it has a huge stone fire-place that will take four-foot logs and really heat the living-room in the wettest, coldest September rain storm; because there is a wide porch over the river; because if I decide to eat some crackers and cheese before going to bed, I don't have to climb into a mackinaw and gum-boots as I do in winter, and cross a clearing in the cold to get them. And most of all I like it because I like to go upstairs to bed, instead of into the next room. For these reasons, we always put off moving out of it in the fall until the last possible moment, and we are rebuilding it so we can live in it all the year. Since Ralph is doing the work himself, for economic reasons, this is a slow process. At the moment the whole structure is balanced precariously on poles over the cellar he has dug beneath it. It looks both dangerous and sloppy, but he says it's perfectly safe, and when you're in a house, its external appearance needn't bother you. In fact, I should think a good way to buy a house would be by the looks of the house across the street, which is the one you see most of.

The house across the street here is the Guide's House, or what would be the servants' quarters, if we had servants. It's called the Guide's House because most people living in a place like this would be summer people, and they would employ a registered guide, who would live in the house across the road. It's a nice little shack, with a living-room and two bedrooms, and Gerrish lives there.

Gerrish works for us, but he is in no sense a servant. He has a guide's license, but that isn't important, because so have Ralph and I. It's a handy thing to own, around here. What Gerrish is, I suppose, is the hired help. We pay him to do certain things, which is the hired part. But since he is practically a member of the family, he does a great many other things for which we don't, and couldn't, pay him. That's the help part. We couldn't ever pay him, for example, for being so good and patient with our four-year-old Rufus, who, not to mince words, is often a pest, un-motherly an observation as that may be. Gerrish has to take his pay for that out of Rufus' adoration of him. We couldn't pay him, either, for being so dependable, and for always giving us a dollar and a quarter's worth of work for every dollar of his wages. We are very lucky to have found him. This is not a place that many people would care to work in. It is remote, not only from movies and stores, but from other people. There is nowhere to go except hunting and fishing, and nothing to see except woods and water. But luckily Gerrish likes it, and I think that he considers the Guide's House, his own undisputed realm, as home. Perhaps that is pay of a kind.

The one building here that looks as though it belonged in the deep woods is Ralph's shop, an old log cabin from long before our day. I can't say much about it, as it comes under the heading of sacred ground. It is full of tools and pieces of board that look like any other boards, but which have something special about them, so that they must never be touched, or even looked at. Hanging from the rafters are old car parts, lengths of rope, chains and boat seats, all of which are going to be used some day for some important project. In the middle is a pile of invaluable junk, and around the edges are kegs of nails and bolts. In my bridal innocence I used, when I needed a nail, to go and take one out of a keg. But it always turned out that I had taken (a) the wrong kind of nail for the job on hand, and (b) a nail that was being conserved for a specific purpose and was practically irreplaceable. So now when I need a nail I find Ralph and ask him to get me one.

He's usually easy to find. I have only to listen for the sound of a motor running. He is completely infatuated with gasoline motors, and collects them from the most improbable places. Once he brought home an old motor that someone had hauled into South Arm for a mooring anchor and then abandoned. It had been under water all summer and frozen into the ice all winter, but he dragged it the seven miles home on a hand sled, brooded over it, took it to pieces and put it together again, and now it runs the saw that saws our firewood.

We have only five miles of road to run a car on, but we are a four-car family. They aren't new models—the newest is a 1930 Model A and the oldest a 1924 Marmon—but they run, and they pay for themselves. All summer long Ralph hauls canoes and duffle across the carry for camping parties, and in the spring and fall the lumber company finds it convenient to hire him to tote their wangans up from Sunday Cove.

This lumber company is our privacy insurance, our guarantee that we won't wake up some morning and find new neighbors building a pink stucco bungalow down the river from us. With the exception of our two acres and a strip owned by a water power company, they own every foot of land for miles around. And they won't sell an inch to anybody. I won't go into reasons and company policy. All that matters is that, come hell or high water, they will not sell.

So here we sit in what amounts to a forest preserve of some hundreds of square miles; and in that "we" the reality differs again from the dream. I was going to live alone, remember. I don't, and that's quite all right with me.

Besides Ralph, Rufus, and Gerrish, there is Sally, Ralph's sixteen-year-old daughter by a previous marriage, and further proof that I am a fool for luck. A step-daughter could be a thorn in the flesh, which Sally certainly isn't. And there are Kyak and Tom, the dog and the cat.

We ourselves wouldn't have named Tom that, but we got him from a lumber camp that was moving out and didn't know what to do with him, so we had to take him as equipped. We compromise by saying that his full name is Thomas Bailey Aldrich, which isn't very suitable. He is the sort of cat that should be called Tom, regardless of banality. He is big and tough and mean, and he'd as soon as not fight the whole family at once. His idea of an average day is to get up at noon, trounce the dog for looking at him, go out and chase a deer away from the clearing, and set out the two miles for Middle Dam, there to visit with his girl, the Millers' cat, after half murdering her other three suitors. Then he comes home, looking so smug you could shoot him on sight, and sleeps until noon the next day.

Kyak, though we love him dearly, we have to admit is strictly an Art Dog. His grandmother was with Admiral Byrd at the South Pole, and his great-grandfather helped carry the serum to Nome. If they could see him, they'd turn in their graves. He is a very good example of the Siberian husky, with a white wolf mask, a rangy big body, and a curling plume of a tail; but he is completely nonfunctional. Try to put a harness on him, and he will lie down with all four feet in the air. Try to teach him to retrieve game, and he will look sorrowful and broken. The only thing he is good for, besides looking beautiful, is a watch dog, and he doesn't even do that well. He barks horribly at nothing, or at members of the family, and then amiably lets strange woodsmen walk right into the house. Then after they are in, and for all he knows, we are lying in a welter of blood, sometimes he remembers his responsibilities and stands outside barking hysterically. There's no use trying to do anything with him, except love him.

Around the blank space on the map where we live are some towns and some things that look like towns, but aren't. South Arm is one of these. We simply call it the Arm, and it's important, because it's at the beginning of the road to The Outside. Once you get off the boat from Middle Dam at the Arm, you have begun to leave the woods behind. There is still a long drive to Andover, the first village, but you can't help knowing that if you follow the road far enough you will land, not at a lonely cove tenanted only by loons, but in Boston or New York, or Butte, Montana. It makes a difference. The Arm itself is not imposing, consisting of a huddle of ramshackle wharfs and a string of tired sheds where people in here keep their Outside cars. But its implications are enormous.

Andover really is a town, with a school, two or three little stores, and a post office, whence comes our mail. Upton is a town, too, and our civic center, where we send Sally to school and where we go to vote. Most of the land around here is wild land, or unorganized territory—just squares on the map labeled C Township, or North C Surplus, or Section 37—but the back line of Upton runs north of us, so technically at least we live in organized territory. Upton has one hundred and eighty-two inhabitants and the loveliest view in Maine.

The only other town that concerns us is Magalloway, which is too small to be on the road map or to have a post office. But it does have the Brown Farm, where our telephone line ends. Let me say at once that the Brown Farm isn't a farm, and our telephone line isn't a telephone line, in the modern sense of the word. It is a fifteen-mile-long piece of wire, frail and uninsulated, strung haphazardly through the woods from tree to tree, and the private property of the lumber company, for communication with their various operations. We are hitched onto it only because once they cut down some of our trees by mistake, and extended this courtesy as reparation and apology. If it hasn't snowed lately, or the wind hasn't blown any trees down across the line, or if the wire hasn't sagged wearily into one of the many brooks it crosses, we can, by cranking three times on the battery-powered telephone which hangs on the kitchen wall, talk to the Millers. Or we can ring four times and talk to Cliff, an old hermit who lives down on Umbagog. Or we can ring twice and get the disembodied voice that is all I know of Joe, at the Brown Farm.

Although not a farm, the Brown Farm is a number of other things, including a hospital and de-lousing station for lumberjacks, a bunkhouse and mess-hall, a rest-cure for work-worn horses, and a store house for the tremendous amounts of food and equipment necessary in the lumber camps. There used to be a clerk in that store house who had a splendid graft. At that time the lumber company was using a brand of canned goods that gave premiums for the labels off the cans:—a pickle dish for ten labels, a baby carriage for five hundred, and, I suppose, a Rolls Royce for a million. The clerk isn't there any more, though. His label-removing activities—they buy canned goods by the car lot—left him no time for his duties; and besides, the cooks in the camps got bored with having to open twenty anonymous cans before they happened on the sliced beets they were looking for. He was about to retire, anyhow. He'd sold the things he didn't fancy himself, and had money in the bank.

Once, seven years ago, I saw the Brown Farm, but I didn't know then what it was going to mean in my life, so I didn't pay much attention. I don't remember what it looks like. I was the school-teacher-on-vacation, and my sister and I and some friends came up through this country on a canoe trip. We went through the Parmachenee section, and then we debated whether we should come back through the Rangeleys and along Rapid River or not. The guide insisted that this was the way to come—that although it involved a lot of work, the country was wild and beautiful and unspoiled enough to be worth a few paddle blisters, pack sores, and lame muscles. So we finally gave in, not too enthusiastically, being travel-frayed already.

And that off-hand decision, in which I didn't even have a major part, was the accident by which I now live in a cabin in the woods. As we walked along the Carry Road, we saw a man splitting wood in the yard of the only house we had seen in days, and we stopped to talk to him. He had just arrived there that morning, and he was about to build his first fire and cook his first meal. He invited us to stay and eat with him, because he felt like celebrating. He'd bought the place for a summer camp during the boom years, but he hadn't been able to come East from Chicago, where he lived, since 1929. Now, however, he'd sold some patent rights and not only was he going to spend the summer there, but if things turned out right, the rest of his life. We were all touched and amused, I remember, by his enthusiasm.

Now that I know Ralph better, I know that there was nothing strange about his inviting us all to spend the rest of the week with him. Since that day, eight years ago, I've known him to invite a week-end guest, whom he liked, to extend his visit from week to week until it lasted more than two years. But at the time I thought, and I guess all the others thought, that he was crazy. We stayed, though.

We stayed, and we had a lovely time. We fished and sun-bathed and swam, and in between times I found out why a man so obviously dry behind the ears should want to bury himself in the woods for the rest of his life. Ever since he was twelve years old, he had been spending his summers at Coburn's, and his winters wishing it were summer so he could go back to Coburn's. Middle Dam was the place in all the world where he was happiest, and he'd always told himself that some day he'd live there permanently. It took a long time and a lot of doing, but finally he'd managed. You see, Ralph, unlike me, has a single-track mind.

My mind, however, did fall into a single track before that week was over. I became obsessed with the idea that if I didn't see more—a lot more—of this Ralph Rich, I'd quietly go into a decline and die. It's a common phenomenon, I believe, both in fact and in fiction. It doesn't need any explanation, if indeed it can be explained. It's seldom fatal, I understand, so probably I'd have recovered if I'd had to. I didn't have to. Almost immediately upon my return to Massachusetts, while I was trying to think up a reasonably plausible excuse for happening back to the Rangeley region at the time of year when people just don't go there, I began getting letters, telegrams, and finally telephone calls, almost daily from Ralph. Then he began spending his time and money on the long and painful trek from Maine to Boston. It was, in short, a Courtship, and ended in the usual manner, with our deciding that this was a lot of expensive nonsense, so why didn't we get married?

I know that everybody who was ever in love has speculated along the following lines, but please bear with me while I do it once again. If, on that trip out of Parmachenee, one of us had stopped on the Carry Road two minutes to tie a shoe string, or if Ralph had split wood just a little bit faster, we would never have laid eyes upon him. He'd have been in the house, and we'd have walked right by. But the timing was perfect, and that's how I happen to live in the woods.

How I happened to be a writer was just as sloppy and haphazard. I wrote a little number about Maine guides, at my sister's suggestion, for *Scribner's* Life in the United States Contest. I finished it in May, and the contest didn't close until September, so I thought I'd try it out on a couple of dogs first. I'd get it back in plenty of time to qualify.

Now this is not mock modesty. I was absolutely stupified when the *Saturday Evening Post* bought it. Ralph was, too. But we rallied sufficiently to write another entry for the *Scribner's* contest, since our first had been scratched, as it were, and it won a prize. This double success so went to our heads that we decided that from then on we would be writers.

We weren't, of course, because being a writer involves a lot more than just thinking it would be nice to be one. We sold our first attempt at fiction—which was probably bad for us as it gave us false confidence—and then we settled down to discover that writing is not all beer and skittles. But I think that now, at last, we are nearly writers. We don't wait for inspiration any more, having found that inspiration is mostly the application of the seat of the pants to the seat of a chair. We stall around, trying to put off writing, which I understand is the occupational disease of writers. We earn most of our living by the written word. And we are utterly impatient with people who say, "I've often thought I could write myself."

It's taken me a great many words, I see, to answer the first questions people always ask us when they come out of the woods and find us here, unaccountably installed in a little clearing that is always full of the smell of pine and the sound of the river. That's a question that always crops up early in the conversation—"Doesn't the river get on your nerves?"—because until you get used to it, the dull roar, like heavy surf, seems to shake the air. It is all-pervading and inescapable, and you find yourself raising your voice higher and higher above it. But after a while, unless the tone changes with the rise and fall of the water, you don't even hear it. You learn to pitch your voice, not louder to carry over it, but lower and deeper, so that it's not shattered by the vibration. And finally all the places in the world that are away from the sound of furious white water come to seem empty and dead.

I don't pretend to know all of the answers. I don't know what to answer when people say, "But isn't the way you live Escapism?" I don't even know, really, what escapism is. We haven't tried to escape from anything. We have only exchanged one set of problems for another:—the problem of keeping out from under car wheels for the problem of not getting lost in the woods, for example; or the problem of being bored to death by one's neighbor for the problem of being bored to death by oneself. I don't know what to answer when someone says, "I should think you'd go insane!" It's too cheap and easy and obvious to retort, "And I should think you would."

But some of the answers, the answers to the easy, matter-of-fact questions, like "Why don't you write a book about it?", I do know. The answer to that is, "Well, I guess maybe I will."

And so I am writing a book about it.

II

"But How Do You Make a Living?"

I ALWAYS LIKE TO KNOW WHAT PEOPLE DO FOR A LIVING. This is probably just plain nosiness, but I like to call it a scientific interest. I like to argue that research is simply snooping on a high plane and that the village gossip is a student of applied behaviorism just as much as was Pavlov, shut up in his laboratory with his unfortunate dogs. So when I run across one who seems to be existing as a lily of the field, neither toiling nor spinning, I like to find out how it's done.

Since we would seem to be in that class ourselves, I consider "But how can you make a living up there in the woods?" a perfectly legitimate question. By no stretch of the imagination could our two acres be rated as a farm. There is no place of business within a day's hard journey of us. We don't like to kill things, so our trapping activities are confined to a trap-line for mice and rats run by Gerrish and Rufus in the kitchen and corn patch. How we keep body and soul together is a mystery to the uninitiated. At times it's a mystery to us as well.

We make a living in a variety of ways. For one thing,

there's the taxi and transport service from Middle Dam to Sunday Cove and way-stations. The rates are a little bit flexible, depending on a number of things. Very often, in winter, woodsmen who are leaving the lumber camps call on us to take them and their turkeys—woods for knapsacks —up to Middle Dam. If all goes well, the charge is a dollar. After Thanksgiving the road gets more and more treacherous as the snow gets deeper and deeper, and it becomes easier and easier to slide off into the ditch. The passenger then is obliged to help get the car back onto the road. If this is a matter of a few shoves, the rate goes down to seventy-five cents. If it requires a lot of snow shoveling and strenuous heaving, the fare decreases accordingly. Sometimes it vanishes utterly. You can't charge a man for spending half the morning with his shoulder to the tail board of a 1929 Essex truck, getting his clothes plastered with flying snow. When that happens, Ralph just decides to make a social occasion of it and spends the rest of the morning visiting with Larry Parsons. So far the situation has never seemed to demand that he pay the passenger for riding.

I always feel a little apologetic about our being a four-car family. After all, with only five miles of road available, it seems a little ostentatious, in view of our faded denim pants and patched work shirts, to be discussing which car to take to get the mail. It was worse, though, when the Packard was running.

The Packard was a 1917 Twin Six touring car, built on the general lines of a pre-Revolutionary four poster with canopy, and I always felt like Queen Mary—a nice feeling —when I sat enthroned in it. I regret the passing of the Packard. I don't like these modern cars that you have to crawl into, bumping your head in the process. I don't like to crouch in a cockpit, no matter how luxuriously upholstered, and peer through inadequate slits of glass at the waist-lines of the pedestrians. I like to stalk into a car, sit regally aloft, and view the country o'er.

I won't regret the passing of the Marmon, known locally as Rich's Big Green "Mormon," at all. It is a 1924 sports touring model, at least half a block long. Because of its tremendous power, Ralph uses it for hauling, and I have to ride in back and watch through the rear window that we don't lose our load. I hate the thing. There is no place to brace my feet and the frame of the car is so long that a twig in a rut turns it into a catapult that tosses me helplessly into the air. The Carry Road is nothing but bumps, so it's like riding in a corn-popper. And besides, I have a sneaking notion that Ralph is just a little bit fonder of the "Mormon" than he is of me.

I'd better make it clear at once that we didn't *buy* all of our four present cars. We came by them through a series of deals—all except the Essex which was given to us by a friend who had become too attached to it to be able to bear the thought of selling it down the river for the twenty dollars the dealer would allow him on a trade-in. He wanted to know that it would have a good home with kind people. Men get so emotional about machinery. And the Marmon was a left-over from the days when Ralph lived on The Outside.

The Model T used to belong to Larry Parsons. Larry is very sensible about cars. When they take to swooning in crises he says, "To hell with it," waits until the ice is safe, tows them out into the middle of the lake, and leaves them to go down into a hundred feet of water during the spring break-up. That's what he was doing to this Model T one winter day when Ralph showed up. Gerrish is unhappy driving anything but a Model T—and I might add that anything but a Model T is apt to be unhappy after Gerrish has been driving it. So Ralph ground the valves on the Parsons' snowboat, did something or other about the Parsons' lighting plant, fixed the plug in the Parsons' bath-tub, which had had to be held up with the bather's toe while the water ran out, in return for the Model T. That is what is known as a deal.

The Model A, vintage of 1930, used to belong to Jim Barnett, the local lumber baron. He had it in here one summer when he was getting out hurricane pine for the government. Under the aegis of several non-mechanical-minded straw bosses, clerks, and government scalers, it developed all the ailments that motors are heir to. During its periods of hospitalization, Ralph did Jim's errands for him, and when Jim moved his camp out, he left the Model A in payment. Ralph spent a happy fifty-nine-hour week investigating its innards, with frequent summons for me to come out and view with horror what some damn-fool butcher had perpetrated on the wiring, the pistons or the timing—I was always properly horrified, as a good wife should be, but I never knew quite at what—and now the thing runs.

People always ask how we got all these cars in here, there being no road from The Outside; and we always tell them that we took them apart, packed them in on our backs over the trail, and set them up again. Gratifyingly often we are believed. Of course we really brought them in over the ice, or rafted them in on scows.

The hey-day of the transport business, with this assorted

fleet of animated junk, is summer. That is when the canoe trips go through here. Some guide book of the lakes, which every camper in the world seems to have fallen afoul of, says that one gets from the Lower Richardson to Umbagog by way of the Rapid River. Anyone who can read a contour map can see that that is impossible. It has been accomplished only twice in history, once by mistake—Captain Coburn, when young, got caught in the current and was lucky—and once by design—some guides from up along the border wanted to make a record, but before they got through they wished they'd never started. Cluley's Rips, a mile below us, is the most vicious piece of water I have ever seen. It's frightening just to stand on the bank and look at it. The water pours into a narrow gut, overhung by rocks and dripping spruces, with such force that it has no time to level out. The middle of the river humps up, green and white and snarling, almost to eye-level of the bank-stander. Cluley, whoever he may have been, was drowned there. That's how you get things named after you in this country.

We profit by the guide book's error. Nobody wants to carry a canoe five miles. It would take all day. We can do it in half an hour, if we're lucky. Sometimes we're not lucky.

The most unlucky day we ever had started out all right. Right after breakfast the telephone rang, and it was Cliff, the old guide and trapper who lives down on Umbagog. Sometimes his last name is Wiggin and sometimes it's Wallace, depending on how he's feeling at the time. He was born with one name, but brought up by folks bearing the other. I'm not sure he remembers now himself which was which. He told us that there were two young men at his

Above: Larry and his snow boat.

Below: Lower Richardson Lake from Middle Dam, looking toward South Arm, where the supplies come from.

place who wanted themselves and one canoe taken across the carry, and that they'd be at Sunday Cove at ten o'clock. That was fine. That would give us time to go up to Middle Dam and bring down forty-eight cases of canned goods that we were laying in against the winter.

Forty-eight cases of canned goods fill our trailer to the brim and weigh enough to be a strain on the trailer hitch. It was unfortunate that the hitch chose to give way as we were going around a down-hill curve. We kept to the road, but the trailer went flying off into the woods, dodging a dozen trees with uncanny intelligence and coming up whango! against a house-size boulder. Cases flew in all directions, exploding as they landed. Cans of milk, figs in syrup, salmon, string beans, sliced peaches, clam chowder and what have you littered an acre of ground. We got out and looked at the wreck and at each other.

Ralph said a few things, and then he said, "Help me get the trailer back on the road, and I'll go home and fix the hitch while you pick up this mess."

It should be easy to pick up a few hundred cans and put them in piles. It wasn't. It would have been easier to pick up a covey of partridges. They were under leaves, behind rocks, down holes. While I was grubbing in the under-brush a can walloped me on the top of the head. Probably it had been lodged in a bush, but it seemed to have leaped from the ground with malicious intent. I had been hot and mad and disgusted and now I was hurt as well. And I still couldn't find three cans. I haven't found them yet. I went home.

It was half past eleven and Ralph was still working on the trailer hitch, he having had his troubles, too. Our clients were still, presumably, sitting at Sunday Cove, and almost certainly thinking hard thoughts about us. Just as we were debating what to do next, they walked into the yard, having got tired of waiting.

The least we could do was to invite them to lunch, with apologies and promises that everything would shortly be under control, and that as soon as we had eaten we would go after the canoe. I walked back to the scene of the wreck, collected some corned beef, spinach, and pineapple slices, and threw together a meal, while Ralph finished the hitch and the two youths went swimming. Then we all had a drink of rum, which we all needed, and things seemed more rosy.

They looked so much more rosy, in fact, that I decided to leave the lunch dishes and ride down to the Cove, too. We boarded the Packard, then extant, hitched on the trailer, and set out. The ride was without incident, *mirabile dictu*. But in turning around at the Cove Ralph stalled the motor, and then we were sunk again. The Packard's weakness lay in weak coils, and it wouldn't start when the motor was hot. We waited for a while for it to cool off, during which time Cookie, Kyak's mother and our dog of the moment, managed to find a porcupine and get her mouth full of quills which we had no tools to remove. The Packard still wouldn't start, so we walked the three and a half long, hot miles home after the current Ford, a Model T touring, since deceased.

I declined an invitation to ride back again and stayed home to do the dishes, de-quill the dog, and lick my own wounds. Pretty soon the whole works was back again—Ford, Packard, trailer and canoe. Apparently the Packard had cooled off enough to start the minute our backs were turned. The trip to Middle Dam was successfully accomplished, with the customers only about a day behind schedule. I will say they were wonderfully good-natured about it. They still wanted to pay Ralph for throwing their trip completely out of gear; but there are a few things left for which we don't take money.

The worst and final repercussion was delayed two days. Then the money for that ill-starred trip arrived by mail, with no return address. There wasn't a thing we could do but keep it. We felt like a couple of curs.

Ralph has hauled all sorts of things across the carry. He has hauled anything that will float, from a rubber fold-boat to a steel, gasoline-powered work boat. He has hauled woodsmen suffering from third degree burns, all manner of cuts and fractures, pneumonia, and delirium tremens, known hereabouts as "the horrors." He has hauled a litter of pigs, bound for the garbage disposal department of a lumber camp. He has hauled news-reel men and their cameras, covering the National Championship White Water Races, and fire wardens covering a forest fire. But the ones I like best and he hates the most are the girls' camps.

He hates the girls' camps because he claims that, in spite of the fact that the girls are always under the auspices of a guide and two or three counselors, you might as well try to organize a handful of quicksilver. I like them, because I like to see the old boy get his come-uppence. He gets them all packed in nicely around their canoes and duffle, and someone decides she has to have a picture of the outfit, but that Tessie's skinned knee and Vera's camp letter won't show, so will everybody please rearrange themselves? Or Muggsy can't find her sweater, so everything has to be unpacked. Or someone has a notion, and the notion spreads, and in a flash the whole works is streaming off into the bushes. It drives him nuts, being, so he says, me raised to the nth degree.

The most recent invasion got even Gerrish down. Ralph went to Middle to get them—fifteen of them from some camp over in Vermont—and stopped here to re-fill his radiator. They swarmed into the yard like a pack of beagles, with an old and completely resigned guide making perfunctory motions of bringing them to heel. While his charges were posing for snap-shots with Kyak, who makes swell local color to show the home folks, he came in to ask permission to build a lunch fire on our land. I asked him how he liked his job. He sighed wearily. "Wal, it ain't no *position*," he said with feeling.

He could have saved his breath about the fire. Gerrish was tarring the seams of a boat and had the tar pot heating over a little fire between two rocks. According to his rather hysterical story, the first thing he knew he was smearing the boat with tomato soup, and then he realized he had somehow become embroiled in a mass culinary operation. He grabbed the tar pot, fought his way clear, and knocked off for dinner. He believes in co-operating with the inevitable.

I was charmed with that lunch, aimed to fill the hollow brought on by ten miles of paddling since breakfast and to generate enough energy to get the whole shebang to the nearest camp-site, ten miles away, before supper. The menu:—Tomato Purée; Cheese Dreams; Lemonade.

Once Ralph got a job with the Geodetic Survey, which was in here for the summer making a contour map of the country. To make a contour map, it seems, you first establish, by some esoteric hocus-pocus with trigonometry, the exact altitude of one point, in this case a stone in Coburn's front yard. (Alt. 1462.27 feet above sea level.) Then, working with surveying instruments, you run in circles from that point, sticking sticks with the new altitudes on them at convenient places along the circumference of the circle. If the reading when you get back to Coburn's stone is 1462.27, you may assume that all points on the circle are correct. You then take any point on the circle and follow the same procedure from there. At the end of the summer the entire country is covered with imaginary circles and actual sticks. Then you start running straight lines across country, re-checking altitude with a barometer at any sticks you may come across—surveyors dignify these sticks by calling them Temporary Bench Marks—and attempting to come out at flags which have been tied according to what system I never did find out, to various inaccessible trees. This is the last step before putting the map on paper, and this is where Ralph came into the picture.

One of the rodmen was taken ill, the appropriation for the survey was almost gone, and the head surveyor was loath to lose time and money waiting for his man to recover. So he appealed to Ralph to help him out, assuring him that all he had to do was stroll through the woods with a string tied to his arm, stop when shouted to, and blaze the nearest tree. He didn't say that they would be working in the B Pond territory.

There is nothing the matter with B Pond. It lies to the south of us, over a beech-covered ridge, and it is lovely and placid and wild. But Ralph loathes B Pond, because the trail over is rough and steep. He'd rather be dead than take a trip over the B Pond trail.

Nevertheless, everyday that he worked for the Survey he

went to B Pond, and he didn't go by trail. That isn't the way the Survey does things. They pick out a point at random, consult their notes and learn that somewhere a mile off to the S.S.W. is a white cloth tied to a yellow birch, take out their compasses, tighten their belts, and start looking for it. The rodman—Ralph—goes ahead, trailing a hundred-yard piece of string. When the end of the string comes abreast of the surveyor, he puts up a shout and the rodman stops and makes his blaze. As soon as the surveyor overtakes him, he sets out again, in theory, at least, letting nothing turn him aside from a perfectly straight line. This would be a cinch on the plains of the West, but this is rough country, and we had a hurricane in 1938.

The results of the hurricane here have to be seen to be believed. Acres of trees are piled up like jackstraws in windrows forty feet high and half a mile long. A rodman doesn't go around these. He goes over and through them. Ralph insists that one whole day he never had his feet on the ground except when he came down for lunch. The despised B Pond trail began to look like a boulevard, especially as he knew it was only a hundred yards off to the west, running parallel to their course. It might as well have been a hundred miles off. It might better have been, because then he could have forgotten it. He tore his clothes to ribbons, and then did the same to his skin. He put a vicious blaze on a little sapling and a porcupine fell out of it, missing him by inches. That's the same as being missed by a twenty-pound ball stuck full of red hot needles. He got three and a half dollars a day and whatever satisfaction went with the chief surveyor's affidavit that (a) Ralph was the best rodman he'd ever had, and that (b) this is the most hellish country he's seen in a career covering every state in the Union.

But I know better than ever again to try to persuade Ralph to take a nice little walk over to B Pond with me.

I have my difficulties, too. I don't much like to cook. I like the results of a morning's hard labor to last more than ten minutes. But once in a while I have to take boarders. This usually happens when I am in the worst possible position to do so. Last spring is a good example.

All three families in Middle Dam had enough food to last, with care, over the break-up and until a load of supplies could be brought in from The Outside. We were feeling pretty good about it, because sometimes we aren't so lucky. Nobody, we fondly thought, could get in to eat up our carefully counted potatoes and beans. We were sitting pretty. I was even entertaining the extravagant idea of making a one-egg chocolate cake instead of a no-egg gingerbread, when the telephone rang. It was Alice Miller, and she was in a dither.

She said, "Louise, how much food have you got? I got a crew of five walked in here along the shore from the Arm to stay over the break-up and do some work on the dam. I ain't got a thing to feed them."

The Millers had helped us out in more pinches than I can remember, and it wasn't often that I had a chance to do much for them. This was a God-given opportunity to lend a hand. I'd peel the larder down to the last bone, and be glad of the chance. If I saved out a dozen eggs and a couple of cans of corned beef, and beans and salt pork and split peas and flour and corn meal, we could eat for the few days until the lake was clear, even if it wasn't a very balanced diet. We had plenty of canned milk and potatoes. I told her what I could let her have.

"Swell! I'll send someone down with a pack-sack!"

She hung up and in due time her emissary arrived. I gave him everything I could spare, and he staggered off up the Carry Road under the load.

Barely was he out of sight when the telephone rang again. A man's voice said pleasantly, "Mis' Rich? This is Ban Barnett. I'm down at Sunday Cove, with a crew of three. We walked in over the old Magalloway trail to fix the Carry Road before the drive comes in, and we'll be right up. We'll stay at your place for two-three days, like always."

"Did you bring any food?" I asked with regrettable lack of hospitality.

"Food? Holy God, Mis' Rich, we had all we could do to get ourselves through that Jees'ly swamp!"

"Ban," I said desperately, "I can't board you. I've hardly got enough food in the house to feed the family. You'll have to—"

He'd have to what? The Millers couldn't feed four more. The Parsons weren't any better off than I was. They couldn't go home, nine miles through the swamp and over a mountain, with nothing under their belts.

"You can feed us," Ban assured me with touching faith. "You got potatoes and salt, ain't you?"

I fed them for three days, and ever since I have had implicit belief in the miracle of the loaves and fishes. We had pea soup, which is very filling. We had baked beans. I sent Gerrish fishing. You can never catch fish when you need them, but he did. We had trout and salmon. We had corn meal mush and molasses. The butter ran out, but we had johnny-cake and the last of the jam I had made the fall before. We had dandelion greens and fiddle-heads, those strange, furry fern fronds that taste something like asparagus and something like swamp water. You boil them and serve them with butter, if you have any butter. My two cans of corned beef made two meals. There are ways of stretching meat enough for three to feed seven, other than Divine multiplication. One can I cut up in cream sauce—a lot of cream sauce—and served on toast. The other I cut up with cold potato—a lot of potato—and browned into hash. The Parsons let me have three cans of tomatoes. One made tomato soup, one went into scalloped tomatoes with bread crumbs—lots of bread crumbs—and the last I strained for Rufus to drink, in lieu of orange juice. You can make one egg take the place of two in scrambled eggs by using too much milk and thickening it with flour. It's not very good, but it's something to eat.

Oh, I fed them. It wasn't according to any known dietetics, but we all survived. And when the ice went out and the first boat came in with supplies, I had left a cup of sugar, five potatoes, three cans of milk, a quart of flour, and one egg.

While I was peeling potatoes paper-thin, diluting canned milk with too much water—we did have plenty of water— and measuring out lard by the quarter teaspoon, Ralph and Gerrish were working with the crew on the road. That's another annual source of income, the reimbursement for which just about covers the taxes. Working out your taxes on the road is routine procedure hereabouts. You spend a week filling in wash-outs, rebuilding caved-in culverts, and leveling out the worst ruts, and the tax sale is forestalled for another twelve months. Oh, you can get along with very little cash money in this country if you know the ropes and are sufficiently adaptable.

I was being very adaptable the day Ted Benson called me up from Pond-in-the-River Dam. Ted is the boss of the dam repair crew that travels about the country from headquarters in Lewiston. They always stay at Miller's when they are in this neck of the woods, and when they are working on Pondy Dam, Alice Miller sends down the makings of dinner, and they prepare it over an open camp-fire. Ted is a Dane, and his name is really Theodore (pronounced Tay-o-dorrr) Bendtsen. He has been in this country ever since, almost half a century ago as an apprentice to the Danish Merchant Marine, he deserted ship at Portland; but when he gets excited he still lapses into Danish on the hard words. He was very much excited on this occasion.

I finally made out that he wanted me to come up to the dam and cook dinner for him and his crew of nine. His long-string-of-Danish cook had been out over the week-end and had too bad a hang-over to be of any use to anyone. It wouldn't be any work at all. Mis' Miller had everything all ready. All I had to do was heat it up. He'd do it himself, only dam repairing had reached a crisis where not a man could be spared. Would I come?

I would be glad to. I like Ted, and I'd like to do him a favor. Ralph had gone to Upton to vote in the state elections, so there was nothing to keep me at home. I locked up the dogs—we had five then; that was when we thought a dog team would be a good idea—put Rufus into a pack-sack—he was too young to walk—loaded him onto my back and went up to the dam.

A fire was already burning under the grate that Ted had

salvaged from an abandoned steamboat and placed on two rocks, and a number of kettles were standing around on the ground. A long-chinned individual named Rush was splitting wood, and Ted was standing by to tell me that the dinner hour was eleven o'clock by the battered Big Ben he had placed conspicuously on a stump. Then he went off down the dam fill, motioning Rush to follow.

Rush put another chunk of wood—only we natives call them "junks"—on his chopping block and reduced it to splinters while Ted moved out of hearing. Then he left his ax in the block and closed in confidentially.

"You want to watch that crazy Dane," he warned me. "I've cooked for him. You know what he does? He gets hungry and comes up and shoves the clock along ten-fifteen minutes. You have to keep an eye on him."

It was half past ten then.

I tied Rufus to a bush and gave him a pannikinful of water and a spoon to play with. Then I looked into the food situation. The big kettle held a boiled dinner—corned beef and cabbage, potatoes, carrots, and turnips. It was all cooked, but it would take at least twenty minutes to heat through again, which left ten minutes in which to make the coffee—at least a gallon in a big, smoke-smudged pot. The grate would hold only one thing at a time. Well, it could be done, with a good hot fire. I set the kettle on and stuffed some dry spruce under it. The flame sprang up with a heartening crackle and I started to unpack the plates and eating tools.

Suddenly I realized that Ted was hovering. He took the cover off the kettle, peered in, put it back, snitched a cookie out of a bag, and wandered back down the dam fill. I looked at the clock. It said ten minutes of eleven. I set it back fifteen minutes and started arranging plates of bread, butter, cookies, apple pie, and cheese in a row on a plank. Alice Miller has a reputation all up the lakes for the abundance and excellence of her fare.

The fire had died down a little, so I put some wood on, saw that the boiled dinner had commenced to steam gently, and took the coffee pot down to the river to fill it with water. When I got back, Ted was again retiring down the dam fill, the clock said five minutes of eleven, Rufus had untied himself and was eating cheese, and there were ants on the pie. I took the cheese away, tied Rufus up, set the clock back fifteen minutes, brushed the ants off, and covered the pies with a clean dish towel. Then I sat down on the stump beside the clock and waited for the boiled dinner to boil. It was quarter of eleven by my time, which by then had nothing to do with any other time on earth.

Pretty soon the big kettle began to rumble quietly, sending out clouds of steam and a delicious odor, and Ted started up from the dam, walking briskly and dangling something in his hand. I took one look and set the clock back five more minutes. It was a two pound salmon, and my prophetic soul informed me, rightly, that he wanted it cooked for his dinner. Boiled, he said, with melted butter on it. I took off the boiled dinner, set the coffee pot on, and went down to the river with an extra pan to get some water for the fish. When I got back the clock again said five minutes of eleven. I set it back to quarter of, edged the coffee pot over to make room for the salmon, and put some butter in a pannikin on the edge of the fire to melt.

Rufus was eating leaves, which might or might not be edible, and although by then I didn't much care which they were, I fished them out of his mouth, getting my finger bitten in the process, and set out the salt, pepper, and vinegar. A loud hissing behind my back indicated that the coffee had boiled over and put out the fire. I took the coffee off, burning my hand, and built up the fire with some birch bark. Ted's fish was boiling, and Ted was coming up from the dam again, so I stuck a fork into it, decided it was near enough done as made no difference, and with no attempt at concealment, shoved the clock along to eleven.

"I guess we're ready," I told Ted, and met his eye. "Right on the dot, too!" I added blandly.

I still take boarders when I have to, but I don't cook out any more. It's too hard on the nerves. I'd rather do something like knitting, which can be confined to the home. I'm a good knitter, and I'm proud of it. I see no point in being modest about things you know you do well. It doesn't indicate humility so much as hypocrisy or lack of perception. So then, I am a very good knitter. I even won first prize at the Andover Fair once for a pair of gloves. Fifty cents, it was, and a blue ribbon. I spent the money, but the ribbon I wouldn't part with for pearls. I can knit while I read, thus staving off boredom and creating an illusion of great efficiency. I can make up my own directions, or I can follow printed directions, which apparently is the harder thing to do, although I don't see why it should be.

I think the difficulty with people who can't follow printed directions for knitting or anything else is that they try to understand them. They read the whole thing through and it doesn't make sense to them, so they start with a defeatist attitude. They try to relate the first few steps to the whole, and there is no obvious relation, so they get discouraged and say, "Oh, I can't learn things out of books. But if you'll just show me—"

You don't have to understand directions. All you have to do is follow them; and you can follow them only one step at a time. What you need is not intelligence, but a blind faith. I never read directions through. I never read beyond the operation I am engaged in, having a simple trust that the person who wrote them knew what he was doing. That trust is usually justified. Oh, there's no trick to following directions, and if I don't teach Sally and Rufus one other thing, I'm going to teach them that. I think it's important.

When I get my own family's sweaters and mittens and socks done for the winter, I knit for whoever will pay me— neighbors, lumberjacks, anyone. Also I sew on buttons and patch clothes for woodsmen, whenever there are lumbering operations in here. I don't like to sew, and I don't sew very well, but I do better than most lumberjacks. Ralph, coming across an article about Father Hubbard, the Glacier Priest, took to calling me Mother Hubbard, the winter I started acting as housemother to the woodsmen. It applied, but not as he meant it to. I'm not a snappy model; I really don't wear Mother Hubbards, but the effect is about the same.

Had Ralph been born a little earlier, he would have been a Yankee horse-trader. As it is, he doesn't do so badly with his car trading, in a country where trading is a religion. Albert Allen, a friend from Upton who has lived all his life in this vicinity, covered the general attitude one day. "Nope," he said, "I'd be ashamed to give it to anybody. 'Tain't good enough. But maybe I can find someone who'll make a trade." No matter what you start with, here, if you stick with it long enough, you'll get what you want. All you need is something to start with. Will Morton, who lives on Rifle Point, off Middle Dam, and who is the oldest working guide in the state, being eighty-two— and one of the best—started out with an electric razor, which one of his sports gave him for Christmas. He ended with a boat, which was what he had in mind all the time. I've forgotten, unfortunately, the intermediate steps.

Ralph's most remarkable operation was the trading of the old Model T touring car. There was a lumber camp over on Sunday Pond three miles north of us then, and one gray November day the clerk of the camp called up and announced that he'd heard Ralph had a lot of cars and would maybe sell one. He wanted it to run up and down Umbagog, now that the ice was safe and the snow hadn't come yet, so he could go out and see his girl.

We'd just acquired the Essex, so Ralph was open to bids on the Model T. The clerk—Mac, his name was—said he'd be over next day to take a look. Ralph spent the intervening time pacing up and down and muttering to himself, trying to decide what price he ought to ask. He concluded finally that he'd ask twenty-five dollars, but would be glad to get fifteen.

The trial run was a huge success. They went everywhere —down to Sunday Cove, across Umbagog to Sturtevant Cove, and up through the woods to the Brown Farm, where they called on Joe Mooney and had a game of ping-pong with the company doctor. Mac was impressed twenty-five dollars' worth, all right, only he didn't have twenty-five dollars to spare. Just as Ralph was about to come big-heartedly down to twenty, Mac advanced a proposition.

"Look, I'll tell you what I'll do. I'll give you fifteen dollars and return the car when the camp moves out."

Every woman occasionally wonders what manner of man she has married. No matter how long she has been living with her husband, once in a while he presents a new face. It's the bunk about women being enigmas and men being just transparent little boys at heart. Or else I'm gullible. I had Ralph down as good old, honest, out-spoken Rich, the guy with the heart of gold; the guy who, offered his price in that frank and open manner, would say, "Oh, hell, fifteen dollars is plenty. She's yours. Drive her away!"

And did he? Oh, my goodness, gracious, no! He hemmed and hawed, while I bit my tongue in an effort not to interfere. Finally he gave in, with the perfectly maddening appearance of granting a favor. "That'll be all right," he said graciously. "When you get through with her, be sure to leave her on this side of the Cove, so I can get her without any trouble." Just like that. And then I swear he went out and measured gas into the tank with a teaspoon, so that Mac could get to the nearest source of supply, but not much further.

That night Mac went to Errol to see his girl. The next day it snowed eighteen inches. The rest of the winter the Ford sat under a drift at Sunday Cove—on this side of the Cove, as requested—and never turned a wheel. In the spring Ralph drove it home. I should think he'd lie awake nights, but he doesn't. He has the horse-trader conscience, I guess.

I haven't. I'm a rotten trader. But I did do one deal that gives me perennial satisfaction. I think I came out all right, but even if I didn't, even if I got gypped out of my

Maine guide Will Morton, the oldest and one of the best.

eye-teeth as Ralph says I did, I'm very happy about the whole thing.

There are three boats and a canoe that go with the place, and of course everybody uses them. But they really were Ralph's boats. I wanted a boat of my own, to use and possibly abuse as I chose. I wanted a boat I could put into a pool downriver and not be asked, "When are you going to bring that boat back to the Pond? I want to use it." So when the Bernier boat—Bernier was a famous builder of the type of boat called the Rangeley boat—began to go to pieces from neglect, Ralph gave it to me. The idea was that I would fix it up myself and it would be mine.

Well, I just didn't get around to it, somehow, and it continued to lie on the shore of the Pond, with the paint flaking off, the wood drying out, and the caulking falling from the seams. And that's where Gerrish enters the picture.

He said to me casually, "Ralph tells me that Bernier boat belongs to you."

I thought I felt a deal coming on, and I'd observed Ralph long enough to have learned some rudiments of the technique. So I just said, "Yeah."

"You ain't going to have no boat if you don't tend to it."

I said, "Yeah," again, and we sat in companionable silence.

Finally he said, "Have a cigarette." Pause while we lighted up. "What'll you take for it?"

"I don't know. What'll you give for it?"

"It ain't worth much. Needs a lot done on it."

"To tell you the truth," I said frankly, "I don't want to get rid of it. I want to cut the stern off square, when I get the price of an outboard motor, and make a kicker-boat out of it. What'll you take for fixing it up for me?" That was in the classic tradition. I'd registered reluctance to part with my property and made a counter offer.

"Half the boat," he said promptly. "I'll do the work and you furnish the materials and we'll own it together. When you get around to buying a kicker—wal, there's places I'd go if I had a kicker-boat."

"Where, for instance?" I asked. I didn't want my half of the boat hauled down to Mount Desert Island along with his.

"Upper Dam. Or the West Arm. I wouldn't take it off the lakes."

So it was a deal. He scraped the boat, caulked the seams, replaced a broken gunwale and put in a new stem and keel. That took a month. Then he gave it two coats of oil and two coats of paint, and it's the best boat on the place. He did a swell job. I don't see why Ralph thinks it was a skin deal. I didn't pay anything for the boat in the first place.

I didn't pay anything for it in the last place, either, and that might be what gripes him. He seems to have a feeling that I should have paid for the paint and oil and steel wool and marine caulking and nails and copper sheathing. But he has a whole shop full of that kind of stuff. I should think he'd be glad—but he doesn't seem to be. It would bother me a lot more if I didn't remember Mac and the Model T.

My sister and I used to play a game called "Husband's Occupation?" It was a simple-minded game that we made up off application blanks of various sorts. One of us would ask suddenly, "Husband's Occupation?" and the other had to think up a possible but not very probable answer. "Flea trainer," for example. Or "Percheron Faulter." Or "Sealer of Weights and Measures." I guess we were easily entertained.

I guess we still are, because I am amused, spasmodically, at being married to a Maine guide. Oh, yes, Ralph's a guide, too, although he doesn't work at it much.

Of course a guide has to be a good woodsman and canoeman and camp cook and emergency doctor, and the State of Maine ascertains that he is, before issuing him a license to guide. But he could never earn a living if he didn't also make the grade with the sports—same as dudes of the West—as "quite a character." He has to be laconic. He has to be picturesque. Maine guides have a legend of quaintness to uphold, and, boy! do they uphold it. They're so quaint that they creak. They ought to be. They work hard enough at it.

Here's the Maine guide. He wears what amounts to a uniform. It consists of a wool shirt, preferably plaid, nicely faded to soft, warm tones; dark pants, either plus-fours, for some unknown reason, or riding breeches; wool socks and the soleless, Indian-type moccasin, or high laced boots. He carries a bandana in his hip pocket and may or may not wear another knotted around his neck. But he must wear a battered felt hat, with a collection of salmon flies stuck in the band, and he must wear it with an air; and he must wear a hunting knife day and night; and he must look tough and efficient. If he has high cheek bones and tans easily, that is his good luck. He can then admit to part-Indian ancestry, accurately or not. Indian blood is an item highly esteemed by sports. Naturally he could do his work as well in mail-order slacks, or in a tuxedo, for that matter; but the sports wouldn't think so. Sports are funny.

"That fellow there," the sport is supposed to say, showing his vacation movies in his Westchester rumpus room, "was my quarter-breed guide. He's quite a character. Never had any education beyond the seventh grade, but I don't know anyone I'd rather spend a week alone with. That's the real test. He's a genuine natural philosopher. For instance, we were talking about the War, and he said —and I never thought of it this way before—." What the guide said he probably lifted from Shirer's book, but translated into Down East, it wouldn't be recognizable.

A few livid scars are a great asset to a guide. It doesn't matter how he got them. Maybe as a barefoot boy he stepped on a rake. The holes make swell bear-trap scars, acquired one night up in the Allagash, when the thermometer was at thirty below and the nearest settlement was fifty miles away. Maybe he cut his hand peeling potatoes. It sounds much better to say a beaver bit him. Maybe he fell downstairs and gashed his forehead. When asked—and he'll be asked all right—he can tell all about his big fight with the lynx. They all make good stories to tell around the evening camp-fire.

Oh, those evening camp-fires! That's when the good guide gets in his dirty work. That's when he sows the seed for a re-engagement next year.

This is the set-up:—Supper—fresh-caught trout with bacon curls, potatoes baked in the coals and slathered with butter, a kind of biscuit cooked in a frying pan and resembling Yorkshire pudding, canned peas and fruit—is over. The sports, pleasantly stuffed and mildly weary from having "helped" paddle for ten or twelve miles, stretch out around the fire. Down on the shingle that natural philoso-

pher, that real character, Bobcat Bill, washes the dishes.
The water glows like blood-stained ebony in the leaping
light, and the firs stand up behind, black and motionless.
Back in the bush a fox barks and a deer crashes away from
the scent of wood-smoke. All around lies the wilderness,
dark and unknown and sinister. Inside the little pool of
light is all that is left of the safe and familiar—the canoes
drawn up on the shore, the piled packsacks and blanket
rolls, the forms and faces of friends. A loon sends its lost-
soul lament over the darkling water, and a shiver runs
around the fire. Then Bobcat Bill strolls up from the lake,
throws an armful of dry-ki onto the blaze, and begins tossing blankets toward the group. In the flash of a buck's tail
the old magic begins to work. The tight little fire-hearted
circle of fellowship is formed. We're all brothers here,
united by our common cause against the power of the
black beyond. We're all valiant, noble renegades from
civilization's chafing bonds. We're dangerous and free!

The loon throws its blood-curdling cry against the
mountains once more, and laughs its crazy laughter.

"Never hear one of them critters a-hollerin'," Bobcat
Bill drifts easily into his act, "but what it 'minds me of one
time I was lost up on them big caribou barrens across the
lake. That's how I come by this here scar on my shoulder.
Reason I was up in there, a feller had met foul play—"

I'm making guides sound like a bunch of frauds, and I
don't mean to. They work hard and they're in a difficult
position. Like all merchandisers, they're obliged to give
the customer what he wants, and it's their tough luck that
the customer wants adventure. Adventure, free of actual
risk, is hard to produce; and the state frowns on the
actual killing off of sports, even by accident. So the guide

has to make the customer believe himself Daniel Boone's contemporary equivalent, without actually letting him stick his neck out too far. A little discomfort, yes. That'll make fine telling back in Westchester. Too much discomfort, no. Actual danger, a thousand times no, not even if he insists with tears and pleading that he really wants to rough it, to get off the beaten track into tough country, to pit his own brains and brawn against death by violence or starvation. It's too easy to meet trouble in this country without deliberately looking for it.

So what's the answer? The answer is atmosphere:—tall tales around the camp-fire, a perpetually grim and watchful bearing, a knife and revolver worn always at the ready. The answer is illusion:—jam into bear's blood, bobcat into Canada lynx, vaccination scar into dagger wound.

Ralph's occasional guiding consists chiefly in taking out fishing parties by the day in this immediate vicinity. That's what he's best fitted for, knowing as he does every fish in the river by its first name, and where it'll most likely be hanging out at two-thirty on any given Wednesday. He always comes home exhausted by suppressed mirth. Sports are funny-ha-ha as well as funny-peculiar.

His prize catch was an outfit of politicians from a medium-sized Massachusetts city. At home they were elaborately teetotal; the W.C.T.U. is a force in that city. But they brought fourteen quarts of Scotch and a case of beer—snake-bite precautions—for their three-day stay in the woods. They managed to get rid of it, and I don't think they dumped it in the river. That would argue a little training somewhere along the line, I should think. They'd never been fly-fishing before, but they'd seen pictures of fly-fishermen. So they had the works:—waders, creels, canvas jackets, tapered lines, collapsible landing nets, everything. Everything, that is, except the ability to cast a fly. Ralph spent the day climbing trees to retrieve flies caught in branches and diving into the river to un-snag them from the bottom. Between times he hauled his sports out of the water—they were great fallers-in—and dodged erratic backcasts. He had a very active day. Along about dusk a great outcry went up. Someone had caught a fish. An enormous salmon, so he said. Ralph netted it. It was a small chub. The chub is a poor relation of the carp family, and we natives look down our noses at them. Even the cats won't eat them. The politician wasn't so choosey. He took it home. Probably he has it mounted over his desk now.

Ralph finally got three of his party put to bed. The fourth—he of the chub—refused to go. He'd tasted blood and he wasn't going to waste time sleeping. Ralph left him sitting on the bank of the river with a quart of Scotch conveniently at hand. It was pitch dark, which not only put him in the legal position of being a breaker of the half-hour-after-sunset law, but also in the impractical position of not being able to see his line. The first consideration didn't bother him. The second he got around by using a powerful flashlight trained on his fly. He caught no fish, but he had fun.

The other thing that we do for a living is write. This is the most important, because we spend the most time on it, and because the larger part of our income is derived from it. Probably if we spent the same amount of time and energy working in a factory or selling brushes from door to door, we'd have more money and fewer headaches. But there are other things we wouldn't have.

In theory, at least, one of the advantages of writing is

that you can work anywhere and any time. You aren't tied
down. Actually this is true only within limits. I have found
that unless I make myself some office hours and stick to
them—8.30 to 11 A.M. and 1 to 3 P.M.—I don't do any
writing. I pick some wild flowers and arrange them, wash
the dog, and make a cake, and then it's too late to start
this morning. So I read another chapter of the book I
started last night and get dinner. After dinner I think I
might as well finish the book and go swimming. Morning
is really the time your mind is clearest, I remember being
told. There's no sense in trying to start writing in the
afternoon. So I'll write to-morrow. I really will.

But I wouldn't if I didn't have my office hours. If I
can't think of anything to write about, I just sit in front
of the typewriter and brood.

I couldn't write anywhere, either. I couldn't write on a
cruise to the West Indies, or in a mining town in Nevada,
or in the bayou country, or any other place where the surroundings were new and unexplored. Putting down words
on paper is a very dull substitute for seeing new things
and people. On my ninety-ninth cruise I could probably
write, or after I'd lived two years in Nevada. The real
meaning of "You can write anywhere" is that you can
choose a place where you're going to like to be and do your
writing there after you've exhausted its other possibilities.
Your original choice is free.

Another reason I like to be a writer, aside from the fact
that I can live in the backwoods instead of off Times
Square, is that I like to see my name in print. This is pure
exhibitionism, and we'll say no more about it. I don't like
exhibitionists, either. And while I'm baring my girlish
heart, I might as well admit that I enjoy having people

look respectful when I say, "Oh, I write." I get a kick out of it, even if I do feel like a fraud.

Feeling like a fraud is one of the bad things about being a writer. You have to be a little disparaging about your work sometimes. Because of its nature, it is so closely tied up with your own personality that taking it seriously verges perilously close to the pompous. So there's a lot of talk by writers about just doing pot-boilers until one is financially secure enough to embark on a really serious work. Frankly, this is hooey. Writing pot-boilers implies writing down, and condescension is immediately apparent to, and rightly resented by, the editor. I believe that any writer who sells enough to eat off the proceeds is writing the very best he can all the time. When he stops, he stops eating.

I've read a lot of first-rate writing, and I have some critical sense; so I know where I stand. I'll never be first-rate. I'll improve with practice, I trust, but I haven't got what it takes to reach the top. However, I hope I'll never make the excuse that "it's only a pot-boiler, after all." Everything I write, no matter how lousy it turns out to be, is the very best I am capable of at the time. My writing may be third-rate, but at least it's honest. You can't be even a third-rate writer without taking your work seriously.

But if you take it seriously, chances are that others will, too, and I enjoy having a fool-proof excuse for not doing the things I don't want to do. If I said, "Oh, I can't. I have to do my mending," the answer would be, "You can do it this evening." If I say, "Oh, I can't. I'm working on my book," there's no argument about it at all. It's wonderful. I hardly ever do things I don't want to do any more. Except write.

Writing is hard work, and don't let anybody tell you otherwise. It's hard on the eyes, the back, the fanny, the disposition and the nail-polish. It's hard on the nerves. Your income is so uncertain. You never know, when you're sweating blood over a story, whether the editor is going to hold his nose, or cheer and send you a check for—

And that's another thing. People don't mind asking a writer how much he gets paid for a story. There must be some explanation for such a breach of good taste in otherwise well-bred persons. I have been coping with the situation by stalling. I say, "Well, that depends. It would be impossible to say. Some magazines pay higher rates than others, and some writers are better than others—" And blah, blah, blah.

But I'm not going to stall any more. The next time anyone asks me how much I got for a story, I'm going to tell them. I might even tell them the truth. And then I'm going to say, "And what does *your* husband earn in a year?" That ought to settle that.

Upon reflection, I conclude that probably the best short answer to "How do you earn a living?" would be "From hand to mouth."

III

"But You Don't Live Here All the Year 'Round?"

WHAT PEOPLE REALLY MEAN WHEN THEY ASK US IF WE
live here the year 'round, is "But good Lord! Certainly
you don't stay in here during the winter? You must be
crazy!" Well, all right, we're crazy. I would have thought
so myself, before I tried it.

I used to hate winter, too. When I was a child it was because winter meant school, and although I got along reasonably well there, school was something to be considered
with nausea. Along about February I used to think of the
stretch of time until June and freedom with such a hopeless depression as I have never known since. It just didn't
seem possible that I could live that long. The only time in
my whole scholastic career that I ever liked school was one
spell when I was in the eighth grade; and the reason for
my change of heart then had nothing to do with my stu-
dies. I fell in love with the boy who sat in front of me,
and since he lived over on the other side of town, the only
time I got to see him was during school hours. It made a

difference in my attitude, but it didn't last very long. In spite of all the sentences I diagrammed for him, and the arithmetic answers I slipped under my desk into his eager palm, come Valentine's Day, he spent all his pocket money on a big lace and ribbon heart for a blonde who sat over in the dumb section, and who didn't know a verb from a common denominator. It soured me on the male for a time, but it taught me a lesson that has been valuable ever since: to wit, men may admire and use brains in a woman, but they don't love them. I reverted to my hatred of winter.

After I grew up, I still hated it, and I think that now I know the reason why. In civilization we try to combat winter. We try to modify it so that we can continue to live the same sort of life that we live in summer. We plow the sidewalks so we can wear low shoes, and the roads so we can use cars. We heat every enclosed space and then, inadequately clad, dash quickly from one little pocket of hot air through a bitter no-man's land of cold to another. We fool around with sun lamps, trying to convince our skins that it is really August, and we eat travel-worn spinach in an attempt to sell the same idea to our stomachs. Naturally, it doesn't work very well. You can neither remodel nor ignore a thing as big as winter.

In the woods we don't try to. We just let winter be winter, and any adjustments that have to be made, we make in ourselves and our way of living. We have to. The skin between outdoors and indoors here is so much thinner than it is even in a small town, that it's sometimes hard to tell where one stops and the other begins. We can't dress, for example, for a day in the house. Such a thing doesn't exist. We have to go outdoors continually—to get in wood, to go to the john, to run down to the other house and put wood on the kitchen fire, to get water, to hack a piece of steak off the frozen deer hanging in the woodshed, or for any one of a dozen other reasons. Outdoors is just another, bigger, colder room. When we get up in the morning we dress with the idea that we'll be using this other room all day. When we step into it we make the concession of putting on mittens—if we're really going to be there long enough.

Everyone in here dresses more or less alike, until it comes to foot gear. We all, male and female, wear plaid wool shirts—two of them sometimes—and wool pants, ski or riding. We wear wool caps and home-made mittens, with leather mittens, called choppers, over them. The choppers don't keep the hands warm, but they keep the mittens dry and prevent their wearing out. We all wear wool socks. And there the great woods schism begins. Everyone has his own pet ideas of the proper footwear for below zero weather. No one will listen to any one else's opinion on the subject. Everyone knows he is right, and no one will dabble with experiments. Feet freeze too easily and frozen feet are too painful and serious to be courted deliberately.

Ralph belongs to the great gum-boot school of thought. Gum-boots have high leather tops sewed on rubber feet. They are loose and roomy, and their addicts wear two or three pairs of heavy wool socks inside them. I guess they're all right, if you like them. Larry Parsons swears by laced, all-rubber knee boots and two pairs of socks. He claims that the leather tops of gum-boots get soaked when there is wet snow, and then where are you? The answer to that is that healthy feet perspire a little, and there is no chance for evaporation through rubber. So by night your socks are going to be wet anyhow, and what difference does it make how you get them wet? The Finnish lumberjacks who brought their equipment from the old country—and there are quite a number of them around here—have a good foot gear, consisting of heavy felt boots, knee high and about an inch thick—too thick to wet through, and much too thick to chill through. They look as though they'd be wonderful, but you can't get them in this country. Some of the native lumberjacks try to achieve the same effect by buying old-fashioned black buckled galoshes, about four sizes too big, and wearing four or five pairs of socks in them. They keep the feet warm, but it's like wearing a bucket on each foot. A few people wear high leather boots, but almost everyone else agrees that they are cold damn things. Nobody would be caught dead in a pair of ski boots. They're too stiff and heavy. Let the city folks have them. They don't know any better.

Myself, I wear one pair of wool socks and the lightest, cheapest pair of sneakers I can buy, and nobody can convince me that this isn't the answer. Everyone else is working on the wrong principle, that of getting more and more layers between their feet and the cold. That's wrong. What they gain in insulation they sacrifice in foot flexibility. Their feet are just two petrified lumps wrapped in wool. According to my system, articulation isn't interfered with, and the blood circulates freely, bringing heat from the body to the feet as a hot water heating system brings heat to the radiators. I haven't been able to win any disciples to my belief, but that's all right. Neither have I ever had my feet frost-bitten.

I seem to have devoted a lot of space to what we wear on our feet in winter, but it's quite in proportion to the amount of time spent talking and thinking about it. It's a very vital matter.

Outside, life takes on pace with the approach of winter. It is the gay season, the season of parties and theatres and all the other things that will help people forget that outdoors something that they can't cope with is going on. Here life slows down, just as the world around us slows down. The leaves fall from the hardwood trees. Spruce and fir and pine stop growing and stand, dormant and black and thick, on mountain-side and lake-shore, their slim tips pointing monotonously to the gray sky. Of course they don't move, but they seem to draw silently in around us. We realize suddenly what we have forgotten: that after all, there are only three families of us—only a dozen puny human souls strung out along the lake and river—against all the forces of nature. To the people Outside, "the forces of nature" is a convenient phrase out of a textbook. To us they are a reality. We know we haven't a Chinaman's chance of controlling them. We only hope we can outmaneuver them.

I always feel like a renegade when the first little powder snow comes. It never lasts long, and it isn't serious, but the proper attitude is the long face, the foreboding shake of the head, and the grim comment that it won't be long now. I would like to act as Kyak does, and go tearing around in circles, scooping up mouthfuls of snow as a fast train scoops up water, and leaping crazily and prodigiously over little snow-covered trees. I don't, partly because any tree I could leap over wouldn't be worth bothering with and I'd probably fall flat on my fanny anyhow, but mostly because I'd simply be too unpopular if anyone suspected my antisocial liking of winter. So I try to remember that in February, when the snow is four feet or more deep on the level and I'm flopping inexpertly around on snowshoes, I'll be cursing the day the stuff was invented and offering my hope of Heaven for a good long look at a patch of bare ground. I turn my attention to the first piece of out-maneuvering that we have to attend to.

That is the circumventing of the freeze-up, our official beginning of winter. That's the fall in-between period, when the lake is just frozen and the ice is too thick to put a boat through and too thin to support a man or a horse or a car. We never know when the freeze-up is going to start or how long it's going to last. The only thing we do know is that while it's going on, we are completely bottled up. The nearest A & P is some forty miles away, but it might as well be in Egypt. Whatever we are going to need over a period of two or three weeks, we have to bring in before the Arm starts to freeze over. Tea, coffee, sugar, flour—I go over the list in my sleep. Oatmeal, canned meat and fish, fruit, and vegetables. And canned milk! Good Lord, if I'd forgotten that again! One year we forgot it and the Parsons forgot it, and the Millers didn't buy any because they keep a cow and didn't have to. So the cow chose that time, of all times, to go dry. We all learned, the hard way, to like black coffee and tea. I still like it, but I don't like to remember how oatmeal tastes without milk on it.

The real problem, though, is fresh meat and eggs and butter. If we bring them in too early and the weather warms up, we have the most horrible phonemena known to the thrifty Yankee heart and soul—good food, slowly spoiling. If we cut the margin too fine, we wake up some morning and find a half an inch of ice—a futile and in-furiating amount—on the lakes. So we watch the barometer and thermometer and stars and the thickness of Kyak's pelt and listen to the weather broadcasts on the radio and rush out at all hours of the day and night to hold a wet finger to the wind. And sometimes we guess right and sometimes we don't. So far we've managed to survive the consequences of errors in our computations, but it's a pretty harassing period to go through, all the same.

Luckily for our sanity, the deer-hunting season furnishes a distraction around freeze-up time. Of course, everyone in here goes hunting. It isn't sport with us, though. We want and need the deer meat. (Only snobs and city people say venison, I early learned.) Hunting is a business with us. There are plenty of deer. In the summer, when it's against the law to shoot them, they stand around the yard under foot in romantic, negligent poses, fairly screaming to have their pictures taken. They come into the flower garden at night, and with great discrimination eat the blossoms off all the more difficult flowers to raise, turning up their delicate noses at such common fodder as zinnias and nasturtiums. Again in the dead of winter when their natural foods are buried deep under the snow, they drift into the clearing to eat hay or excelsior or cardboard boxes out of the dump, or anything else they can find. We couldn't shoot them then even if the law allowed; they are too gaunt and pathetic—"too poor," as they say up here. Anyhow they wouldn't be fit to eat. They've already been driven to browsing on cedar, with the result that they taste like furniture polish. During the hunting season, when they are fat and sleek and it's legal to kill them, every deer in the country remembers a man he has to see about a horse back in the thick growth on the highest ridges. It's uncanny. Ralph estimates that by the time he has caught up with one and shot it and dragged it out, estimating his time at the current local wage of thirty-five cents an hour and taking into account expenditure of shoe leather, ammunition, and wear and tear on clothes, but with no charge for loss of temper, the meat comes to about ten dollars a pound. He doesn't like deer meat, anyhow, so probably his figures are padded. He says he'd rather eat an old goat and be done with it. So he goes out only when I drive him out, almost at the point of his own gun.

Larry Parsons was in the same frame of mind one year. We were up there one afternoon when he came in from hunting. He'd been out all day, and he was a rig. His shirt was torn, his face was scratched, and frozen mud caked his boots and pants. He told us in no uncertain terms that that was definitely that. He didn't give a damn if he never shot another deer. For all of him, every unspeakable deer in the State of Maine could go climb a tree—an interesting possibility, zoologically speaking, only Larry wasn't speaking zoologically. He was speaking from the heart. He had been over at Black Cat, got into a swamp, crawled through blowdown for two miles or more, and when he went to eat his lunch, found it gone from his back pocket. So he was through. He'd eat potatoes and salt if he had to. He'd eat nothing, if it came to that. But never, never, so help him Hannah, would he step foot out of the house again, after a deer.

At this point Al, who had been listening with the look of sympathy we all learn to assume to cover up the fact that we are inwardly estimating just how soon it will be safe to broach the subject of deer hunting again, squeaked and pointed out the back window. In the middle of the clothes yard stood an eight-point buck. Larry shattered every existing record in oath-breaking. The kitchen floor smoked as he crossed it. He missed the first shot, and the buck obligingly turned broad-side. He couldn't miss the second time. It must have been a feeble-minded buck. From the eugenic viewpoint, it was undoubtedly better for the race that he didn't live to propagate his kind.

The real excitement of the deer-hunting season isn't hunting deer, though. It's hunting deer-hunters. It's always the same, every year. Any night that Ralph comes in at sunset and says, "It's going to turn cold tonight. We'd better get in some extra fire-place wood," I know what's going to happen. We go out into the lovely still dusk for the wood, but I can't really appreciate the black silhouettes the pines on the western ridge make against the orange and apple-green sky, nor the wreaths of steam that begin to rise from the river as the temperature of the air drops below that of the water. I'm too busy wondering how soon the telephone will start ringing.

It usually starts just at full dusk. It may be the Millers calling, or Cliff Wiggin, or the Brown Farm, but it all amounts to the same thing. "Say, you ain't seen anything of a couple of hunters, have you? Yeah, they're stayin' here. Went out this morning and they'd ought to have been back an hour ago. Well, sort of keep your ears open for signals, will you, and call me up if you hear anything—"

We'll hear something, all right. Just after we've decided that, thank God, they're lost in some other neck of the woods and aren't our responsibility, and have changed into slippers for a quiet evening in the home, Kyak will look interestedly out of the window and indulge in a short "woof." We'll go out onto the porch to listen. Sure enough, faint and far away will come the sound of three grouped shots, the universal woods signal of distress. It's a signal that can't be ignored. I don't know what would happen to a person who turned a deaf ear to three shots, but I more than half believe that the nearest tree would fall and crush him to a pulp. It should, anyhow.

Ralph groans, gets his gun, fires the two answering shots that mean, "O.K. I hear you. Now for the love of Mike, stay where you are and keep on signalling," and starts pulling on his gum-boots again. I go to the telephone to report that the missing have been spoken. Ralph collects his compass, a lantern, his gun with lots of cartridges for signalling, and sets forth into the night.

If lost hunters would only stay put, they'd be fairly easy to find. But they rarely do. If they're inexperienced enough to lose themselves in the first place, they're inexperienced enough to get panicky. The thing to do, once you know you are lost, is to find a good, safe place to build a little fire, build it, fire the three shots, light a cigarette, and sit down and wait. If the shots aren't answered wait a while till you are sure it's late enough for searchers to be out looking for you and shoot again. If you've plenty of shells with you, continue to do so every five minutes; if not, space your volleys further apart or until you hear someone shooting for you. But *before* you have used up all your cartridges, resign yourself to a night in the open and make the best of it. They'll be looking for you in the morning—you don't have to worry about that. They'll come shooting, and you'll answer with the cartridges you've carefully saved, and before ten o'clock you'll be back in camp eating bacon and eggs and drinking hot coffee.

This is such a sane and easy program to follow, but no lost hunter that we ever encountered ever followed it.

They all do the same thing. They start travelling as fast as they can, usually in the wrong direction and always in circles. I've been lost, and I know the feeling. It is hard to be sensible—not to be driven by a nameless terror and urgency—but you have to be sensible. You can't go ramming around in the woods in the pitch dark. The least serious thing that will happen to you is that you'll become completely exhausted and demoralized. Much worse things can happen. You can fall in a hole and break a leg. You can trip and shoot yourself. One hunter over on B Pond ridge went running through the woods at top speed, smacked into a tree, and knocked himself cold. It's better, even if harder, just to sit down and wait.

The procedure for finding lost hunters is always the same. First comes a period of swearing at anyone dumb enough not to get himself out of the woods before dark. (This phase runs concurrently with the assembling of paraphernalia.) Because we live so near the river, the next thing that Ralph does when he has to go out hunter-hunting, is walk up the road to where it's quiet so he can hear the shots as plainly as possible and determine their direction by compass. Then he fires two answering shots and starts off in that direction and keeps on walking until he hears some more shots. He re-checks his direction, finds that the lost one has wandered four points to the northeast, say, corrects his course, fires two more shots, hoping that they will toll the quarry in his direction, and keeps on walking. This may continue for an hour or it may continue most of the night. The first time it happened it was fairly exciting, but after years of it it has become a nuisance.

In the meanwhile I have kept the tea kettle boiling so

that when Ralph gets home, complete with hunter, they can have something hot to drink before going to bed. My inclination, after a half a dozen experiences, is to go hastily to bed as soon as I see their lantern up the road, and let them get their own lunch. Six times is enough to hear the same old story, and it always is the same old story.

After the hunting season is over and the lakes have frozen, we can settle down to winter, which consists not of the problem, primarily, of how to keep ourselves amused, but of the much more interesting problem of keeping ourselves warm and fed.

The first thing that has to be dealt with is the wood situation. You don't have to ask anyone what he's doing for busy-work from November until January. He's getting in his year's supply of firewood. What else would he be doing? The wood has to be cut after the leaves have fallen, but before the snow gets too deep and makes it hard to get around in the woods. It has to be sawed into four-foot lengths, split, and piled for hauling when the snow gets deep enough. The hauling is usually done with horses and sleds, although we use a car and have to build a road for the purpose. It's amazing how good a road can be built out of brush and snow over the roughest terrain. Brush is thrown into the holes and wet snow piled on top. Then it is trodden down and smoothed off. You wouldn't think it would hold up a rabbit, let alone a car or a team of horses and a heavy sled loaded with a couple of cords of hardwood. But as soon as the weather settles down to a steady cold, the whole thing freezes as solid as a rock. It seems to have the permanence of the Appian Way. I'm always surprised when I run across an old hauling road in summer to find it nothing but a series of skids, brush piles, boulders and deep holes. It seems impossible that we ever rode on it smoothly where now it's difficult even to walk.

We put up eight or ten cords of wood, all of it since the hurricane being blowdown along the Carry Road. That is not an editorial we. Gerrish and Ralph do most of the work, but the proudest moments of my life are those occasions upon which Gerrish sidles up to me at lunch time and mumbles, for fear of hurting Ralph's feelings, "You got time to come out this afternoon and give me a hand? I got an old son of a bitch of an old yellow birch to saw up." You see, I'm a much better hand on a two-man cross-cut saw than Ralph is. Gerrish says I'm better than a lot of professional woodsmen he's worked with. This sounds like frightful bragging, but I don't care. It's really something to brag about.

Excellence on a two-man cross-cut has nothing to do with size and strength. It's wholly a matter of method. A two-man cross-cut is a saw blade four and a half or five feet long with a removable handle at each end. The sawyers take their stances at either end and pull the saw back and forth between them. That sounds easy, and it is easy if you can just remember to saw lightly, lightly, oh, so lightly. Ralph's trouble is that he hates to saw wood and he wants to get it over with as soon as possible; so he bears down on the saw, instinctively, I suppose, since intellectually he knows better. A lot of people who know better do the same thing. It doesn't make the saw cut any faster, and it makes it run an awful lot harder. It makes all the difference between pulling a four-pound weight back and forth or a forty pound. A very common admonition from one sawyer to another in this country is, "Pick up your feet, will you?" That is probably meaningless to the uninitiate, but a good sawyer resents it very much. It means that his partner is saying that he doesn't mind riding him back and forth with every stroke of the saw, but he does consider it unnecessary to have to drag his feet along the ground, too. It's the obscure local way of telling a man he's bearing down on his end of the saw and it's an implication that he doesn't know his trade.

I don't know how other sawyers manage to retain the fairy touch, but this is how I do it. First I make sure that I'm going to be comfortable, even if this involves shoveling holes in the snow for my feet and lopping off sundry twigs that might switch me in the face. Then I take my end of the saw and pay very close attention to what we're doing for the first inch or so. It's important to start the kerf straight. If it slants or curves appreciably the friction becomes terrible when you get half way through the log. By the time the cut is well started I've got into the swing of the thing and don't have to think about it any more. Particularly do I not think about the fact that we are sawing a log in two.

These are the things I do think about. First, I think with satisfaction how good this particular exercise is for the waistline. I can feel the muscles roll and any accumulated ounces of superfluous padding melt away. Then I look around the woods and think how lovely they are in winter, with the lavender shadows of the bare trees lying like lace on the snow, and the evergreens standing up black and stiff all around. Everything is as still and sharp as an etching in the thin winter sunlight.

About then Gerrish says "Whoa." We have long since agreed that when either of us says "Whoa," we'll finish the stroke we're on and do one more. This gives both our minds a chance to come back from the vacuum they've been wandering in. This whoa of Gerrish's indicates that we're more than half way through the log and it's time to drive a wedge in the kerf to prevent the saw from being pinched. I sit back on my heels while he drives the wedge, and consider taking my top shirt off. Putting up your own wood is certainly the way to get the most heat out of it. It warms you twice—once while you're sawing it and again while you're burning it. I take my shirt off and pick up my end of the saw again.

Now I think of the deer who will be coming in at night and how glad and surprised they'll be to find a new tree down. They can browse all night long in the moonlight on the buds which yesterday were forty feet above their reach. We'll see their tracks in the morning. I look at the sawdust that is coming out in little spurts from our kerf with every stroke of the saw. If it happens to be a white birch with a red heart, the sawdust is lovely on the snow—pale gold and soft warm rose. White birch is the least satisfactory of the hardwoods for firewood, but it makes the prettiest sawdust. Firewood's excellence in order is this: maple, yellow birch, beech, and white birch. White birch is the most expensive to buy, though. People from the city think it's pretty and romantic, and that puts the price up. I'm just thinking about that when the saw drops and we're through the log. Gerrish hasn't had to tell me to pick my feet up, either.

After the wood has been cut, rough split, and hauled into our yard, it has to be resawed into stove length and split into two sizes, a large size for the heater and a small size for the kitchen stove. The sawing is done by power.

We have a circular saw rig, run by a Model T motor
that Ralph fished out of the lake and reconditioned. It's
certainly a lot more satisfactory than the old-fashioned
hand buck saw, but I refuse to have anything at all to
do with it. It terrifies me. Just the sight of the saw spinning viciously around, its teeth a bright blur in the sunlight, and the sound of the queer, inhuman rising shriek
it gives as it rips through a piece of wood, make the cold
shudders run up and down my spine. I'm really and truly
afraid of it. It's unreasonable, I know; but some fears lie
beyond reason.

I like to help split the wood, though. It's frozen to the
core by now, and splits easily. It's fun to stand a chunk—
pronounced "junk" here—up on the chopping block, give
it a clip with the axe, and watch it explode. Occasionally
a knotty piece will give trouble, but the mere fact of reluctance to split puts the whole thing on a personal basis.
So! You won't, huh? Well, we'll see about that! All right.
I don't have to use an axe. I can use a maul, if you're
going to be that way. There! Dammit!

It's invigorating to win a fight, even if it's only against
a stick of wood.

We're still fussing around with one or another phase
of the wood question when Christmas comes along.

Christmas in the woods is much better than Christmas
on the Outside. We do exactly what we want to do about
it, not what we have to do because the neighbors will
think it's funny if we don't; or because of the kids, who
will judge our efforts not by their own standards but by
the standards set up by the parents of the other kids.
We don't have any synthetic pre-Christmas build-up—no
shop window displays, no carol singers in department

stores, no competition in the matter of lighting effects over front doors. At the intersections where the deer-runs cross the Carry Road, no Santa Clauses ring bells in the interest of charity. We didn't even have a Santa Claus until last year. We thought it would be nice if Rufus grew up knowing who gave him presents and bestowing his gratitude in the proper places. So we had never even mentioned the name of You-know-who. However, a visitor at Millers let him in on the secret, explaining to him that Santa Claus is the man who brings things for little boys. Rufus knew very well that Larry Parsons brings in everything we get from the Outside. Q.E.D., Larry is Santa Claus. He still persists in this belief, which makes him perfectly happy and we hope it does Larry, too.

We don't even have a Christmas tree. It seems a little silly, with hundreds of square miles of fir and spruce, from knee-high babies to giants of eighty feet on all sides of us, to cut one down and bring it into the house. It seems almost like vandalism to shake the ice and snow from its branches and hang them with pop-corn strings and cheap tinsel. We have our Christmas tree outdoors, for the benefit of the birds, hanging suet and crusts on the branches of one of the trees in the yard.

But we do have Christmas, just the same, and since we are so far from stores and last minute shopping, we have to start planning for it a long time ahead. With no chance to shop for gadgets, we have to make quite a lot of our presents, and the rest we get from what is known here simply as the Mail Order. I give mittens, hand made by me with the initials of the recipient knit into the design across the back. These don't cost much over and above my time, and no one in this country ever had too many

pairs of mittens. For people who live Outside I try to
think up things that they couldn't buy in stores. After
all, it would be simple-minded to send out and buy something, have it mailed in here, wrap it up, and send it out
to someone who, doubtless, lives almost next door to the
store where it was bought.

I make little mittens about an inch long and sew them
onto a bright fourteen-inch length of cord, as children's
mittens are sewed onto a cord. These are bookmarks, in
case you haven't guessed. To city people who, I know, have
fire-places, I send net bags full of the biggest and best
pine cones I can find, to be used as kindling. I make
balsam pillows. I know these can be bought at any roadside stand north of the Maine border. But mine don't have
pictures of Indians stamped in ink on cheap pink cotton cloth, along with the excruciating sentiment, "For You
I Pine and Balsam." I collect old-fashioned patchwork
quilt patterns from any source I can find them, and use
them to make my pillow covers. In the old quilts, each
unit is usually from twelve to fifteen inches square, and
that makes a very good size for a balsam pillow. I make
them, naturally, by hand, and they look very simple and
expensive. They don't cost very much either. And I do
love the names of the old patterns—Star of Bethlehem,
Wedding Ring, Flower Garden, Log Cabin. They have a
nice homely sound. You can think of a lot of things to
make out of nothing, if you have to.

But making presents isn't half of Christmas in the woods.
I'll never forget the year the lake didn't even begin to
freeze until well after the tenth of December. We'd ordered our Mail Order, and presumably the Andover Post
Office was harboring our stuff until someone could go out

to get it. Finally, the day before Christmas, it was decided that an expedition should go on foot, get the stuff, and then, if at all possible considering the thin ice, drive it all in in Larry's old Model T which was down at the Arm.

We had living with us then a friend named Rush Rogers. He and Ralph and Edward Miller and Arch Hutchins, who was working for Larry, joined forces and set off down the ice on foot dragging a couple of sleds behind them to haul the stuff in on if the ice proved unsafe for the car. They got to the Arm all right, and from there into Andover was easy in Miller's Outside car.

Sure enough, all our stuff—we'd sold a story a short while before and were having a fat Christmas that year—was at the Post Office. In fact, since the Post Office was small and space at a premium during the rush season, our packages were all piled in the front window like a display, and the population of Andover was standing outside guessing at their contents. The Middle Dam delegation continued on to Rumford, stocked up with groceries and Christmas Cheer, picked up the mail and packages on the way back, and arrived back at the Arm in the afternoon. The mail and supplies filled the Ford to bulging. Arch wedged himself into the driver's seat, Edward stood on the running board to watch the high-piled packages, and Rush and Ralph tied the two sleds behind in single file and sat on them. I wish I could have seen them. The sleds were hardly big enough to accommodate their rears, and they had to hunch their knees up under their chins and hang on with both hands for dear life. Arch was driving the old Ford as fast as it would go, snow and ice chips from the chains were flying into their faces, so they couldn't keep their eyes open, and the sleds at the ends of their lines were

slewing with terrific swoops. As a final touch they held
their bare hunting knives in their teeth so they could
cut the sleds loose if the car went through the ice ahead
of them. Edward told me later that they were the fun-
niest-looking rig he ever saw.

The ice was really too thin to be safe. It bent and bowed
under the weight of the car, and rolled up ahead of them
in long flexible swells. But Arch followed the rules for
driving a car on thin ice—keep the doors open, go like
hell, and be ready to jump—and they got home all right,
only a little late for supper.

Then started one of the most hectic evenings I have
ever spent. First, everything had to be unpacked; and when
the Mail Order packs, it packs, what I mean. Corrugated
board, excelsior, paper padding—they certainly give it the
works. We decided that Ralph would do the unpacking in
the back bedroom, with no lamp. He could see enough
by the light through the open door. We didn't want any
fire on Christmas Eve, and all that packing material around
loose was definitely a fire hazard. Rush would assemble
all of Rufus' toys that came knocked down—and that year
most of them did—but first he had to put the new batteries,
which were in the mess somewhere, into the radio so I
could hear the Christmas carols.

I would re-wrap packages prettily. I started out with
our present to Renny Miller, a five-cell flashlight, which
we thought might come in handy for him. A flashlight is
an awkward thing to wrap neatly, but I did a fairly good
job and went on to the next thing. Rush was back of
the chimney doing something to the radio wires, and in
a minute he said, "Hey, Louise, where's that flashlight
of Renny's? Lemme have it a second, will you?" I un-

wrapped, let him have it a second, and wrapped it up again.

I'd barely got the bow tied satisfactorily when a yelp came from the back room, "Good-night, there goes a box of blocks! Hey, Louise, lemme have that flashlight of Renny's a second, will you?" I unwrapped it, let Ralph have it a second, and wrapped it up again. The back bedroom, I noted in passing, looked as if a brisk breeze had swept through it. I wrapped up the snow gliders we'd got for the two younger Miller children and looked around for Rush. He had disappeared, so this looked like the opportune time to tie up the mittens I'd made him, and the checked wool shirt that was Ralph's present to him. I got out a suitable piece of Christmas paper and some silver cord.

Then came a rapping on the window, and in the glow of the lamplight I saw Rush's face, framed in icicles and spruce branches. He didn't look like Father Christmas, though. He looked like a man in distress. "Hey, Louise, I can't see a thing out here by this aerial. Bring out that flashlight of Renny's a minute, will you?" I unwrapped it again—carefully, this time, as the paper was getting a little shabby at the creases—and took it out. In passing through the back room I observed that the brisk breeze had risen to gale velocity. I could still see the top of the bureau and of Ralph, but the bed had been drifted under. I held the flashlight while Rush did whatever he had to do. We went back into the house and turned on the radio. A very satisfactory rendition of "Holy Night" rewarded us. I re-wrapped Renny's present, decided it looked pretty moth-eaten, undid it, got fresh paper and ribbon, and did it up again.

"Holy Night" changed to "Oh, Little Town of Bethlehem," and I listened with pleasure, wrapping up presents, while Rush started to put together Rufus' bounce horse. As the music came to an end, I woke up to the fact that Ralph had been shouting for some time from the back room. "Hey, Louise! Bring that flashlight of Renny's—"

Before we went to bed that night I had wrapped that darned flashlight nine times. I had become a much better flashlight wrapper by midnight than I had been at seven o'clock.

At midnight we had some sherry and crackers and cheese. Because this was Christmas, Ralph had a raw egg in his sherry—which I think is barbarous—and Rush brought me a magnificent treat—Camembert cheese, which Ralph considers equally barbarous. We were exhausted and silly and we had a lot of fun. It was the best Christmas Eve I ever had, in spite of the flashlight.

After Christmas, what we call "the long drag" sets in. One day is very like another. The sun rises late over a snow-covered world. It's worth while to get up, even with the thermometer twenty below zero, to see a winter sunrise. The eastern sky flames with red, and the whole world turns rose. The steam, rising from the churning open water of the river, has been freezing all night long on every tiniest twig and spill from the water level to the tops of the tallest trees. Walking down to the kitchen over the squeaking snow is like walking through a fabulous wood where all the trees are wrought silver encrusted with diamonds. It's a marvellous sight, all the more breath-taking because it lasts so short a time. As soon as the sun is up and the wind begins to stir, it is gone and the trees stand again in their winter grays and dark greens.

Getting breakfast in winter is something. The kitchen stove won't hold a fire over night, so in the morning everything in the place is frozen—the wood, the water in the pails, the bread, the butter—everything. Everything you touch is colder than ice—the metal pans, the copper on the drain board, the iron of the stove-cover lifter. You learn very quickly not to take your mittens off until the place has had a chance to thaw out. I can get a whole breakfast wearing my mittens. I think it would be very good training for those occupations, such as surgery, for example, which require unusual manual dexterity.

Dusk draws in early in the winter. We come in for the night about four o'clock, light the lamps, and settle down. I know all about the inconveniences of kerosene lamps. You can't tell me a thing about filling them every morning, about trimming the wicks, about keeping the chimneys bright. But they give such a lovely, soft, golden light that it's worth the bother. I love lamplight.

During the short space between sunrise and sunset, there are a lot of things that have to be tended to. There are the daily chores, chief of which is filling the woodboxes, bringing in the water, and shovelling snow. Snow shovelling sounds like a trivial occupation, but it isn't. It's hard work and it's maddening work. The paths and steps have to be shovelled out, but all the time you're doing it, you know in the back of your mind that (a) it'll probably snow again during the night, and (b) if you could only wait until spring, you wouldn't have to do it at all. I get tired just thinking about shovelling snow. I hate futile activity.

But keeping the paths clear hasn't half the headaches

of keeping the road to Middle open for a car. We can't even choose our time for doing that. We start out in the car as soon as it begins snowing as if it meant business. You can always tell. A really serious snow starts in with fine flakes, which hiss against the windowpane and sting the face. The wind starts moaning up the river, and first the further ridges, then the nearer, then the trees across the river, disappear in a ghostly pall. Probably blizzards start as often at ten o'clock in the morning as at seven o'clock at night, but my impression seems to be that it is always dark when we start out to break out the road. Undoubtedly this is a hangover from my first trip.

It was cold that evening, I remember—too cold, we thought, to snow. We never knew when the sun set; gray afternoon merged slowly into black and starless night. We brought the wood and water in, had supper, fed the dogs, pulled down the shades against the biting cold, and drew up around the lamp with our books. The fire roared softly in the stove; a dog whined in his sleep; outside a tree cracked now and then in the falling temperature. It was a good evening to be inside.

Suddenly Ralph said, "Listen to that wind!" We pulled aside the curtains and peered out into the night. At the bottom of each pane of glass was a little line of white, curving up at the ends. Even as we looked, the lines thickened and something like a handful of smoke momentarily clouded the glass. Ralph dropped his corner of the curtain. "Snow," he said, and reached for his gum-boots. "I'll go get the car started. You'd better put some wood on the kitchen fire. I'll meet you up at the road."

By the time I had put on my sneakers and mended the fire, Ralph was ready to go. He had a cant dog, a couple of shovels, some rope, some empty burlap sacks, and a lantern in the back of the old Model T. I climbed in beside him and we started off. It really didn't seem to me that this was necessary. Only about an inch of snow had fallen so far, and it was crisp and mealy. Why didn't we wait awhile?

I found out. As soon as we got out of the shelter of the buildings, the road vanished. Everything vanished. The headlights showed us only a thick white wall that swayed in the wind, and pretty soon we couldn't even see that. I got out onto the running board and scraped the windshield clean, and we went a few more rods. Then I repeated the performance, and we went on again. It was just like living and trying to work in a heavy, smothering black bag. I hadn't the faintest idea where we were. None of the trees along the side of the road looked familiar. Even our voices sounded odd and muffled. We must be, I thought, about halfway by now. I got out to see if I could find the ruts, and sensed rather than saw something even blacker than the surrounding blackness off to the left. It was the wangan. We'd come only a third of a mile.

Halfway up Wangan Hill we fell off the road. The front left wheel went down with a sickening slump, the rear wheels raced, and there we were. We didn't say anything. We didn't have to. We just lighted the lantern and got out to look. The bottom of the car was resting on the frozen snow shoulder of the road, and neither of the rear wheels had traction. We had to dig the pan and axles free and get her back into the ruts somehow. We did. Don't ask how. I don't know. All I remember is lying for what seemed like hours on my stomach with snow drifting over me, scraping away at that frozen shoulder. Then

I remember shoving for dear life while Ralph gave her the gas. I remember also Ralph's giving me a little lecture on the asininity of anyone my age not being able to drive a car. If I could drive and he might shove, then we might get some place. This annoyed me, as I do feel like a fool to be the only woman east of the Rockies who can't drive a car, and I gave an awful heave. Out she came and I leaped aboard.

The snow had made three inches while we were fooling around, and any last trace of ruts had vanished. Indeed, it had become hard to tell where earth ended and air began. There was only one thing to do. I took the lantern and got out and walked, leading the way. I hadn't thought of it when I decided upon sneakers as the ideal winter foot gear, but this was a place where they were of unparalleled value. No one else could have felt the ruts with the soles of their feet. I walked along one rut, making a track that Ralph could keep a wheel in. That was all he needed to keep him on the road. We made Middle all right—everyone there was in bed—turned around and started home again. The return trip was comparatively easy. Our own tracks were still faintly visible.

We went down to the kitchen, made some coffee, drank it, ate a doughnut apiece, stoked the fire and started out again. It was after eleven o'clock, and snowing harder than ever. We fell off the road three times, and on the return trip the car dragged in the middle all the way. We drank some more coffee, ate some more doughnuts, and set out again. This time we were piling up so much snow with the front of the car that we both got out and stumbled and slid a hundred feet up the middle of the road to break down the crown, came back and rode the distance we had walked, and repeated the performance, until we saw Miller's back pasture gate in front of us. Then we shovelled out a place to turn around in and came home. It was after three o'clock by then, and neither of us could remember a time in our lives when we hadn't breathed snow, and had snow down our necks, up our sleeves, in our faces, and most especially dragging at our feet. And it was still snowing, and we had to keep on making these ghastly expeditions into uncharted space. We set out again.

I can't remember whether this trip, or the next, or the next, was our last. They all blur into one long eon of wallowing and pushing and shovelling, of roaring motors and spinning rear wheels and boiling radiators, of blowing snow and moaning wind, of brief periods in the warmth and light of the kitchen, of scalding coffee, of changing soaked mittens and socks for mittens and socks not quite so wet, and of wishing first that I could go home and go to bed, and, along toward the last, that I could just go to bed under the nearest bush. Somewhere along there, though, we found ourselves standing beside the Ford, tacitly acknowledging that we were licked. We'd shovelled and we'd pushed. We'd practically willed her along the last quarter mile, when she'd been out of the ruts more often than she'd been in. The snow was just too mealy to provide traction, and now it was just too deep to plow through. The last inch had been our undoing, and now we might as well drag ourselves home and go to bed. Ralph drained the radiator. The Ford would keep until spring just where she sat.

I looked around. I could see a little now. The woods were getting, not lighter, but a little less solidly black. I could see a gray smear running away in two directions

from where we stood. That would be the road. I could see
strange humps and fantastic figures that were trees standing around us in the thinning snow. Yes, thinning. The
flakes were falling much slower now. They were big and
feathery, and lacked the vicious drive they'd had all night.
The storm was definitely letting up. We took one more
look at the car, and Ralph shook his head. It was just too
late to make any difference. We were on foot now until
spring. We might as well accept it.

"Where are we, anyhow?" I asked.

"Top of Birch Hill."

It could have been worse. It was less than a mile home.
We could have had to walk all the way from the Parsons'
front door. We blew out the lantern and started home
through the first beginnings of a beautiful clear dawn.

On foot for the rest of the winter! That's where we
always end. Sometimes we're on foot in December, and
again we manage to keep the wheels rolling until February, but sooner or later we have to get down the snowshoes from their pegs on the porch and start walking the
mail.

When we first came to live here, mail was definitely
catch as catch can. The Post Office at Coburn's is a summer office, open only from May 15th until October 1st,
and before and after those dates, Middle Dam ceased to
exist as far as the Government was concerned. If anyone
happened to be going Outside, he took the community
letters and brought in whatever postal matter the Andover
Post Office had been storing for us. Sometimes we got
mail every week. In the dead of winter or when conditions
were bad we were lucky if we got it twice a month. Now,
however, we have a Star Route to Middle Dam, and we

get mail every Tuesday and Friday. It's wonderful for everyone, except possibly Larry, who is the mail carrier. There are times, I imagine, when he'd just as soon stay home as go trekking off down the lake with what he sometimes refers to as "the Christly mail." It's all right while the boat is still running, or after the lake is frozen and he can use his snowboat—an ingenious device that looks like a Black Maria, with skis in place of the front wheels and caterpillar treads behind to furnish the driving power. But in between times he has to carry the sacks around the shore on foot, and that's something else again. The first year he was mail carrier Ralph had two great over-size tires come for the Big Green "Mormon," and, of course, they arrived during the freeze-up. Ralph told Larry he was in no hurry for them and to leave them at the Arm until the ice was safe, but Larry is too conscientious for his own good. He carried and rolled them all the way up from the Arm. That's the kind of a guy Larry is.

On Mondays and Thursdays, then, one of us has to walk to Middle to take up the out-going mail, and again on Tuesdays and Fridays, someone has to go up to bring down the in-coming. I myself don't mind the trip, even on snowshoes, those inventions of the devil. It isn't like breaking a trail through fresh snow. We take pains to tramp down a good, wide, level float up the middle of the road, and in between storms this float is packed so hard that we can sometimes go all the way bare-foot. Bare-foot, I probably don't have to explain, is simply woods for "without skis or snowshoes." It's nice to get away from the house for a while and to visit Al Parsons and Alice Miller, and there's always a lot to think about and look at along the road. There are the woods themselves, which I like better in winter than in summer, because I like the type of design that emphasizes line rather than mass. The bare branches of the hardwood trees look exactly like etchings. There are strange vistas of hill and pond which the foliage blocks out in summer, and which therefore have a rare, new appeal, like glimpses into a far and beautiful country. The view through the bare tree tops from the top of Birch Hill might be a Swiss view, I decide, and the deep black slash between the ranges where the Arm stretches south through its narrowing valley might be a Norwegian fjord. Then I wonder why we all like to pretend that we're somebody else, somewhere else. Why is it more fun to think I'm a Norse woman looking over a fjord than to admit I'm me looking over into South Arm? Probably, because part of being me, looking into South Arm, lies in pretending I'm a Norse woman? This is very involved and gets me nowhere. That's the sort of footling conjecture that I indulge in while walking the mail.

Another great source of entertainment on these mail walks is the tracks in the snow. Sometimes they are just tracks—the clear-cut, chiseled hoof marks of deer, a rabbit's big, spreading pad-marks, with a little dent behind them where its maker squatted in the snow, or the precise line of prints left by a trotting fox. Sometimes they tell of tragedy. You follow the delicate embroidery of a wood-mouse's trail for a quarter of a mile, and then it ends like the snipping off of a thread. Two feathery swept places in the snow, where the wings of an owl brushed as he swooped, tell why. Or you may come to a churned-up, blood-stained spot, with the tracks of a rabbit and a wild cat leading into it, but only the wildcat's tracks leading out. You don't have to have a dictionary to translate that story. Once in a while we see a bear track, but not often. The bears ought to be, and usually are, sleeping somewhere in the winter.

Actually, the only track that has the power to startle us very much is the track of man. We fancy that we know about where everyone belonging to Middle Dam is, at any given hour of the day or night. Moreover, if anyone comes down the Carry Road, it's usually to see us. There isn't any other place to go, in winter. So if nobody has stopped at the house, and yet here's this track on the road—well! It couldn't be any of the Millers. They're all working on their wood. It can't be Larry. He doesn't wear L. L. Bean gum-boots, and only Bean boots have this chain tread. It might be Dorian, who works for Larry. He was talking last week of getting some new boots. But he's supposed to be sawing ice. Maybe it's one of the company timber cruisers, come in from the Outside. Or maybe it's the game warden. Or maybe— It doesn't strike us as odd at all that we have so changed our way of living from that in which we were brought up, that bear and deer and wildcat tracks are all in the day's walk, while a stray human boot-print throws us into a dither.

But that's not all of walking the mail. After we get to Middle there are people to see and talk to. There are all the Millers and both the Parsons, and whoever is working for the Parsons at the time. They may be doing almost anything, but whatever they're doing, it's worth while stopping to watch. Al will probably be sewing or cooking. She's one of the busiest people I ever saw. She's never sewing ordinary things. She runs a gift shop in the summer, for the benefit of Coburn's sports, and she'll be making a very trick apron, or a particularly useful laundry bag. If she's cooking, it won't be just cake and pie and cookies. It will be doughnuts that contain orange juice and grated rind instead of milk and spice—a very tasty dish, by the way—or a spice cake, the basis of which is canned tomato soup, or coconut-chocolate candy, made largely of leftover mashed potato. She gets around among the pages of the women's magazines, all right.

If it's right after New Year's, all the men of Middle Dam will probably be cutting ice. Cutting ice is a man-sized chore. Over two thousand cakes have to be got in for the hotel, so-called, and on top of that there's Larry's own personal ice and Miller's ice. Then they branch out. They go up into the Narrows and fill the ice houses of a couple of summer camps up there, and they fill Mrs. Graves' ice house at the Arm. It's a lot of work, and more involved than would seem at first glance.

First of all, they have to arrange to have the ice the right thickness, a matter that can't be left to Nature alone. This is one of those cases of circumvention. The ice, during the first part of January, is about a foot thick, and that isn't quite thick enough. Before spring it may be three feet thick, but freezing under the insulating blanket of snow that covers the lake after the first of the year is very slow. So in order to speed it up, the snow must be scraped off the cutting area. A couple of below-zero nights after the ice is clear will do the trick. Then the ice field has to be scored for the cutting lines like a pan of fudge, with a tool that looks like an old-fashioned spike harrow with the spikes set sixteen inches apart. Then the cutting begins.

The cutting used to be done with a hand ice-saw, until Larry decided that that was unprogressive. He got hold of a machinist on the Outside who dreamed up an ice-cutting machine for him. This consists of an old Model A motor on steel runners, with a chain-driven circular saw out in front and a handle like a baby carriage handle out behind. The operator walks behind, pushing the rig and raising and lowering the saw as desired. The scored grooves in the ice act as guides for the runners. This ought to have been much easier and faster than hand sawing; and it would have been, if, instead of sawing ahead in a straight line, the thing hadn't inexplicably insisted on sawing backward in a circle. Ice sawing was suspended until the creator could be brought in to take the bugs out of his darling. He came in one week end, toiled long and earnestly, and left Sunday night with assurances that everything was going to be all right, now.

Monday morning ice cutting was resumed. Larry drove his reconditioned labor saver the length of the ice field, parked it for a moment while he organized the hauling and storing brigades, and turned back just in time to see what happened. Ralph was at Middle at the time, and saw it, too. He says it was one of the most impressive sights he ever witnessed.

Larry had unwittingly left the ice cutter on the edge of a triangular floe of free ice, formed by two accidental and invisible cracks and the open water alongside of which he had been sawing. It was a big floe of a thousand square feet or more of ice—too big to be noticeable to a man just walking across it. But it wasn't too big to be affected by the weight of the machine bearing down on its edge. As they looked the point of the triangle rose majestically, and the opposite side dipped. The ice cutter clung for a moment and then started slipping into the lake. It was the slow-motion quality of the thing that made it so impressive. The whole works just hung for a long moment. Then the cutter disappeared into twenty feet of icy water, and the floe settled slowly back. The lake stretched without blemish two miles to the further shore.

They got it out later all right, and sent it out to be overhauled. It's still there, and they're still cutting ice with a hand ice-saw at Middle Dam.

They had some trouble putting the ice in at the Arm one year, too. When a cake of ice has been cut free, naturally it floats and can be hauled up out of the water, loaded on a sled, and taken up to the ice house. The first cake they cut from the ice field at the Arm didn't float, though. It disappeared, leaving a hole. So did the next. Larry stuck his head down the hole to see what went on. He found that he and his men and horses were standing on a sixteen-inch piecrust of solid blue ice, over some three feet of air, with another layer of ice below. The lake had dropped three feet after the top layer had frozen and the lower level had frozen subsequently. Ordinarily the ice would follow the water down, but the ice was so thick it just arched to the shore instead. Larry was relieved to know that the laws of natural science hadn't suddenly been revolutionized. All the same the situation was annoying. One man had to crawl down into the air space and lift up the pieces as they were sawed so they could be hoisted to the top. It was a nasty, cold, cramping job. Nature can think up simply abominable little tricks to pull off unexpectedly.

Some winters we have lumber camps in here. Nobody has to have the general nature of a lumber camp described to him. Literature and the movies have done that quite adequately. They haven't shown, however, what it means to be neighbors to a lumber camp; to have as the boon companions of one's four-year-old son a bunch of the hardest and toughest teamsters, sawyers, border-jumpers and general roustabouts that ever came down a tote road; to find that one is suddenly confronted with a choice of stopping talking or learning an entirely new language—a language consisting of such terms as "bucking up on the landing," "sluiced his team" and "shaking out the road hay." Being what I am, I chose to learn the new language.

I also had to learn to differentiate between a day man, a stump cutter, and a member of a yarding crew. A day man gets paid by the day and does whatever the boss tells him to. He may cut firewood, swamp out roads, pile up brush and tops, anything. A stump cutter is an individualist. He works alone, felling his own trees, limbing them out, sawing them up into four-foot lengths, piling the pieces neatly for the convenience of the scaler, and getting paid by the cord. He's usually pretty good. That's why he works alone. He can make more money that way than he could at day rate or by pooling his ability with that of someone else. Sometimes, however, he's hard to get along with and no one else will work with him. A yarding crew consists of three men and a twitch horse. One of the men cuts down the trees and limbs them, one drives the twitch horse, dragging—or "twitching"—the entire trunk of the tree to a cleared space called a yard, where the third man saws it up with a buck saw and piles it. A good yarding crew can cut and pile an awful lot of wood in a day.

Besides these classifications of woodsmen, who comprise the main population of the camp and who sleep in a long low bunk-house, there are several specialists. There's the boss and the straw boss, who have their own little shack, not because they feel exclusive, but because the men like to sit around their bunk-house in the evening and bellyache about the weather, the food, the administration of the camp, or the way the trees grow, or any one of a thousand other things. The presence of authority would put a definite damper on this favorite of all indoor sports. And while talk is cheap, like other cheap things—air and water, for example—it is invaluable. A man who has cursed the boss all evening to his confreres is almost always a man who goes to bed feeling at peace with the world, and who wakes up ready to put out a good day's work. So the boss lives in his own little hut, dropping over occasionally to join in the poker game that runs continually from supper to bed-time and all day Sunday.

In another little hut, known as the Office, live the clerk and scaler. The scaler, as his name implies, scales the wood for the men. That is, he estimates with the aid of a long marked rule called a scale rule the quantity each man cuts, keeps a record of the scale for the landowners, and reports each man's cut to the clerk, who pays the man accordingly. The clerk keeps the camp books, pays the men, orders supplies, tends the wangan—the little store where tobacco, candy, clothes, saw-blades and axes are sold—and runs the punch board, which is always a part of the camp picture. The clerk and scaler are men of at least some education, and I think they enjoy living alone, because they like to sit up nights and read, and in the bunk-house lights have to be out at nine o'clock.

Behind a partition in the kitchen, which is also the dining-room, and which is by law a separate building, live the cook and his cookees, or helpers. They don't mingle much with the rest of the camp. They're too busy, for one thing. For another they have their discipline to maintain.

If arguments start they're apt to start in the dining-room. That's one reason why no talking is allowed in the dining-room, aside from simple requests to pass the butter, please. And I mean "please." I've eaten a lot of meals in lumber camps, and I've been amazed at the prevalence of "please" and "thank you." I wish my own family were always so punctilious. The other reason for no talking is that the cook doesn't want the men dawdling over their meals. A large percentage of our woodsmen are Canadian Frenchmen, and they can't talk without gesticulating. This means they would have to put down their tools and stop eating, which would slow up the meal considerably. The cook contends that they can do their talking somewhere else. All he wants them to do is eat and get out, so his cookees can get on with their dishes.

Somewhere high on the social scale comes the blacksmith. He sometimes lives with the boss, sometimes with the clerk, and sometimes with the men, depending on his type. He makes the sleds that are used to haul the wood, keeps the horses shod, repairs tools, and is usually an amateur veterinary besides. He and the feeder—woods for stableman—are responsible for the health of the horses, but if anything beyond their ability arises, they take the responsibility of calling a real vet. The feeder waters and feeds the horses, cleans the stable, and keeps an eye on the pigs. Every lumber camp has five or six pigs. They are brought in in the fall, cute little tricks with curly tails, fed all winter on the tons of excellent garbage that are the inevitable by-product of catering to a hundred men or more, and sent out in the spring to be slaughtered. By that time they are simply enormous.

Every lumber camp also has cats. In the fall the cook

brings in a cat to keep the kitchen free of mice and the stable free of rats that come in in the bales of hay. It is always a female cat. If I didn't know our Tom, I'd be inclined to believe the flat statement of an old friend, Beatty Balestier—yes, Kipling's brother-in-law, but he'd kill you if you mentioned it. Beatty told me once when I was trying to locate a tom kitten, "There's no such thing. All cats are female cats, and all kittens are the result of immaculate conception." My observation of lumber camp cats inclines me to believe he had a tenable argument there. But be that as it may, by spring every lumber camp within a radius of ten miles of us has at least a dozen cats—the original and three litters. All the kittens, regardless of their mother's complexion, are black and white. No wonder Tom is such a smuggy.

When a lumber camp first moves in, all the men look alike to me. They're all big and tough-looking and most of them need a shave, which they won't get all winter. They all dress more or less alike, in layers of shabby sweaters and shirts, ragged pants, and wool caps. They all walk along the road with the same swagger, carrying their axes and saws over their shoulders, swearing at their twitch horses, and dropping their eyes upon meeting me. After a while I begin to get them sorted out and those that I meet regularly I start speaking to. The first time I do this the same thing always happens. The man starts obviously, raises his eyes to look at me, looks all around to see if by any chance I mean a couple of other guys, and looks back at me. Then his face lights up in the warmest and friendliest of smiles, and he answers. If he can't speak English, he answers in French or Russian or Finnish. It doesn't make any difference. We both know what we mean:—"Hello, stranger. I'll never get to know you very well. We haven't much in common, but we're both here on this snowy road, with the woods all around us. Stranger, I wish you well." They do wish me well, too. Lumberjacks have a reputation, I know, for being brawlers and roisterers and general trouble-makers, and I guess when they are on the Outside, with their systems full of rot-gut, they often deserve this reputation. But I have never met a lumberjack in the woods who didn't treat me with complete respect and friendliness—and I've met a lot of lumberjacks. What they do Outside, I neither know nor care.

Sometimes, though, we get indications that some individual's conduct before he crossed our ken might not bear the most rigid inspection. This was true, we gathered, of one of Rufus' bosom pals, a big part-Indian named Tony. Tony looked like a ruffian, and was sweet. He rode Rufus on his horse, stopped in the yard to play with him, took him on walks and brought him presents, like partridge feathers or a length of chain carved out of a single piece of wood. I used to worry about these friendships of Rufus' —for Tony was only one of many. After all Rufus was only four and some queer customers do get loose in the woods. I suppose it was the stock maternal stewing. Ralph told me not to worry, and after a while I came to believe him. I'm glad I did. The risk was negligible, I know now, and what Rufus gained in knowledge and poise was considerable.

Then one day the feeder came down to the house at noon simply bursting with excitement. "We got a G-Man, Mis' Rich," he announced, as one would announce the outbreak of a rare and fatal disease. And sure enough, an F.B.I. agent had walked into camp from Upton—a long, hard walk, but you know the F.B.I.—looking for some man. The man had been there, but had left the week before. (I don't know, to keep the record straight, what he was wanted for, or whether they ever caught him.) So the G-Man had some lunch and walked out again. He wasn't in camp more than an hour. But the fact that he came at all was enough.

When the cutting is a mile or more from camp, some of the men carry their lunches with them rather than walk clear in and back again. Tony was one of these. But the man that worked with him preferred to walk back for a hot lunch. He came back to the job that afternoon and told Tony that there was a G-Man in camp. Tony went on with his work but kept deep in the spruce thickets along the back of the cut. When knocking-off time came, he turned his horses loose, with a slap on their rumps to get them started, and let them go into camp, alone—a thing they always did, anyhow. He, himself, didn't go home to supper. He stayed up on the mountain-side, hungry and all alone in the cold and dark until the middle of the night. Then he sneaked into camp and snatched a few hours' sleep. The next morning, bright and early, he was at my kitchen door to say good-bye to Rufus. I didn't recognize him, at first. He'd shaved off the luxuriant beard he'd been nursing along all winter. He didn't know where he was going, he told me cheerfully. He was just going.

These seemed, and still seem to me, to be over-elaborate precautions for complete innocence to take. I still wonder sometimes what Tony had on his conscience.

This visit of the G-Man and Tony's oddly coincidental flight were a source of discussion all the rest of the winter. Nothing is so prized in the woods as a good juicy morsel to hash over. Here is a community of men, practically cut off from the world. Most of them can't read. They have one thing in common—work. They have to talk about something and they'll talk about anything. They'll talk about the number of birds that flew out of a thicket, or the deer they saw eating road-hay—the hay spread on icy places in the hauling roads to prevent loaded sleds from overrunning the horses—or the super-intelligence of their own twitch horse. They'll talk about the snow, which is damned for hindering the cutting, or lack of snow, which is damned for hindering hauling. They'll talk about the food—it was always better at the last camp they were in—or the shelter. That was always better, too. The roof was either higher, permitting better ventilation and air circulation, or lower, conserving heat; or else the floors were warmer, or the lice less numerous. But most of all, they like to talk personalities. In short they like to gossip. They'll take the fact that a man changed his underwear in the middle of the week instead of waiting until Sunday, the conventional underwear-changing day, and make almost an international incident out of it. It's fascinating to observe.

Occasionally there's something worth talking about. Once in a great while someone goes crazy and tries to kill himself or someone else. That's good for a month's talk. Once Rufus got lost, and I, in desperation, called up and asked the clerk if anyone there had seen him. Every man available set out to look. He was finally discovered about five hundred yards from the tar paper shack where the horses are taken to eat their noon-day meals; or as the man who found him said, "About two and a half good twitches." A good twitch is the distance a horse can drag a full-length pulp log without resting. Distances are frequently measured in twitches or fractions thereof by woodsmen. It's a habit I've got into myself.

This search for Rufus furnished talk for a week. Once a big Swede known as Bow (pronounced as in bow-wow, which is what his brother is called, incidentally) decided to relieve the monotony by putting a set-line through the hole in the ice where the horses were watered at lunch time, and catching himself some fish. The fact that if the game warden had caught him, he'd have probably spent the rest of the winter in jail only added spice to the venture. For days he tended his line night and morning and never caught a thing. Then one evening his luck changed. There was something—a considerable something—down in the water at the end of his line. His shouts brought the whole camp onto the ice in time to witness the landing of the fish. It was fish all right—a can of salmon with the label still adhering, in case proof were needed. They're still talking about that, in the woods.

Sunday is the day of leisure in a lumber camp. That's the day the men do their washing, file their saws and sharpen their axes, get their hair cut, and attend to any other odd personal jobs. It's horse-shoeing day, too, except in emergencies. Sometimes the blacksmith lets Rufus "help" by holding the horse's foot for him. This is a great treat for Rufus, but considerably less of a treat for the blacksmith, I would think. What the horses' views are, I have no way of knowing. Sunday afternoon is recreation time. Then the big stud poker game really gets going, and the Russians and Poles start their interminable gloomy hands of *spadowiecz,* a game completely incomprehensible to non-Slav. Then if the ice is good, the athletically inclined join Ralph and Rufus and me in skating on the

Pond in the cove where we keep our boat in summertime. We can't skate for sour apples, but neither can anybody else, so we all have a lot of fun and make a lot of noise falling around on the ice. Then those who can carve, work on their ornamental bottle stoppers and birds in cages, mysteriously cut out of a single block of wood. Then those that are big enough and tough enough to get away with it knit on socks and sweaters.

I never can quite make up my mind whether I like to have the lumber camps move in or not. I really like it best when we're here alone. I've heard enough of the popular Freudian lingo that people in general sling around so carelessly to know that I am no victim of agoraphobia. I like to know that I have miles of unpopulated space around me. The lumber camps don't bother me, but I know they are there. Worse, I know they are cutting down the trees. I feel a great regard for trees; they represent age and beauty and the miracles of life and growth. I don't like to see them destroyed, especially as the cellulose made from them can just as well be made from corn stalks. On the whole, I'd just as soon that the lumber camps went somewhere else.

On the other hand, there are nice things about them. It's nice to have not-too-close neighbors once in a while. But the thing I enjoy most about them is a perfectly silly and inconsequential thing. Our winter bedroom is right next to the road, and I like to hear the men and the horses going to work before we get up. Once in a while a man will whistle or sing, but mostly they go quietly, with only the jingle of a chain, the blowing of the horses, and the squeak of the frozen snow to mark their going. The whole thing doesn't last fifteen minutes, and it really isn't anything to get starry-eyed about. I just like it; that's all.

Winter, to look forward to, is a long, dark, dreary time. To live, it's a time of swirling blizzards and heavenly high blue and white days; of bitter cold and sudden thaws; of hard work outdoors and long, lamp-lit evenings; of frost patterns on the windows and the patterns of deer tracks in the snow. It's the time you expected to drag intolerably, and once in a while you stop and wonder when the drag is going to begin. Next week, you warn yourself, after we've finished doing this job on hand, we'd better be prepared for a siege of boredom. But somehow next week never comes. There's always something to keep it at bay.

Then one day there's a patch of bare ground on a sunny slope, the dog starts going wild with the smell of spring, and someone says that the break-up ought to come early this year. The break-up! But Good Heavens, the lakes only froze up a couple of weeks ago. Well, a little more than that, maybe. Let's see— Why, it's time to tap the maple trees and overhaul the cars and clean house! The next thing you know, the smelts are running and the loons have come back into the growing patch of open water in the Pond-in-the-River. There's an ant hill in the flower garden and a dandelion blossom up by the road. Gerrish has begun talking about a good mess of dandelion greens, cooked with salt pork. It's time to clean up the vegetable garden and paint the boats, and the consensus is that the ice will be out by next Tuesday.

Next Tuesday!

Where has the winter gone?

IV

"Isn't Housekeeping Difficult?"

No. Housekeeping in the woods is—for me—not at all difficult. I'd like to let that statement stand unqualified, testimony to my enormous efficiency and energy. Too many people know the truth about me, though, to make that advisable. The truth is that under the most favorable circumstances—circumstances including linoleum floors, vacuum cleaners, washing machines, and automatic water heating systems—I would still be a rotten housekeeper. My friends would indulgently call me a little bit careless, and my enemies would label me down-right slovenly. My enemies would be the nearer right.

Here I can be a rotten housekeeper, and it doesn't make much difference. After all, this is the woods. People don't expect quite so much in the line of shining silver, polished glass, and spotless woodwork. I can, with a clear conscience —or fairly clear, anyhow—ignore a lot of persnickety details. I can be sensible about these things. I can refuse to allow myself to become the slave of a dustpan and brush. I have learned, because I've had to, to spend money wisely. Now I am learning to spend my time wisely; and I don't think it's very wise to spend two hours waxing the living-room floor on a lovely day when I could be out fishing. If I say this often enough and fast enough, I can convince myself that almost no effort beyond attending to the bare necessities of food, clothing, and shelter is really required of me.

We do have to eat. That I will concede. So I spend a large proportion of my housekeeping time in getting ready to cook, cooking, and recovering from cooking. It makes me tired just to think about it.

This is supposed to be the Independent Life, but as far as getting supplies goes, we're dependent on quite a number of things, ranging from Larry Parsons to the weather. Except during the short summer months, Larry is the one who goes to Rumford and hauls our supplies in by car and boat, and whether or not he goes depends on the weather, the state of the lake, and how much else he has to do. Once Larry goes, whether I have the ingredients to cook what I want to cook, or must, instead, cook what I have the ingredients for, depends on how bright or dull we were while making out the supply list. We try to put in supplies for a week at a time in the summer, and for a month or more, at a time, in the winter. In making out a list of that length, it's very easy to leave off two or three items that are absolutely essential. There is no way of rectifying these errors. Once a thing is forgotten, it's forgotten until next time. Then you find to your surprise that a lot of things you thought were essential aren't essential at all. It's very enlightening.

Try to make a list of all the groceries you're going to be needing for the next four weeks. Go ahead. It won't cost you anything. You aren't in my boots. If you leave off eggs, you won't have to go without, as we do. Remember that fresh fruit, meat, and vegetables won't keep forever, and plan accordingly, listing canned goods for the last part of the month. Remember also all the boxes and bottles in the kitchen that aren't empty, but will be next week. Those are the things I always forget—the vanilla and salt and nutmeg. I used to forget the staples, too, going on the assumption, I guess, that one always has sugar, flour, and tea. It didn't take me very long to learn this little fact of life— one doesn't. Now my lists start with the staples—eggs, butter, milk, oatmeal, cornmeal, molasses, coffee, split peas, beans, salt pork—you go on from there. Next I do the perishables—oranges, bananas, lettuce, whatever vegetables are in stock and good. I leave that to Sam Swett, the manager of the A & P, who, fortunately, is most trustworthy. Rumford is no Babylon, rich in exotic viands. I have to take what I can get. (Once in my ignorance I ordered artichokes, and got back a little note saying, "I heard of these, but I never see one.") Meat next—beef, pork or lamb to start the month with, and then a ham, always, which is only semi-perishable. Then the canned goods—meat, fish, fruit, and vegetables. Then the odds and ends, like cheese and spices and macaroni and rice and cocoa. It sounds easy enough, but I always forget something, like a lemon. So instead of having Eggs Benedict, as I had planned to have as a special treat, I end by having plain ham and eggs which are no treat at all.

I've just been over the foregoing list, and there is a very serious omission, which I'll bet a button no one spots. Of necessity, everyone in the woods makes his own bread. I've left off yeast, which means that we eat corn bread or baking-powder biscuit until Larry goes out again. Almost everyone thinks he likes hot breads, and they are all right once in a while. But they get terribly, terribly tiresome, both to make and to eat, after a week.

The usual supply difficulties are intensified twice a year by the fall freeze-up and the spring break-up, those periods when, as I've explained before, you can't get out of here because the ice isn't safe to cross but is too thick to put a boat through. Cold weather, though, isn't an unmixed curse. When it really gets cold, with a cold you can depend on not to waver, then you can stop vilifying the temperature and begin to use it. You can make ice-cream, for example, following any good recipe and putting it outdoors in a pan to freeze. This involves running out every half hour or so, to stir the custard and scrape what has frozen away from the sides, but it's worth the bother to me. I've loved ice-cream from my childhood, when a cone was an event. I still love it enough not to be too bitter about the fact that here in the woods we almost never can have it in summer, when the weather is hot, but must wait until the time of year when scalding soup and hot buttered rum would be the reasonable man's choice.

The important use of cold, though, is to keep food. Early in December we buy a case of butter—thirty-two pounds— and freeze it. This will last us until spring and the final pound is exactly as sweet and fresh as the first was. We buy meat in quantities and freeze that, too, It's wonderful to know that in the Arctic regions of the summer house living-room, fifty pounds of pork loin dangle from the ceiling, out of reach of dogs and cats, awaiting our pleasure. Frozen meat is all right to eat if care is taken to thaw it slowly. Otherwise it will be tough. And, of course, it can't be thawed and frozen again and thawed and eaten. You're apt to die horribly if you're not careful about that,

I understand—although so far my knowledge of that is hear-say.

Like everyone else in this country, we freeze up a deer whole, if we're lucky enough to get one, and if we get it late enough in the season. We let it hang long enough to be tender—about two weeks—in an above-freezing place, and then we hang it out in the woodshed. There are two advantages to using the woodshed for a cold storage room. One is that it is cold. The other is that we're no butchers, and we need a lot of room and a lot of tools to get a steak off a frozen deer. I found a chart in Fanny Farmer for the guidance of housewives in buying beef, and while a deer doesn't seem to be constructed exactly like a cow, still we can get the general hang of the thing from the chart. So we always take Fanny to the woodshed with us when we're going to butcher. Then we lower the corpse from where we've hoisted it to the peak of the roof, and lay it across the chopping block. By using an axe, the buck saw and once in a while the two-man cross-cut, we manage to worry off what will pass as a roast or a steak or a collection of chops.

If we get the deer early in the season before it's cold enough to freeze it, the problem of keeping it is complicated considerably. The liver and heart are eaten first, by me. Ralph won't eat what he inelegantly calls "guts." Then we save out two or three of the choice cuts to be eaten fresh, and I have to can the rest. The steaks I fry for about a minute, first on one side and then the other, in a good hot spider, so they'll brown. Then I roll each slice in a tight little roll, pack the rolls into jars, semi-seal, and boil the jars in a washboiler full of water for two hours and a half. After the jars are removed from the boiler, I complete the sealing, stand them upside down to cool, scrutinizing them at intervals for tell-tale air bubbles which mean leaks and consequent spoilage, and finally put them away. Later these can be unrolled and broiled or fried as ordinary steaks; but unless they are lightly fried before canning, they'll be nothing more than plain boiled meat.

The tougher cuts, such as the forequarters, I hack up and boil in large kettles. Next day I cut the lean meat from the bones, pack it tightly into pint jars—pints are better for our size family—fill the jars with gravy, partially seal, and go on from there with the same routine as above. This meat can be used in the winter for meat pies, pot roasts, hash, or just plain meat and gravy.

That takes care of the bulk of the deer, but there are still the neck, horns and hoofs to be accounted for, and we're the Thrifty Riches. A live deer, grazing by the riverside, is a beautifully proportioned thing; but the minute that it's dead something happens to its neck. It doubles in length apparently. There's a lot of meat on it, but the meat's no good. It's tough and stringy and can be used for only one thing—mince meat. It makes the best mince meat in the world.

This leaves only the horns and hoofs. No, we don't make our own gelatin. Ralph uses sections of horn for decorating hunting knife handles, and makes gun racks and coat hooks out of the hoofs and thin lower legs. They are bent at the ankle, dried and cured, and driven into holes bored in the walls. We have a dozen or more of them over the house, and they look very nice indeed and are very handy.

And that's that, as far as a deer is concerned.

I always think I'm going to can some partridges, too, but

I never have yet. We don't get very many, and they're so small that it takes several to even make a decent meal. So we never have any left over to can. I've never tried salting fish, either, although it can be done, I guess. We eat them fresh, in season—fried, if they're pan trout, or baked if they are big salmon. Those, and smelts in the spring of the year, are the only kind of fish we get here, except chubs and suckers, which aren't fit to eat. We've never tried eating porcupine, either. We've never had to. We don't kill them, though, even when we find them chewing our houses down. They are edible, and they're the only animal that an unarmed man can kill for food. They're so slow and stupid that they can be clubbed to death if necessary. No woodsman will kill them wantonly. Someday he may be in a spot where a porcupine will save him from starvation. Some states—Montana, for example—have game laws to protect the porcupine, for this very reason.

In Maine, as in all other parts of the world, there's a lot of talk goes around about the excellence of the native country cooking. In Maine, as in all other parts of the world with which I am familiar—not so many, I'll grant you, but enough—this is largely eye-wash. There are a few fine country cooks around here, but most of the food is very undistinguished in character. Most local cooks have two ideas about what to do with food. They either fry it— and I think the steady diet of fried food in Maine accounts largely for the high incidence of chronic indigestion and stomach ulcers—or else they make a chowder out of it. We have a by-word in our family. When confronted with the disposal of almost anything from a dead fish to a pair of worn-out pants, someone is bound to say, "It'd make a nice chowder!" That really isn't stretching the point much, either.

I'm indebted to the local cooks for another expression. That is "smitches and dabs." We have a meal of smitches and dabs about once a week, usually on wash day. This consists of a smitch of this and a dab of that. In other words, that's the meal that cleans up the ice box. It's a family institution by now, and a very useful one. Sometimes these left-overs are just warmed up separately and sometimes they are combined into one dish. You dump some odds and ends of meat, any stray vegetables, a can of beef broth—to make gravy—into a baking dish, top the whole with biscuit dough, bake, and you have a shepherd's pie. Or you put left-over salmon, peas, ham, and a can of mushroom soup into a dish, cover with buttered crumbs, and again bake. I suppose this is some kind of a casserole, but it doesn't really make much difference what it is. It comes under smitches and dabs in our family.

We have Desperation Dishes, too. These are things we eat when we run out of food, for one reason or other. A stand-by, of course, is baked beans, which we have every Saturday night anyhow. In a minute I'm going into the proper baking of beans in detail. It's a subject that deserves attention. Baked beans can be terrible, or they can be swell. In our family Gerrish is the judge. He's a baked bean expert from away-back. If he says after the first forkful, "Your hand slipped a mite this week, didn't it, Louise?", I feel like crawling under the table. But if he says, "You hit it about right this time," my chest swells to the button-bursting point.

Even good baked beans can become tedious. I remember one year when the lake didn't finish freezing and we couldn't get in any supplies, we had them twice a day for ten days. One of these days was Thanksgiving, too. In honor of that day I invented another Desperation Dish. Besides beans, we had in the house a very small can of Vienna sausages and a half a bottle of ketchup. I put a layer of cold baked beans in a baking dish, sprinkled lavishly with ketchup, and arranged half the sausages on it. Then I repeated, ending with a layer of beans, and heated the whole until it bubbled gently. It was really pretty good. We have it now every once in a while, even when we aren't desperate. Desperation Dishes often turn out much better than you'd expect.

Now about the baking of the beans. Baked beans have to be baked. That sounds like a gratuitous restatement of the obvious, but it isn't. Some misguided souls boil beans all day and call the lily-livered result baked beans. I refrain from comment.

We use either New York State or Michigan white beans, because we like them best, although yellow-eyes are very popular, too. I take two generous cups of dry beans, soak over night and put them on to boil early in the morning. When the skins curl off when you blow on them, they've boiled long enough. Then I put in the bottom of the bean pot, or iron kettle with a tight-fitting cover, a six-by-eight-inch square of salt pork, with the rind slashed every quarter of an inch, a quarter of a cup of sugar, half a cup of molasses, a large onion chopped fairly fine, and a heaping teaspoonful of dry mustard. This amount of sugar and molasses may be increased or cut, depending on whether you like your beans sweeter or not so sweet. This is a matter every man has to decide for himself. The beans are dumped in on top of this conglomerate, and enough hot water is added to cover, but only cover. The baking pot should be large enough so there's at least an inch of free-board above the water. Otherwise they'll boil over and smell to high heaven. Cover tightly and put into a medium oven—about 350° is right. They should be in the oven by half past nine in the morning at the latest, and they should stay there until supper time, which in our family is at six.

So far there is no trick in making good baked beans. The trick, if it can be dignified by such a term, lies in the baking, and like a great many trade tricks, it consists only of patience and conscientious care. You have to tend the beans faithfully, adding water whenever the level gets down below the top of the beans, and you have to keep the oven temperature even. If you're lazy, you can put in a lot of water and not have to watch them so closely. But to get the best results, you should add only enough water each time to barely cover the beans. This means that you'll give up all social engagements for the day, as you can't leave the baby for more than half an hour at a time. I think the results are worth it—but then, I haven't anywhere special to go, anyhow. My beans are brown and mealy, and they swim in a thick brown juice. They're good. I always serve them with corn bread, ketchup and pickles.

Another Desperation Dish is Mock Tripe. It is an old home recipe of that almost legendary Norwegian guide, Travis Hoke, and is very useful in disposing of otherwise unusable odds and ends. If you have a fresh salmon you can put its skin in a light brine until you are ready to use it, or the skin of a baked fish, carefully removed, will serve as well. Save the daily leavings of the oatmeal pot and spread them out about a half inch thick to dry. When you have amassed a sufficient quantity and it is covered with a heavy brown crust, season well and wrap in the fish skin. Dredge this with flour and put it in your roasting pan with a small amount of water or milk, cover, and bake at least an hour in a medium oven. The result is truly amazing.

Every cook is supposed to have some short cuts or labor savers that experience has taught her. I ought to have a million, for Lord knows I have learned to cook in a hard school. But I have only a measly little list of discoveries. The first is that an egg beater can be used for a lot of other things than the beating of eggs. I'd almost rather throw my stove away than my egg beater. I use it to take the lumps out of gravy or chocolate cornstarch pudding or cream sauce. When the cereal sinks in a leaden mass to the bottom of the pan, because I didn't have the water boiling briskly, or didn't stir it enough, I beat it up with the egg beater, and it comes out smooth and creamy. I beat mashed potato with it, and squash. I beat anything and everything with an egg beater, and I always put it immediately into a deep pan of cold water to soak. Otherwise all the time it saves will be spent in washing the thing. It's devilish to get clean if it is allowed to dry.

My second little device is a pane of window glass which I put over my open cook book. I'm a messy cook, splashing flour and milk and batter and egg yolk all over the table. If they splash on the book, the pages will stick together and you can't use that recipe again, as I have found to my sorrow. If they splash on the glass, that's all right. Glass washes.

My third and last contribution to the culinary world is a way to crumb fish or croquettes or cutlets or what-have-you easily and quickly. I put my crumbs or flour in a paper bag, drop in the object to be crumbed, close the bag and shake violently. This doesn't sound like much of an invention but it saves an awful lot of mess. When you're through you have nothing to clean up. You just shove the paper bag into the stove and burn up the scanty leavings.

Now I'm probably going to discover that all these things are common practice among cooks everywhere, and that I'm just tagging tardily along behind my brighter sisters.

There are two factors which complicate the cooking situation for me. One is that I never know how many people I am going to have to feed. I always have to allow for at least one more than the family, in case anyone drops in. In the woods the first question you ask anybody, no matter what time of day he arrives, is, "Have you eaten?" This is absolutely obligatory, and the reason is easy to see. A man can't drop into a dog cart for a hamburger or a cup of coffee, if he's hungry. He expects the population to feed him, and in return he expects to feed whoever drops in at his place. It's an understood thing, just as it is understood that in winter, no matter whose house you go into, if they are not at home you immediately look at the fires and add wood if necessary. You do this even if you are a stranger to the householder. It may be serious to let a fire go out. So we feed game wardens and fire wardens and timber cruisers and lost hunters and stray woodsmen and anyone else who happens along, and they tend our fires as required. Once we even fed the census taker, a gentleman whom, by the way, we were very much surprised to see come staggering out of the snowy woods. We'd figured that we would be among the submerged and forgotten one percent, when it came to census taking.

The other difficulty I have to surmount is the kitchen itself. In the country, and even more in the woods, a kitchen is much more than a place to cook. It's the place where people sit, for warmth or sociability, or to do odd jobs. We have the usual kitchen furnishings—straight-backed chairs, table, work bench, sink, ice box, stove and woodbox. We also have a comfortable rocking chair and a pile of books and magazines. Half the time, when I'm cooking, I'm also hurdling over someone's legs, or a dog or cat, or a pile of guns and coats. Or I may have to walk around a landing net that has been left by the stove, or an inner tube that Ralph is patching in the middle of the floor. In all seasons except summer, I have to dodge a line-ful of wool socks, hung up to dry, and skirt two pails of water left by the end of the stove to keep warm for car-starting purposes. Often my pots and pans have to find what space they can around a soldering iron thrust into the firebox and my pot roast is shoved back in the oven to accommodate a pair of newly oiled boots that must be dried.

I used to try to keep the kitchen sacred to legitimate kitchen activities, but I finally gave it up. No matter how often I chased Gerrish and his tackle-mending or Ralph and his car-repairing or Rufus and his fleet of trucks into the living-room, they always insidiously filtered back. Actually there's an advantage to having them right there. If they're in the room they can't very well pretend not to hear me when I start hollering to have my water pails filled or some wood brought in from the woodshed. And I might as well break down at last and admit that I like having them underfoot. The few times that they stayed in the living-room when I sent them there, I felt like a social pariah out in the kitchen all alone with my efficiency.

To augment our larder, we have a vegetable garden, and believe me, please, that's quite a feat when you start, as we did, with a little plot of land which has excellent sun and drainage, but which also has a growth of brush and evergreens all over it, and under that nothing but thin, acid woods soil studded thickly with rocks and boulders and solidly interlaced with a mat of roots. Our garden is splendid now, but it's taken us eight years to get it that way.

The first year was spent in cutting the brush and trees and removing the roots and the worst of the rocks. This was honest-to-God hard labor, particularly as we didn't have the right equipment for it. Ralph and Gerrish and I have spent a whole day getting out a boulder that weighed more than the three of us put together. The first step, always, was to trench around the thing so we could get at it, and Ralph and Gerrish did this. Then they collected an assortment of chains, levers, and cant dogs, and summoned me. My part consisted solely of lending my weight on the end of a twenty-foot beam that served as a pry, or dodging around the edges of the operation with an armful of blocks of assorted sizes. "Over here! Over here!" Ralph and Gerrish would shout in chorus, their faces red and strained with lifting. "For God's sake, stick a block under her before—" I'd thrust a block in to hold what they'd gained and they'd relax, panting and perspiring, to get their breaths and plan the next step. The general modus operandi was to lift the boulder up with levers to ground level, building a scaffolding of blocks under her as she came—I'm catching this "she" habit, too—and then roll her across an extremely precarious bridge of planks to solid earth. Then we worried her onto a stone-drag and dragged her away behind our then current work car, the old twelve-cylinder Packard. Frequently, with only six inches to go before we could roll her out, the entire scaffolding would collapse and drop the boulder back to the bottom of the pit—a perfectly maddening thing to have happen. I do believe in the malevolence of the inanimate, and of all inanimate objects, stones are the most malevolent. In the first place the stones in our section lack symmetry, so if you apply pressure where you think it will do the most good, they are just as apt to roll to the left onto your foot, as to the right where you plan to have them roll. In the second place, they are ponderous, and once they start rolling, you can't stop them. All you can do is jump clear and start swearing. In the third place—and this to my mind is the worst of all—after they have flopped the wrong way and have ruined an entire morning's work, they just lie there. There's something about the bland face of a stone, lying in the middle of a pile of wrecked scaffolding at the bottom of a hole, that makes you want to throw yourself face down on the ground and kick and scream.

We got enough rocks and roots out of the ground that first year so that we could plant a few things in the cleared spaces. But we didn't get them all out, by any means, and haven't even yet, in spite of a yearly session with them. We put in peas and string beans and carrots and beets and corn. Ralph and I were no gardeners but Gerrish had had a garden in one place or another ever since he wore diapers, so in most things we bowed to his superior wisdom. But when it came to corn, he and Ralph disagreed. Ralph contended that the growing season as far north and as high as we are is too short to allow corn to reach maturity, and that it should be started in the house and transplanted into the garden as soon as the weather was warm enough. Gerrish announced categorically that one did not transplant corn. It wouldn't grow, and even if it did, there was no point to it. The season was plenty long enough.

They argued two or three days about this, and then they decided that they'd divide the corn patch, and each would take half to cultivate as he saw fit. Ralph made himself some nice little starting flats, filled them with dirt, and started his corn in the house. Gerrish put his corn away in a drawer and forgot about it until the ground warmed up.

Ralph's corn came up very nicely and he tended it as if it were black orchids. On the same day that Gerrish put his seed into the ground, Ralph transplanted his thriving little shoots. They looked very green and tender and brave out there in the cold world, and he covered them carefully every night, to guard them against a spring frost. They didn't grow very much at first. I suppose they were getting themselves acclimated. After about a week, Gerrish's corn started to come up, and that's where the double-dealing entered the picture.

Gerrish came home from fishing one evening with a whole string of chub. Nobody eats them, so I couldn't imagine why he had saved them, or why he was hiding them so carefully under the back steps. He didn't mind telling me, after swearing me to secrecy. He'd remembered that the Indians used to plant their corn over dead fish, for fertilizer, and he was going to tunnel into his corn hills and put dead chub where they'd do the most good. He'd show Ralph how to raise corn.

Well, a promise is a promise, I know, and I usually try to keep mine. But this was supposed to be a controlled experiment, and I've been brought up to respect the scientific attitude. I couldn't let that go. I told Ralph—swearing him to secrecy, of course—and that night he went chub fishing, with some success. Thereafter the two of them spent a lot of time sneaking fish corpses into the garden and burying them under their respective corn hills. I used to help them both, which was probably traitorous of me, but it afforded me a lot of fun.

We had corn off both sides of the patch on the very same day, and there was nothing to distinguish the one from the other. Now we plant our corn by the Gerrish system. It's a lot easier.

Oh, the troubles we had that first year! No sooner had our vegetables broken ground than the deer started coming in at night and eating the plants. We decided at once that we had to fence the garden, but it was going to take a little time to get the fencing material in from the Outside. In the meantime something had to be done. For a while we worked days cutting and setting fence posts, and sat up nights with a shot gun. But you can't keep that up forever. Then the game warden told us to spread some blood meal around. This is a packing house product that is used primarily for fertilizer. The smell of blood is supposed to frighten the deer away. It didn't, though. On the contrary, I think it attracted them. Then someone told us that if we made a little tent in the garden and kept a lighted lantern in it all night, the deer would keep their distance. The tent material had to be thin, so the light would glow through, and the color had to be changed often, so the deer wouldn't acquire the contempt bred by familiarity. We tried that—we'd have tried anything—and rather surprisingly it worked. At least, it worked for a week. Then one morning we went into the garden and found the tracks of a dozen deer, all converging on our little tent. Apparently they'd held a meeting and decided on a mass investigation. They hadn't touched any of the vegetables, though. I guess they were too intrigued with the light to bother about anything else.

That very afternoon the wire for the fence came, and next morning we put it onto the posts we'd set so fast that it smoked. And that was that.

That wasn't the woodchucks, though, that crawled through the mesh of the wire. We had to set traps for them. *That* wasn't the heavy rain, either, that gullied out the slope of the garden and washed out half the crop. We had to terrace the whole slope, the next year, to prevent a recurrence. But neither fence nor traps nor terracing was any answer to our basic problem, the problem of the soil. It's taken us all these years to lick its thinness and acidity and infertility. We've spaded in tons of manure which we've hauled from Miller's and various lumber camp stables, to add humus and give body to the soil. We've bought hundreds of pounds of lime and raked it in, to counteract the acidity which is always a characteristic of forest mold. We've scattered hundreds of pounds of commercial balanced fertilizers, too. What we've accomplished, really, is to make arable earth out of the rubble heaps of sand and clay and gravel that the great glaciers dumped here ages and ages ago. It may not be a becoming attitude, but all the same, we do point with pride to our vegetable garden. I consider that my skill with a spading fork is just as much a part of my housekeeping ability as is my urban sister's nose for a bargain in canned goods. They both result in putting better, cheaper vegetables on the family table.

The clothing problem causes me very little concern. One of the reasons I like to live here is that I don't have to bother to try to be a snappy number. I couldn't, anyway, no matter where I lived; but in civilization I'd at least have to make the effort, in fairness to Ralph and Rufus. I couldn't humiliate them by putting them in the position of having to answer, when someone asked, "Who's that funny-looking woman?"—"Oh, that's my wife" or "my mother," as the case might be. And, boy! would I be miserable! I can't stand having things tight around my waist or neck or wrists, and you can't be stylish unless you have your clothes anchored in a few places, at least. My idea of an ideal costume is slacks worn low on the hip bones, and a cotton shirt with the sleeves rolled up and the neck band unbuttoned. I can wear that here. I look thoroughly sloppy, but here it doesn't matter. Ralph and Rufus love me—I hope—for my good nature. There wouldn't be even that about me to love if I had to try to be chic.

This is what my entire wardrobe consists of at the moment.

- 1 pair of blue denim pants
- 1 pair of canvas pants (my garden, fishing, and berry-ing pants)
- 1 pair wool whipcord jodhpurs (Ralph hates them)
- 1 pair wool ski pants
- 3 cotton shirts (the 59¢ variety)
- 3 wool shirts
- 4 pairs of cotton ankle socks (17¢ a pair)
- 3 pairs of wool ski socks (I made them myself—39¢ each, but worth a lot more)
- 2 sweaters

1 wool jacket
1 denim jacket
1 bathing suit and cap
3 changes of underwear and nightclothes
1 very old bathrobe
1 wool bonnet and mittens to match
3 pairs of 79¢ sneakers
1 pair of leather moccasins
1 large kerchief, to use as hat, scarf, berry pail, dog
   leash, depending on the circumstances.

I did have a belt, but I never wore it, so I gave it to
Gerrish. And I have a .22 revolver, but I don't suppose
that comes under wardrobe, really, even here. I've also got
a tweed suit and a pair of silk stockings and some shoes in
case I have to go Outside in a hurry; but it's been a long
time since I've even looked at them. They've probably
perished of dry rot by now. The last time I had to go out
in a hurry was when Kyak became suddenly and terrify-
ingly ill and needed to be taken at once to the veterinary.
It was at night and raining pitchforks, and I had no time
or inclination to dress up. I wore my fishing pants and
Gerrish's raincoat, which was just as well. The only people
besides Ralph that I saw were Larry Parsons and the vet.
I didn't really see Larry. He was running the boat, but it
was so dark and foggy that he had to make the trip down
the lake by compass, and all I could distinguish of him
was a dark shadow up in the bow and a faint blur of features when he inhaled on his cigarette or turned the flashlight onto the compass. And later in the car it was almost
as dark. The vet was too much interested in Kyak's symptoms to bother about what I had on. I'm sure the next time

an emergency arises, the conditions will be duplicated. So I don't have to worry about my Going Out Clothes.

Ralph's wardrobe is about like mine, except he has gumboots for winter and work shoes for summer and a canvas parka and a mackinaw. He prefers canvas pants the whole year through and refuses to have riding or ski pants. Rufus wears overalls and cotton shirts, or sun suits, for summer, and ski pants and sweaters in the winter. Once when he was very little I did buy him a little wash suit, with shorts and frilled shirt. He looked perfectly adorable in it the one time he had it on. But he and his father and Gerrish all pronounced it sissy, and I could never get him to wear it again. Sally is the best-dressed member of the family. She goes Out to school, so she has to have the usual quota of dresses, presentable shoes, and street coats. At her age, too, these things would matter, I suppose, even if she never went Outside.

There are a few general aspects of the clothes situation that interest me very much. One of them is the growth of ski pants as a national institution. When I was a child, ski pants were absolutely unknown in this country. I realize that they were introduced along with the vogue for winter sports, and that is not surprising. What surprises me is their acceptance by non-skiers of all ages. It has apparently reached the point where everyone owns a pair of ski pants, just as everyone owns a skirt or a pair of trousers. This really is a tribute to the practicability of the garment. People in general don't own baseball caps or football pants. The most non-athletic types own ski pants.

Another thing that interests me is the false notion held by almost all city people that you can get wonderful bargains in the country. Ralph, for example, owns a very handsome red-and-black-checked shirt, made of wool material so thin it tailors marvellously. He calls it his sporting shirt, and wears it only on special occasions. Occasions special enough for the sporting shirt usually involve people from the city, and before long someone will get up the courage to ask, *"Where* did you get that shirt and how much did you pay for it? I want one like it."

The answer is, "My sister-in-law gave it to me for my birthday and she got it at Jordan Marsh's in Boston and I've no idea what she paid for it."

The let-down is always tremendous. "Oh, I hoped you were going to say that you got it at some cross-roads country store for two dollars. You always hear about the wonderful things that people pick up back in the sticks for practically nothing—"

Yes, you do. But there aren't any wonderful things in country stores, for any amount of money. The stock in a country store consists of cheap clothes, cheap food, cheap everything. Usually they cost more than the same article in the city. Cheap things are all that country people can ordinarily afford. If you want marvellous things, you have to go to the luxury trade stores in cities, and pay accordingly. You can't get something for nothing, even in the country. I buy homespun yarn from various farmers' wives around on the Outside, and I pay very little for it. It's all wool, from sheep reared on the place. That sounds like one of those marvellous bargains; but it isn't. It's worth exactly what I pay for it. It's harsh, and it's unevenly spun, and there are only two colors—gray and a tan mixture. For my purpose—work socks and mittens—it's quite all right. But when I want to make a sweater, or a nice pair of socks for

Rufus, Kyak, and Ralph.

Ralph, I send away to the Mail Order for some decent yarn.

The truth of the matter is that in spite of the literary convention of bursting barns, overflowing larders, and cellars crammed with luscious preserves and delicious smoked hams, in spite of the accepted version of the countryman as being clad in the warmest and best of wools, the thickest and softest of leathers, and the deepest and darkest of furs, country people are clothed much more shoddily and poorly than city people, class for class. In short, the country standard of living is very much lower than the city standard. This is actually not as hard on country people as it would seem to be. You don't mind cheap clothes if everyone else is wearing clothes just as cheap. There are other things that contribute to health besides a balanced diet. There are fresh air and sunlight and lack of nervous tension. I think, probably, whether you're better off in the country or in the city depends, in the final analysis, on where you'd rather be. You're best off where you're the happiest.

As I have said before, we do all our purchasing from the Mail Order—more formally, from Sears, Roebuck and Montgomery Ward. Having been brought up in a medium-sized town within easy reach of Boston, I never had a chance to become familiar with the great American institution of the Mail Order until I came to live in the woods. Now, I couldn't get along without it. It's wonderful as a source of supply, and their catalogs are a fascinating source of entertainment. We sit by the hour looking at the illustrations and reading the descriptions of the thousands of items in the enormous twice-yearly catalogs, and we buy anything from motor parts to ankle socks from

Sears' or Ward's. If, for my sins, I ever have to live at the corner of 42nd and Broadway, I shall still trade with the Mail Order. I'm completely wedded to the idea.

Everybody in this country is thoroughly familiar with the Mail Order. I show up at Middle in a new pair of slacks, and Alice Miller says, "Oh, those are those Ward's slacks. A dollar ninety-eight. I was thinking about getting me some, only in brown." Or somebody comes in from Upton sporting a new hunting shirt, and I can put the price tag and percentage of wool on it with the accuracy of a purchasing agent. Fifty percent wool, and two seventy-five in the big catalog; but he paid only two forty-nine for it. They had them on sale in the latest flyer. There are no secrets between Mail Order devotees.

I never realized how revealing a filled-in order blank can be until one day I happened on the sample order blank in the back of the Sears catalog. This is a facsimile of an order, made out in full, for the guidance of the customer in making out his own order. Very likely the name and address at the top of the blank are fictitious, but the order itself looks genuine. I read it through carefully, and I felt at once that I knew the woman who made it out as well as I know myself.

The goods were to be sent to John T. Jones, R.F.D. No. 1, Tipton, Iowa, but Johnny Jones didn't make out the order. Mrs. Jones did that. She hadn't been married very long, I think, and she didn't have very much money to spend. But she had ideas. She wanted her house to be nice. She lived in the country in Iowa, but she didn't want to let herself go. She wanted to look smart like the town girls. I know just how she conned the catalog night after night, between finishing the supper dishes and going to bed, to be sure she was getting the best possible value for her money. She made a lot of selections and jotted them down —the names of the articles and the prices—on an old envelope, before she made her final choices. I know, because I have done the same thing. She had only thirty dollars to spend. I know that, because the order came to $29.42. That's just about as close as you can come to a specified sum.

I know that this order was important to her, because it is written so carefully and neatly in ink. The penmanship is obviously not her note-to-the-milkman hand. It's her very best penmanship, stiff and careful, with the t's crossed accurately. That's the way I write when I make out an order to Sears' or Ward's. That's the only time I do write that way.

This is what she bought. Four yards of rose-printed chintz, a dusty rose chenille bedspread, and a pair of dusty rose curtains. You see? She was fixing up a bedroom, with spread, curtains, and dressing table to match. Probably it was for the spare room; she'd at last saved enough to redecorate it as a real guest room. None of the articles is the best grade—that I remembered from my own perusals of the catalog. But they're the best she could afford. She wanted her house to be nice.

Then she bought three pairs of flag-red ankle socks— that's how I know she must be young, and therefore newly married—and a green suit, Cat. No. 55H7186, which cost $15.50. I remembered Cat. No. 55H7186. It's a nice suit, very young and dashing. She hesitated a long time before she spent that much money on a suit, I know, but in the end she remembered how proud of her Johnny always acted when he took her to the movies Saturday night before they were married. In the end she sacrificed I don't know what—a two-quart double boiler, perhaps, or an extra pair of sheets—to keep him acting that way.

The last item was a Craftsman hammer, for ninety-eight cents. That was for Johnny. She had a little over a dollar left, and he'd been fussing about that old hammer with the loose head out in the shed— Oh, I know Mrs. John T. Jones of Tipton, Iowa. Perhaps she is just someone dreamed up in the advertising department of Sears' Chicago office! But she's me, too, and a million other women like me, scattered from here to the Rio Grande, who do their shopping through the magic of the Mail Order.

All my life I've had a very clear idea of the kind of living-room I'd like to have. It's the living-room so often described in English novels or novels of country life among the gentlefolk in Virginia or the Berkshires. Everybody knows the room well, with its wide windows, its books and flowers and faded chintz, its open fire and comfortable shabby chairs and sleeping dogs. It sounds attractive and comfortable. It's comfortable, all right, but not necessarily as attractive as it's made out to be. I know. That's the kind of a living-room we have in the summer house.

The trouble with faded chintz, let me tell you, is that instead of looking soft and old and precious, it looks like chintz that should have been replaced two years ago. The trouble with the dogs is that instead of lying in front of the fire and lending atmosphere, they lie in the middle of the floor where you fall over them. Or else they lie in the shabby chairs and look so hurt when you try to oust them that you can't bear it, and you'd almost sit on the floor yourself rather than cause them pain. The trouble with the open fire is that it throws embers onto the rug—a screen holds in the embers, but holds in the heat, too—so that eventually you decide to take up the rug altogether and have a bare floor—unless you've already taken it up because it's too hard to keep clean, what with the men-folks of your family, and the dogs and cats, tracking in mud, sawdust and snow. There's nothing the matter with the flowers and the books and there's nothing the matter with the shabby chairs, if you can accept them as shabby chairs and don't try to make something interesting out of them. BUT —and this is never taken into consideration in the novels— if you're the kind of weak-minded person who will put up with faded chintz and dogs in shabby chairs in the first place, you're too weak-minded to put your foot down there. You allow the corners of this interesting room to become jammed with fishing tackle and guns; the table and mantle are soon buried under a mound of fly-tying material, magazines, odd pieces of rock, and work gloves; the floor is littered with toys and tools; and several pairs of boots for all types of weather are parked at the end of the couch. In short, the place is a mess. The only thing that can be said for it is that there is nothing in it that can be hurt by the roughest usage. It's a room you can let yourself go in, for what that's worth. It's a room where you can put your feet up and relax.

That's the kind of a home Ralph and I have made for ourselves in the backwoods, and that's the kind of marriage we've managed, together, to make, too. There are drawbacks to living off the beaten track, but there is one thing that more than offsets any number of drawbacks: if you can stand this life at all, your marriage has a much greater chance of success than it would have anywhere else. I believe that a great many marriages fail because there is no true dependence between the partners thereof. Somehow, when a well-dressed, well-fed, sleek and contented male says to me—and there have been such occasions in my palmy youth, believe it or not—"I need you!", I just can't quite believe it, much as I'd like to. It's nice to hear, but it's silly. When, however, Ralph comes into the house with the sleeve of his shirt torn and blood dripping from a gash on his arm, and shouts at the top of his lungs, "Damn it, where are you? I need you!", he's obviously telling the truth. He may be interrupting me in the middle of something that I don't want to leave, but that doesn't make any difference. He does need me, and he needs me right then. There isn't any doctor he can go to to tie him up. There isn't any restaurant where he can get his meals, or any laundry to wash his shirts. I'm necessary to him; and by the same token, he's necessary to me. It's a terribly trite thing to say, I know, but most of us have to be needed to be happy.

Is it, then, necessary to live the hard way, just so you can feel you are needed? For me, yes, it is. I know myself too well to be able to delude myself that my wit or my beauty or my wisdom or my intelligence could ever become indispensable to anyone. I have to have things demonstrated in material terms that I can understand. And I have found this to be true: that the material makes a very good and solid foundation for a dependence that cannot be defined, an inter-dependence of mind and spirit which we might never have known had we not first had to depend on each other for the tangible, demonstrable things.

We've managed to make a good marriage. This I say with all humility. It's a marriage in which there is nothing that can be hurt by the roughest usage. It's a marriage that you can let yourself go in, a marriage in which you can put up your feet and relax.

V

"Aren't the Children a Problem?"

THE TRUE YANKEE ANSWER TO THE QUESTION, "AREN'T THE children a problem?" is, of course, another question: "Aren't children always a problem, no matter where you live?" If they aren't, I've wasted a lot of time in my civilized past listening to the bridge table chat of the young mothers of my acquaintanceship. Unless my memory plays me false, parenthood anywhere from the heart of Texas to the middle of Manhattan is one long coping with maladjusted personalities, crooked teeth, allergies to goose feathers, and lamentable traits inherited from the other side of the family. In short, certainly children are a problem, only in the woods the details of the problem aren't quite the same as they are on the Outside.

The problem starts with getting them born. Of course, with Sally, I skipped this. She's my step-child, and sprang into my life, full-panoplied, as it were, at the age of twelve. I skipped not only the actual giving birth, but also the house-breaking and habit-forming. This advantage is offset to an extent by the fact that I'm responsible for her not only to her father and my own conscience, as I am with

Rufus, but also to her mother as well—no mean responsibility. It would be bad enough to have something happen to your own child. It would be almost impossible to have to go to another woman and say, "So sorry, but I let your daughter get drowned." That's the chief reason that the first thing I did about Sally when I took her over was to insist that she learn to swim. All in all, though, I would say that I came by Sally in the easy way.

Rufus I got the hard way, on the 18th of December at 2.55 A.M., with the thermometer down to 10° above zero. That's a night I won't forget in a hurry. Neither will Ralph, I imagine. Ralph has always been the type that, if he heard it rumored that the wife of one of his friends was going to have a baby eight months from date, took to crossing the street and raising his hat politely from the opposite sidewalk, when he met her. He was taking no chances of having to ride in a taxi with her to the hospital. The mere thought caused him to break out in a cold sweat. Well, the night Rufus was born he didn't have any time to worry about what might happen in a taxi. He was much too busy coping, single handed, with what was happening right then and there. In spite of the temperature, though, he was doing his quota of sweating. I can see him now, with a wool cap pulled down over his ears, his mackinaw collar turned up to meet it, and his mittens on, reading by lantern light a little book called, "If Baby Comes Ahead of the Doctor." Perspiration was running down his face. You see, he knew the doctor couldn't possibly get there for ten hours or more.

Nothing is more tiresome than the details of some other woman's pregnancy, but just bear with me for a minute. I've been wanting to say this for a long time. I don't believe most women need be miserable at all. There are two simple preventive measures to take. First, they can stop regarding themselves as being for the period, interesting and unique and fragile, and treating themselves like rare porcelain. It's very bad for them. No wonder they feel rotten. A coal heaver would feel rotten too, if he kept telling himself that he ought to on general principles. And second, they can just not listen to their married friends' and maiden aunts' tales of the terrible things that may happen to them. Some of the things that otherwise sensible women tell prospective mothers are enough to frighten the wits out of anyone. They won't let you remember that these ghoulish tales are the exceptions and that most babies are born with some discomfort, it's true, but not much else. Personally, I'd almost rather have a baby any day than go to the dentist. My friends tell me that this is just because I was lucky. I think I made my own luck. I felt swell, so why should I alter my normal behavior and curtail my normal activities? And—this I will admit was just plain luck —I was so situated that there were no married friends and maiden aunts to scare the pants off me. Result: I had a very pleasant pregnancy, thank you.

End of Lecture on Prenatal Care, by Mrs. Rich. Thanks for listening.

I was supposed to go out to Rumford to have Rufus; but then he wasn't supposed to be born until the first of the year. The idea was that I would stay in over Christmas, and then in a leisurely way, betake myself to the hospital to wait the necessary week or ten days. Consequently we hadn't moved out of the summer house which is without heat upstairs. Ralph was going to move the things in my absence. In the meantime I pursued my program of

"Business as Usual," and the usual business of a lovely day such as the 17th of December turned out to be, was sliding on the Pond. I never saw such a beautiful winter day. It was warm and sunny, and the ground was covered with a light fluff of snow, which was blue in the shadows, and gold in the sun, and faint rose and purple on the distant hills. On the Pond it had blown into tightly packed patches which were white, as snow is supposed to be, against the sky-reflecting deep blue of the glare ice. We'd started to go to Middle Dam, but when we saw the Pond, we went there instead. The sliding was perfect. We could run on the snow islands and slide across the intervening spaces of ice to more snow. Cookie went with us—she was alive at the time, Kyak's mother—and she had a lovely time, too, racing and barking and falling down and scrambling to her feet. We all fell down dozens of times before we completed the mile circuit of the Lamonts' island, which may have had something to do with Rufus' premature arrival. I don't know. I felt quite all right.

All I know is that I woke up in the middle of the night, out of a sound sleep, with a stomach-ache. Only it wasn't a stomach-ache. It was an emergency, and there were no lights on the Ford, and I didn't have a bag packed. I woke Ralph up, and he went down to telephone the Millers and, of course, woke them up, while I wandered around with an old pair of slippers in one hand and a cake of soap in the other. I couldn't seem to think where I'd put my suitcase or what I should put into it. Pretty soon it became obvious that it didn't matter. I got back into bed just as Ralph came up with the information that the Millers' Ford had no lights either, and since it was pitch black outdoors we wouldn't be going anywhere. This didn't upset me as much as it would have fifteen minutes before. I'd already come to the same conclusion but for an entirely different reason.

I don't want to give the impression that I was calm and unruffled through this whole proceeding. I wasn't. But I took one look at Ralph's face and saw that he was ten times as alarmed as I was. I'd never seen him really alarmed before, and it was the best thing in the world that could have happened to me. I suddenly felt very brave and confident. I remembered that lots of babies are born without benefit of the medical profession, and that the best thing in a crisis is to keep busy. I was busy enough myself. All I had to do was to give Ralph something to occupy his mind.

"You'd better heat up a lot of water," I said. I didn't know quite what for, but I remembered that in books people always heat water under similar circumstances.

He went away and I could hear him rattling away down in the kitchen. By and by he came back and said that he wanted a nice wool blanket to warm over the stove before he put it in the laundry basket. "Got to have some place to park the kid," he explained, and I stopped worrying about him. He was functioning again, that was plain. I told him where to find the blanket, in between pains, and he went away again. When he came back, five minutes later, he was a father.

Usually a father has no immediate responsibilities toward his new off-spring aside from running up to the hospital once a day for a viewing—and of course paying the hospital bill. Ralph's responsibilities, on the contrary, were immediate and pressing. There was the little matter of the umbilical cord to be cut and tied, first of all.

"And don't you wash new babies?" I asked.

"Nope. You grease them." I don't know to this day how he came by this piece of knowledge, but he was right. Perhaps he read it in the *Reader's Digest*. That's where much of our information originates. He folded his new son in a bath towel and went away with him, while I lay in bed and worried. What did he know about greasing babies and tying cords? The new baby was crying, too, a little but furious bellow. I could hear him from away upstairs. What was his father doing to him? Or wait a minute—you were supposed only to worry, weren't you, if they didn't cry. So probably it was all right. It was criminal, I decided, for a grown woman to arrive at motherhood knowing as little about the whole thing as I did. By and by Ralph came back.

"Did you get him greased all right?" I asked anxiously.

He looked offended. "Certainly I did. I should hope, after all the pistons I've oiled in my lifetime—" Pistons, mind you!

"What did you use?" I asked, horrified, "Motor oil?"

"Olive oil, naturally."

"Where did you get it? We haven't any olive oil."

"I've got a can. I use it to make fly-dope out of."

Well, why not, after all? If early experience molds a child's life, I could see from where I lay that I was going to be the mother of another mechanic and fly-fisherman.

"He's all right and he's all there," Ralph went on. "Fingernails, toenails, hair, everything. I went over him carefully. And, my God! is he homely!" He threw out his chest. "I never did like pretty men, anyway," he added complacently. "He's got a grip like a wrestler, and Cookie likes him, so I guess he'll get along all right. And say. What am I supposed to do with all that hot water?"

Oh, yes. The hot water. Well— "Why don't you make some coffee?" Suddenly I was starved. "Make me a sandwich, too—a ham sandwich with a lot of mustard."

Alice Miller came down in the morning, as soon as it was light. Lying in bed, I could hear her laughing down in the kitchen. She laughed all the way upstairs. "What do you suppose Ralph used to tie his cord with?" she demanded before she was halfway into the room. "A piece of rope! That poor little kid! The knot's bigger than he is. I guess I'll call the doctor in Rumford when I get home and tell him there's no need of his coming way in here. No sense in spending twenty dollars for nothing—"

And so Rufus missed his chance of having a doctor look him over. I guess it didn't do any harm. He's never seen a doctor from that day to this, except in a purely social capacity.

I frequently read in magazines articles which begin:—
DO YOU REALIZE—

That blank percent of the homes in America have no running water?

That blank percent have no bathrooms?

That blank percent of our children are born with no doctor in attendance?

These appalling figures show that the huge army of the underprivileged—

I cluck my tongue, suitably appalled for a moment until true realization hits me between the eyes. "My God," I think, and then I am truly appalled. "That's *us* they're talking about! Why—*we're* the underprivileged! Why—Why—"

But are we? I'm not stupid enough to recommend that all, or even any, children be born with only their fathers in attendance. But because it happened to Rufus doesn't make him underprivileged. In fact, I would say he was especially privileged—not in that he was held up by the heels and oiled with piston-oiling technique, but because from that moment on, his father has had a very special feeling for him. All normal fathers love their children, we will assume. They all feel a responsibility toward them. But—and I think I am not being merely sentimental when I say this—that early, primitive responsibility that devolved upon Ralph toward Rufus left its mark. Fatherhood is necessarily a less intimate relationship—physically at least—than motherhood; but Ralph can't think of himself only as the guy who buys Rufus' food and clothes and administers spankings. Fundamentally he is always the guy who tied his cord and greased him, when there was no one else to do it. That is something I wouldn't want Rufus deprived of, for all the hospital treatment in the world.

Nor can I bring myself to believe that our children are hopelessly handicapped because they take baths in washtubs in front of the kitchen range, read by the light of kerosene lamps, and sleep in unheated bedrooms. We'll give them a bathroom and steam heat and electric lights when we get the house rebuilt; but perhaps we'll be making a mistake. Soft living isn't important to them now, because it never has been. They're never going to be miserable because of physical inconveniences. Perhaps the best thing we can give them in a world where the possession of material things becomes more and more precarious, in a world of marching armies and destruction-dealing skies, is a tough-fibered indifference to heat and cold and comfort and discomfort.

What can we give our children then, that won't be outmoded, that won't, under some eventuality that we can't foresee, prove to be a handicap to them? I don't know the answer to that one. Once I would have said "Ideas and Ideals." But I grew up in the years after the first World War, when perpetual peace was supposed to be the easily attainable ideal. I was trained in that ideal, and I believed in it with all the sincerity of which I was capable. Perhaps it is still attainable—but if it is, it will be by some different means than those I was taught to trust in. I don't want my child ever to feel as lost in the world as I do right now; nor do I want to inculcate in him the doctrine of force and aggression at no matter what sacrifice of the rights of others.

We can give him a happy childhood to remember, a way of life that he will be willing to die to protect, if the need arises. That sounds like a grim and Spartan gift to a little boy, but it's not as dangerous a gift as the belief in pacifism and universal well-wishing to which my generation was exposed. I don't want to raise my son to be a soldier—but if he has to be one, I want him to be a good and capable one. I want him to know what he's fighting for—and Freedom and Democracy won't mean a thing to him, unless they are all tied up with memories of things that he has loved ever since he can remember—things like the sound of the river, and the way Kyak lies and dreams in front of the open fire on a crisp autumn evening, and the picnics we've held at Smooth Ledge. The name of his country won't be worth fighting for, unless he can remember from experience that his country is the place, not of equal opportunity, not of universal suffrage, not of any of those lofty conceptions so far above a little boy's ability to comprehend, but the place where he walked with his father down a woods road one evening and saw a doe and twin fawns; or the place where he came in from playing in the snow and found the kitchen warm and fragrant and his mother making pop-corn balls.

That's all that I can give him; that's all that I dare to try to give him—something that he will love enough to want to preserve it for himself and others against whatever danger may threaten from whatever quarter, and the toughness and courage with which to fight for it. To bring him up untouched by war, insofar as is possible in a world where no one is completely unaffected by war today, is about the only contribution that I know how to make for the future.

Even here I am working in the dark. He won't remember the things I expect him to remember. I don't remember from my own childhood the important things that happened; but I can recall a hole in the ground among the roots of a maple tree that grew in front of our house. It was a small hole, about as big as a pint measure, but there was something about it. It was moist and smelled of earth and water when I lay on my stomach and thrust my four-year-old face into it. It was everything that was mysterious and marvellous to me then, and somehow it still is. I couldn't have explained to anyone then what that little hole in the ground meant to me, and I still can't. But the memory of it makes me wonder what Rufus is carrying around in his head that he can't share, and never will be able to share, but which will affect him. Sometimes I get a clue. Sometimes I see him lay his hand on a rock with a special gesture, or I find a piece of broken china that he has carefully hidden away, or I hear him talking to himself about a rabbit. But since I, myself, loath nothing quite so much as having someone prying into my thoughts and feelings, there is nothing I can do but wonder.

I wonder, too, if all the houses he ever reads about in books will be this house, just as all the houses I read about are in the end the house in which I grew up. It was a low, white, old-fashioned house, and some of the houses in books are huge mansions. But no matter how carefully the author explains the arrangement of the rooms, no matter if he goes to the trouble of drawing a floor plan, when his characters go from the drawing-room down long corridors into the dining hall, in my mind's eye they pass from our little living-room through a door to the left directly into the low square room where we ate. I only hope that Rufus won't spend his life picturing lords and ladies taking baths in the middle of the kitchen.

Of course the biggest problem we encounter in bringing up our children in the woods is their formal education. They do have to go to school. Even if there weren't laws requiring their attendance, even if we were quite capable —which we aren't—of giving them a solid foundation in the three R's, we would still have to send them. One of the most important parts of education is learning to get along with other people, and we just can't supply a society of their peers for them to rub up against. Rufus has seen so few children of his own age that he has no idea how to act with them. He lets them walk all over him, he's so happy to be with them. So we'll shortly have to ship him out to his grandmother's where he will learn among other things, I hope, to stand up for his rights. It's going to be rather a painful experience, so the sooner he gets it over with the better.

I certainly hope the school authorities don't start out by giving him an Intelligence Test before he's learned the ropes. If they do, his I.Q. will be about 50. (I don't believe in I.Q's. anyhow. My own is up in the near-genius group, and nobody knows better than I the abysmal depths of dumbness I can plumb. I just happen to have a very good memory for the sort of things they ask on Intelligence Tests.) But poor Rufus! All the questions dealing with such common things as running water, electric lights, hens, and railroad trains will leave him completely in the dark, and they don't ask how to tell a fox track from a dog track —a difficult thing that he can do easily—or how to use a birch hook, or how to employ a cant dog to its utmost efficiency. I suppose that is what the textbooks dismiss blandly as Feeble-mindedness by Deprivation.

Sally's education has been somewhat peculiar. The first twelve years of her life she lived in Southern Illinois and attended school regularly. Then she came with us for a while. Just as she was getting used to our peculiar mode of life, her mother sent for her to come to Liechtenstein— a small country between Switzerland and Austria, in case you didn't know—and she spent two years there and in the West Indies. She didn't go to school at all, but she was being educated, nonetheless. She learned, among other things, not to giggle when a Count kissed her hand, no matter how much it tickled, how to get through the customs with the least trouble, how to wear clothes, and how to order a meal in German. Then came the War, and Sally came back to us. She goes to school in Upton now, boarding with the Allens, who are among Ralph's oldest friends. She certainly ought to be adaptable. She's had a varied

enough experience. I think that she is. When she was
fifteen, her birthday party was held in the bar of a hotel
in Haiti, closed to the public for the occasion. When she
was sixteen, her birthday party was held in Allens' kitchen
—open to the public for the occasion, I judge. Apparently
everyone in town attended. As far as I can tell, she enjoyed both parties equally.

The school in Upton is a two-room school, and I'd forgotten that such a thing existed. If I'd remembered it, I
would have delivered a speech beginning, "Well, in this
day and age, with all the fine schools available, no child
of mine—"; I would have been wrong. Sally learns as much,
if not more, in what is known as the Upstairs Room, where
Grades 7 to 10 inclusive sit under one teacher, as she could
possibly learn in the biggest and best-equipped school in
the country. Her Mr. Flanders is a very good teacher. The
excellence of a teacher has nothing at all to do with his
background, or the amount of salary he is paid, or anything else except his own personality and inherent bent.
A good teacher is born, I am convinced, and his presence
would make a good school out of a woodshed.

But Sally gets more than book learning out of going to
school in Upton. She gets, for the first time in her life, the
sense of being a member in a community. This is a thing
more easily acquired in a small town than in a large one,
and it's very important to feel, I believe, that you are a
member of a whole. There's time enough, later, to be an
individual. Later, when she gets out into the world, she
will be "different" because she went to a rural school. It
will make a good story. It will set her apart. We all want
something to set us apart from the rest, to make us interest

ing. It doesn't have to be very much. I, myself, derive a great deal of satisfaction from the fact that I'm the only person I ever encountered who grew up in a family where they had family prayers every morning after breakfast. My sister and I are probably the only people in the world who grew up in a household where the immutable winter Sunday morning breakfast was oyster stew. Ralph says now that he wishes that on the night of Rufus' birth he'd thought to move me out into his work shop. It couldn't have been any colder than the bedroom was, and Rufus might then have had the distinction of being the last American child to be born in a log cabin. Not that it would have made any difference—unless he wants to run for the Presidency of the United States some time, which God forbid—but it would have been something to talk about. That's what I mean.

So Sally, some night in the future when she's sitting in the Stork Club all done up in gold lamé—also God forbid—can smile reminiscently and say, "You know, I got my education in a rural school in the backwoods of Maine." I think the effect will be very piquant.

Right now, though, she's having too much fun to worry about being different. She belongs to the 4H Club, and goes to church and teaches a Sunday School class of infants, and has a boy-friend. In fact, she has a different one every time we see her, practically, which makes it nice. If she stuck to one I'd probably think I had to worry about its being serious. In short, she's living the usual life of a small town American girl, only she's getting a lot more out of it than most small town girls do. She's been around enough to value it at its true worth.

Probably I ought to be able to draw some valuable de-

ductions and conclusions from my special set of circumstances in regard to the problem of child-raising. I'm sorry
to say that I can't. The only conclusion that I've come to
is pretty general and pretty trite. All any parent can do is
to stagger along as best he is able, and trust to luck.

Left: Rufus's first picture. Jonesy, the crew's cook, is holding him.

Below: Rufus and two of the pups with Rollo, the skunk.

VI

"What Do You Do With All Your Spare Time?"

THIS IS WHAT I CAN'T DECIDE:—WHETHER I DON'T HAVE ANY spare time at all, or whether most of my time is spare time. Spare time, as I used to understand it, was the time left over from doing the necessary, unpleasant things, like correcting Sophomore English themes or washing out silk stockings in the bathroom. It was the time I frittered away on useless, entertaining pursuits, like the movies or contract bridge. Now almost everything I do—except cooking —is fun, and it is also useful. There is no line of demarcation between work and play. It makes it hard to explain what I do with my spare time.

Take the matter of smelting, for example. I happen to be among those who consider going smelting a form of sport. Gerrish agrees with me, but Ralph thinks it's hard work. Therefore, since someone has to stay home and mind the fires, he's the one to do it, while Gerrish and I sally forth into the night.

Smelts are not, unfortunately, the most co-operative of

fish. In this country they're about the size of average sardines—the Norwegian kind—and normally they live deep in the lakes, where you never see them. In the spring, however, after the ice is out of the brooks but before the lakes break up, they run up into the brook mouths to spawn. We stand on the bank with dip nets, dip them out into pails, take them home, and eat them. The hitch—and never let anyone tell you that Nature hands over anything without a string attached—is that they don't start running until after dark, and they're extremely coy about the whole thing. You can never tell what night or what time of night they'll pick to run, so you have to be there every night.

We do our smelting at the Head of the Pond, where the upper river empties into it. That's almost two miles from the house, and of course the road is deep in soggy snow at that time of year, so we have to walk. Right after supper Gerrish and I start out, leaving the dishes for Ralph to do, because if we are going to get there before dark, so that we can collect fuel for a fire to keep warm by, we've got no time to waste. It wouldn't be so bad if we had only ourselves to consider, but we have to take lanterns and buckets and nets—fine-meshed dip nets attached to long handles. The walking is terrible, the kind of walking where you can go along fine for a few steps on an old snowshoe float, and then you sink in suddenly to your knees. It's much harder and more nerve-racking than just plain wallowing to your waist at every step, but if you leave the road and start wading in the soft snow at the side, you find there is a foot of running ice water underlying it, and that your boots aren't quite a foot high. It's a most disconcerting discovery to make.

After a while, though, we get there, coming out of the

gloom of the path through the pines onto the shore of the Pond. The snow has shrunk back from the water, here where the sun can reach, and the ice has receded beneath the insistent attack of the current from the river. We stand on bare gray rocks and look out over an open stretch of fretted gray water to the dirty white line of the ice pack. All the delicate and subtle coloring that is a part of the winter landscape—the faded gold of dead grass heads, the fine red lines of the stems of low bushes, the orange of a fungus on a stump, the lavender of distance—has been drained away by the dusk that lies on the surface of the Pond and the darkness that lurks in the enfolding hills. There is nothing at all to be seen but gray—a hundred different tones of gray, from not-quite-white to almost-black. It's dreary and desolate and lonely, and I love it.

In the middle of the river is a little, low, rocky, scrub-covered island, and that is the best place to establish our base, because from it we can cover both channels. We take our impedimenta across, leaping precariously from rock to rock, and then start collecting a pile of firewood. The fire started, we sit down close to it, shivering a little in the penetrating wind that blows across the ice, and talk for an hour or so, while we wait for full dark. The flames leap up, staining the black water crimson. The river gurgles over a reef of gravel with a soft, incessant chattering sound. Off in the open water toward the ice pack a loon, the first of the year, raises its dismal, wailing hoot. A fox barks back in the woods. Finally we light our lanterns and go down to peer into the water.

If luck is against us we see just the clear water, deceptively shallow in the lantern light, running swiftly over the clean stones. We blow out the lanterns and go back to the fire to wait a while, not really expecting that things will be different in half an hour, but because, since we're there, we might as well make sure that tonight is not the night. Our initial opinion that there's no sense in hanging around usually proves to have been correct, so we leave our paraphernalia under a bush and go home. That's one nice thing about living in the woods. You can leave anything anywhere, for any length of time, and be sure of finding it when you come back to it.

But if luck is with us we see the smelts running up against the current, millions and millions of them, like a long black snake, and the fun begins. We scoop frantically, and the fish that were black in the water turn to living silver as we lift them out, struggling in the nets. Water streams from them like silver fire in the unsteady light of the lanterns, and we call back and forth to each other, "Come over here! There's millions of them—" or "How're you doing over there?" We get excited and careless, and misjudge the depth of the water, so that our boots are soon full. But it doesn't make any difference. The pails are filling, too, and the smelts are running thicker than ever. Gerrish freezes suddenly, like a dog going into a point. "Gosh, I think I heard a salmon jump! Let's come over here early tomorrow night and bring our rods." I agree. Suddenly I don't see how I can wait until even tomorrow to feel a three-pound salmon fighting on the other end of a line.

The pails are full. We put out the fire, leave the nets and one of the lanterns, and start home. It is inky black in the woods, and sooner or later, usually sooner, whichever is carrying the remaining lantern falls down and breaks the chimney. Then we flounder around an interminable time, running into trees, falling down and spilling the smelts, gathering them up by the light of matches—until the matches give out—and listening to the loons laugh with a laughter that suddenly has an extremely personal note to it. Eventually, we see the lights of home, and stagger in, exhausted.

Why is this so much fun? I don't know. It just is, if you happen to like it. Even if you don't, it's worth while to go smelting. After the winter's diet, the first fresh fish of the year taste wonderful. Gerrish and Ralph clean them for me, cutting the heads off and slitting the bellies, and I dip them in a thin batter and fry them in deep fat until they're brown and crisp. They look like French-fried potatoes, and served with lemon juice or tartar sauce, taste like manna. We have them every day during the brief fortnight they are running.

The very last time that we go, Gerrish and I always bring home twenty or thirty live ones in a pail of water. These we dump into the wangan spring hole as we go by, to save as bait when we go trolling at B Pond. They'll live there indefinitely, I guess. I've never had a chance to find out. Most of them escape down the brook before very long.

Along about smelting time is usually sugaring-off time, too, and this I don't particularly relish. I like the new maple syrup all right, and I don't have to do any of the work. Ralph and Gerrish tap the trees, going back into the woods across the road on snowshoes, and carrying the pails and spiles by the armload. It takes them about all one morning to get the tapping done. Then one or the other of them goes out morning and evening with two buckets on a shoulder yoke, and brings in the sap. In good years we make enough syrup to last us through the whole twelve months. It's good syrup, too—heavy in weight and delicate in flavor.

Good sap weather is clear weather in which the temperature during the day rises to above fifty and drops well below freezing at night. The sap is supposed to be drawn by the warmth and sun up into the branches daily, and driven by the cold back into the roots at dark. I say *supposed*, because this is the old country-man's explanation of it, and I've gone through life discovering that, no matter how reasonable these homely bits of scientific data sound, often they are completely wrong, and the real explanation is something involved and improbable. That may not be the case here. I don't know anything about it. I'm just protecting myself.

Our equipment is mostly homemade. Some of the spiles are just wooden spouts that Gerrish and Ralph have whittled out by hand. They are driven into the holes bored into the south side of the tree trunks, and the sap drips through them into the pails which are hung beneath. These are simply No. 10 tin cans in which we have bought fruit or vegetables, with covers roughly fitted to them to keep out rain and snow. The rain and snow doesn't do any harm, but it makes that much more water to evaporate before we have syrup. Our evaporating pans are a series of large shallow cookie pans, which we put on the kitchen stove top. They're the reason why I don't like the sugaring-off season. Every time I want to put a stick of wood in the stove, or toast a slice of bread, or heat a flat iron, or fry an egg, I have to move one of those damn syrup pans. If I hang up a pair of mittens over the stove to dry, the chances are that sooner or later they'll fall into a syrup pan.

Briefly, the whole thing is a nuisance, and before we're through, I wish to Heaven I'd never heard of maple syrup.

It's nice to eat, though, on griddle cakes, for supper. Sometimes we boil it down a little more, beyond the aproning consistency which is the standard weight for syrup—syrup is said to apron when it runs off the side of a spoon in a solid sheet, or apron, instead of in rivulets—and pour it hot onto dishes of snow. It congeals as it cools to a thick gumminess, and is wonderful to chew on. It's fun to give it to Kyak for he loves its sweetness so, but at the same time gets his jaws all stuck up, to our great amusement. This over-cooked syrup makes a marvellous sauce for vanilla ice-cream, too. A common country dessert that we sometimes have is fresh raised doughnuts and hot, new syrup. Each member of the family has a cereal dish of syrup, and dips the doughnut into it as he eats. This is not very elegant, but it's very good. Lots of people have hot baking-powder biscuit with butter and new syrup for breakfast, during the syrup season, instead of the more conventional griddle cakes and syrup. Probably this is good, too. I wouldn't know. I have trouble enough getting breakfast on the table without going into hot baking-powder biscuits.

I know one man who drinks a full cup of new syrup every night before he goes to bed, for its medicinal properties. He says it accomplishes the same thing as sulphur and molasses, but a lot more pleasantly. That may be so. I know that all over the countryside here, woodsmen and farmers and trappers drink maple sap out of the pails at the trees. They seem to have a craving for it, which isn't accounted for by its taste. It hasn't much more taste than spring water; it has only what I can best describe as a green

feeling in the mouth. I believe, therefore, that it is a
natural spring tonic which supplies minerals or vitamins
or some other elements that have been lacking in ordinary
country winter diet. I can't see, otherwise, why men who
usually drink no more than four or five glasses of water
a day suddenly take to drinking two or three quarts of
maple sap.

To complicate matters in the spring, our semi-annual
moving day rolls around. My mother always says that two
movings are as good as a fire, when it comes to eliminating
unnecessary possessions, and she's about right. All the
things that have been collecting in the winter house against
a sudden unforeseen need—the leaky gum-boots, the nests
of cardboard boxes, the crop ends of boards, the links of
chain, and the broken toys—I suddenly see in their true
colors, and take them down to the dump. Of course Ralph
and Gerrish and Rufus trail me like a pack of hounds and
salvage most of the trash, uttering outraged cries of horror
at my vandalism, but I manage to accomplish a little thinning out. To take care of the remaining worthless treas-
ures—and of what use is a felt hat with four holes in the
crown and no brim to speak of, or a piece of rubber belt-
ing six inches square?—I have instituted in the kitchen
what is known as the culch corner. This is a sort of exter-
ritorial ground for junk. Anything that's been put in the
culch corner—a wide corner shelf with a box on it—I can't
touch, much as my fingers may itch to pitch it out. There's
everything there—old bolts, old wrought-iron cut nails, bits
of unrelated metal, old wool, wiping rags, coffee cans,
broken hack saw blades, a divorced work glove or two,
parts of a dog team harness, lengths of fish line, a coil or
two of synthetic gut leaders (known woodswise as "sympa-

thetic gut"), and some odd wooden wedges. It's a mess, but it's better to have this one big mess in the corner of the kitchen than a patina of messiness spread all over the house. I didn't, by the way, name the culch corner. Culch is the New England word for that clutter of partly worn out or obsolete objects that always gathers, like moss, on a non-rolling household. I don't know who first used the term culch corner, but it stuck. Now we all call it that.

It's nice to be down in the summer house again. There's more space to move around in, and the river is nearer and louder. We wake up in the night and hear it, and for a night or two mistake it for the sound of wind and rain. But real rain is different. It starts slowly, with individual drops striking the roof only three feet over our heads, in an almost ceremonial roulade. Then it comes faster and faster, with the full symphonic orchestration of rising wind in the trees and the river's roar. The walls of the summer house are not ceiled like those of the winter house, and the storm seems much nearer to us when we're living down there. Paradoxically, this makes us feel that much warmer, and safer, and more protected.

There's always one thing I forget on moving day. We manage to shift all the favorite chairs, and the lamps, and the radio, and the typewriters, and footstools, and personal belongings, and ash trays. But come bed-time, Ralph always says, "Where's my sleeping hat?" He thinks his head gets cold at night without it, although he goes around bareheaded all day. It's always in the same place—hanging on the head of the bed in the winter house bedroom. Sometime I'm going to establish a record and remember it—unless he establishes the same record first.

As spring moves into summer, the berries start getting

ripe. All through the woods, wherever there is enough of a clearing to let the sun in, acres and acres of raspberries and blueberries come into fruit. I never can quite believe that this dour and grudging country has suddenly suffered such a complete reversal of form. This princely generosity seems just too good to be true. I feel we must go berrying right now, right this minute, before all the berries vanish again.

Ralph loathes picking berries. I used to try to sell him on the idea that since for once we were getting something for free, it was his *duty*— But my wifely pep-talks never raised his enthusiasm above a Laodicean luke-warmness, which started cooling the first time he tripped and stretched his six-feet-two in a bramble patch, and from then on declined rapidly to absolute zero. So I gave up. He just isn't the type. Fortunately, Gerrish is the type.

Gerrish always refers to me as She, just as he always refers to Ralph as The Boss. He'll say to Ralph, "She claims She wants to go ras'berryin' t'morrer mornin', so if you ain't got nothin' special in mind—"

Ralph never has. He's only too thankful that I don't try to enlist him.

To get to the best raspberry patch, we have to take a boat and row about a mile across the Pond to where the dead stub of an old "punkin" pine stands on a ridge, dwarfing with its towering height the by no means insignificant growth along the shore. From the boat, the shore line is an unbroken wall of forest, but we know that if we land near a maple a little to the left of the stub, and scrambled up a steep, spruce-covered slope to the foot of the pumpkin pine, we'll come out into an old, overgrown birch cutting. Here the raspberries grow on tall rank canes among the rocks and fallen trees and rotten birch tops and around clumps of young spruce and fir. It is a quiet place, sheltered from the wind, and when we arrive there early in the morning, it is wet with dew and laced with long shadows from the surrounding forest. It is cool and full of the stir of birds and the scoldings of red squirrels and little striped chipmunks. That's why we always go there early. Later, when the sun is high, the place is like a furnace, breathless and so hot that even the birds and squirrels retire to the shade of the woods. It is silent then, and dead, except for the hum of insects; but the heat and stillness account for the size and quality of the berries. If you stand still and listen, you can almost hear them grow, swelling and stretching as the rich red juice fills them.

The minute we get into the clearing, I find that I am alone. Gerrish has vanished. I hear a dry stick snap somewhere, but the bushes are so high I can't see him. It would be useless to call. He wouldn't answer. Like me, when he goes berrying, he wants to berry, not stand around doing what he calls "jawrin'." When his pail is full, he'll whistle and I'll go down and meet him at the boat. My pail will lack a half an inch of being full. Gerrish takes a proper pride in being the best and fastest picker he ever saw, and there's nothing I can do about it, try as I will.

The raspberries hang on the underside of the canes, glowing like jewels against the green of the leaves. They are dead ripe, and will drop off at the lightest touch. Raspberries are the most care-demanding of all berries to pick. They mash easily, so they must be handled lightly. Even setting the pail down too often and too hard will result in a shapeless mush in the bottom. That's why Gerrish and

I suspend our pails from our belts; thus we'll have both hands free to pick and avoid constant jarring of the berries. The canes have to be lifted delicately. It's infuriating to raise one and have all the fruit tumble off to be lost among the rocks and debris on the ground.

I don't know where Gerrish goes after he shakes me. I keep away from the south side of the cutting. That is, by tacit consent, his stamping ground. I don't even know what's over there. I have my own beat to patrol, working slowly up a vague remnant of hauling road near the middle of the clearing to the top of the ridge, and coming back down along the edge of the woods on the north side. At the top of the loop the earth is thin and shallow and the bushes aren't very big or productive, but I always go there just the same. There is an outcropping of ledge there, gray and weathered and warm with sun under the hand. I love stone. I won't try to explain why, because I don't know. But everybody loves the feel and quality and essence of some material. It may be leather, or wood, or fine porcelain. It may be satin or bronze or tweed. Whatever it is, there is almost a spiritual kinship between that substance and that person. That's the way I feel about stone, and that's why I always go up to the top of the raspberry patch.

We're not the only ones that pick berries. The birds eat them, of course, and the foxes. Bears love them. One day I followed in the path of a bear down my north side of the cut. I could see by the bent bushes where he'd been ambling happily along, stripping the canes as he went, minding his own business and thinking his own thoughts, even as I was doing. Suddenly I came to a place that looked as though a tornado had hit it. The undergrowth was all flattened out, the ground was torn up, and a couple of saplings were broken off. Right smack in the middle of the devastation, dangling from a low branch, was what was left of a big hornets' nest, gutted and destroyed by one furious sweep of a huge paw. The poor old cuss had evidently been attacked by a squadron of dive bombers before he knew what it was all about. I could see where he had started for the Pond. He certainly hadn't stood on the order of his going either. Every jump must have been ten feet long. I'd like to have seen him, clearing rocks and bushes and fallen trees like a bird on the wing. There, but for the Grace of God, might have gone Louise Rich. Well, better him than me. I have only two legs, and it would have broken my heart to have had to jettison a pail half full of raspberries.

On the way back across the Pond, I always think about the delicious jam and preserves I'm going to make out of our twelve or fifteen quarts of berries. This is purely mental exercise, but it makes me feel smug and thrifty, and I might as well enjoy the feeling while I can. In our family everybody, even the dog, will eat raspberries until their eyes pop, so there aren't ever enough left after twenty-four hours to do anything fancy with. I do, though, usually manage to squeeze out a couple of pies, making a special effort to have the crust flaky and sprinkling flour over the berries lightly before baking to prevent the juices all stewing out. Too much flour is bad. It takes all the juice up. With the remnants of crust I make turn-overs for between-meal snacks. If the weather is sultry and the berries start to mold, I stew them up with sugar for supper-sauce, to be eaten with cake or cookies. Then if there are still some left, I make jam, to be put away against the winter.

There is really only one dessert to be made out of raspberries, when there aren't enough to go around. This is a sort of cooked up-side-down shortcake. In the bottom of a cake pan I melt a little butter, add about a half a cup of sugar, and a cup or two of raspberries—whatever I have left after saving out a cupful. Then I mix up a good short biscuit dough, using two cups of flour, four teaspoons of baking powder, a generous third of a cup of shortening and a half a cup of milk. This I roll out about a half an inch thick, cover with the raspberries I've held out and some more sugar, roll up into a jelly roll, and slice into inch slices, which I put cut-side-down in the pan. I bake in a hot oven and serve hot with milk or cream and the hot cooked berries from the bottom of the pan. It's nothing, really, to write home about, but it accomplishes its purpose, which is to keep the family from hollering too loudly and long about the inferior desserts that are being handed out to them recently.

Blueberries are more common and therefore much less highly esteemed than raspberries. We don't have to go on any boat trips to get plenty of blueberries. They grow all along the Carry Road, and in a half an hour I can pick enough for a couple of pies, some blueberry muffins, and a little spiced blueberry jam. The only trick about pies is to add a little salt and lemon juice to the berries to give them zip. Blueberries are apt to be flat. The only trick about blueberry muffins is to roll the berries in flour so they won't sink in a sodden mass to the bottom of the batter. Blueberry jam is easy to make. Add sugar to the blueberries, pound for pound, and boil until the mixture starts to thicken. Then add cinnamon, nutmeg, and allspice—a pinch of each to the pound—and pour into glasses.

It jellies readily—I think there must be a lot of natural pectin in blueberries—and is good with hot or cold roasts and fowl.

There are plenty of other things to do, too, to fill in spare time. Before the ice goes out all the boats and the canoe have to be overhauled and painted. Usually one or more of the boats has sprung a leak somewhere and we have to find out just where and repair it. Usually, too, someone' during the preceding season—probably I—has left a boat improperly secured on a windward shore, and it has chafed badly on the rocks. This rough spot has to be sandpapered smooth and oiled before the painting can begin. Any broken thwarts and gunwales have to be mended, and missing irons replaced and oarlocks repaired. Anchor ropes have to be examined for frayed places, and Ralph's trick anchor control gadgets have to be gone over to see that they are in working order. These rigs, which he invented and made himself, are very clever The rope feeds over a pulley wheel in a bracket bolted on the bow and back through a special casting attached to the rower's seat, which allows the rope to be locked any where by a cam lever. If you're handling a boat alone in a current, jockeying for the right fly-casting position, it's a great advantage to be able to drop your anchor without leaving the seat or missing a stroke. It's also a great ad vantage, when you have somehow become involved with a six-pound salmon who is either going to break your rod or run your line all out unless you do something and do it fast, to be able to up-anchor without putting your rod down.

I like to paint boats. Ours are all painted the same, like our houses, which are a soft Nile green with buff doors and window sashes. Our boats are green outside and buff inside. The basic principle—to put on several thin coats instead of one thick coat—applies to boats as well as to any other paint job, and you have to be careful not to let drops form along the edges of the strakes. But after a while you can paint automatically and let your mind wander where it will. It's sunny and sheltered down on the boat float, and it's a nice place to be in the early spring. The birches along the shore of the Pond are beginning to show the faint and tender green that is so different from the black-green of the conifers, and the maples are blossoming red. The water, in the patches where the ice has gone out, is a deep indigo blue, and the ice pack in the distance is a line of snowy white. The wind smells of spring.

Ralph spends the before-break-up period, which is also the period when the road is hub deep in mud and therefore impassable for anything but foot traffic, in overhauling the cars. This I won't attempt to go into. I don't know anything about it, except that it involves lying in mud and dirt under the cars, and coming into the house with simply filthy hands, and moving my potatoes to the back of the stove, where they stop boiling, so that some motor part or can of oil can have the place of honor. It also involves dozens of trial runs around the loop of the driveway, and a great deal of breathless listening to what sounds, to my untutored ear, like a perfect performance, and then a flood of language and another taking down of the motor to locate the seat of a murmur that may some day develop into a bad chest cough. It's a very trying period for everyone except Rufus, who crawls under the cars right along with his father, and sticks his nose into gudgeon grease, and gets his clothes plastered with mud and oil, and has a wonderful time.

About two years ago Gerrish and I took up fly tying. There were several reasons for this. We thought it would be nice to have a hobby for our evenings, for one thing. For another, flies are expensive to buy if you fish as much as we do. We're always losing flies, or having them ruined by a big fish, and it's always the fifty-cent types that meet with grief. It runs into money in the course of a season. Besides that, it was getting embarrassing for us to have to look respectful when city sports said, "Oh, of course I tie all my own flies!" as though that were a feat beyond such inept souls as we. So we took up fly tying.

I, myself, didn't intend to become a slave to the habit. I thought I'd just dabble in it, but it didn't work out that way. We were too proud to ask anyone how to go about tying flies, so we got ourselves a book of instructions and a batch of feathers and set out to teach ourselves. Gerrish gave me fair warning before we started that he couldn't learn things from books. He had to be shown; but if he could just see someone actually *do* a thing once, then he could do it all right the next time. I can follow printed directions fairly well, so the idea was that I would follow the book and Gerrish would follow me, and in that way we'd both learn. We both did, but what started out as a hobby became almost an obsession, especially with Gerrish. He's a rabid fly tyer now, and I might add, a very good one. He makes a much better fly than I do, for all that his hands are bigger and look clumsier than mine. The heads of his flies are small and smooth, while mine sometimes get beyond me and turn out large and rough. That's where the amateur betrays himself.

We thought at first that we'd be satisfied if we could make a few streamers and some of the simpler stock patterns of wet flies. We weren't going into anything complicated. We weren't even going to consider tying dry flies. We knew our own limitations. Neither of us was going to invest a lot of money in equipment. Ralph had a small vise he'd lend us, and I had nail scissors and some odds and ends of embroidery silk and yarn for bodies. There was plenty of black thread around the house, and some silver and gold string left over from Christmas wrappings, and Ralph had some beeswax in his sailmaker's outfit. He also had shellac, and we could probably find plenty of feathers and fur around the woods. All we'd have to buy was two or three dozen hooks and maybe a few feathers not indigenous to this soil, such as jungle cocks for eyes. We wouldn't have to spend more than fifty cents, all told. That's what we thought, at first.

That state of mind lasted about a month. During that month we saw everything in the light of possible fly-tying material. We brought home dead birds, and the tails of deceased flying squirrels we found, and quills out of other people's feather dusters. We clipped stiff fur from Kyak to make buck tails, and went hunting with my .22 revolver for red squirrels. (We never managed to get one.) We hounded chance acquaintances from Upton to bring us in hen feathers and hackle feathers from roosters the next time they came. And we tied up enough Plymouth Rock streamers to last us a lifetime. We had plenty of Plymouth Rock feathers, you see. Then we faced the truth. The bug had got us. We'd have to buy some more equipment—not very much, of course; just a few necessary things. After all, this was partly an economy measure. We'd just spend a dollar or two.

Last spring our feather bill was over fifteen dollars. We'd already spent five or six dollars on special scissors, a pair of hackle pliers, a bottle of head varnish, a special wax preparation, and a box of assorted hooks. Heaven knows what our bill would have been if some friends hadn't presented us with a fly-tying vise. That's what fly tying can do to you. It can make you lose all sense of proportion. We even lost our pride. When a professional fly tyer, Frank Walker, of Oxford, Maine, came to stay at Millers' that summer and offered to show us a few tricks of the trade, we forgot all about our lofty ideas of independence, and spent all one Sunday afternoon with him. He's an old man, and he's tied thousands of flies, over the course of years. He's found short cuts and practical methods that the books never dreamed of, and that it would have taken us twenty years to dope out for ourselves. And even if I never intended to tie a fly in my life, I would have enjoyed watching him work. It was really something to see him tie a Black Gnat on a No. 14 hook, with his big hands, a little stiff from rheumatism, moving slowly and delicately and surely around the almost invisible little object in the vise. Great skill and competence in any line is always impressive.

It's hard to tell exactly where the great fascination of tying flies lies. Of course, there is the satisfaction in creative work. It's fun to take a pile of raw materials and make something out of them. The more demanding the work, the greater is the satisfaction. It's fun to finish shellacking the head of a fly, hold it up, and be able to think,

"There! I'll bet nobody could tell that from a bought fly!"
You feel so pleased with yourself.

But that's only the beginning. People are easy to fool.
The real test comes when you try the fly out on a fish. If
you can catch a fish on a fly you tied yourself, then you
can commence to regard yourself as a fly tyer. Still, there
are always a few fool fish about that will rise to anything,
so it's better to get several strikes on the fly before you
indulge in too much own-back patting. But that isn't the
end, either. Pretty soon you start regarding the copying
of the proven, standard patterns as mere tyro's work. Anybody can copy a fly, you think. Most people know the Yellow May is good at this time of year in these waters. So
there's nothing remarkable about catching a good fish on a
Yellow May, no matter who tied it. Now if you could think
up a new pattern that would catch fish, that would really
be something.

So you start watching the fish. Tonight they're rising to
some silvery gray little bugs that are flying up the river.
If you could tie a fly that looked something like that, with
perhaps a touch of yellow in the body— You reel in and
go home. By working fast, you can get it done in time to
try it out before dark. Perhaps it won't catch fish. All
right; maybe if you used a little tinsel in the tail— There's
no end to it, as you can see. And there's no feeling quite
like the lift you get when eventually you hit on the right
combination, and a walloping big trout comes surging up
out of the shadows and grabs your very own fly, the fly you
conceived and executed all by yourself.

One of the things that always surprises people who visit
us, anticipating, prepared for, or resigned to—according
to their various natures—a period of total quiet, is the num-

ber of excursions and alarums which preclude any chance of monotony. Something is always cropping up, and you never know when you get up in the morning what will have happened before you go to bed at night. It may be nothing more momentous than a visit from the game or the fire warden, but they always have something of interest to offer.

Our fire warden lives with his wife and dog on Pine Island at the upper end of the Narrows between the two Richardson Lakes, and he and Ralph are kindred souls. They both collect junk. Fortunately, where Ralph collects car motors, Amby Hines collects motor boat parts, so they don't chisel in on each other's rackets. I haven't been up at Pine Island lately, but I gather that Amby is running into the same trouble that Ralph is—not enough space to store his loot and a wife that objects to having to clamber over a pile of cold metal when she gets out of bed in the morning. She won't let him make a junk pile out of her boudoir. (I won't let Ralph, either, but he does, just the same.) Amby is really in a worse position than Ralph. The Island isn't very big, and he's used up about all the available space. He's loath to start a boat motor dump on the mainland. "They'll rob 'em off me," he explains matter-of-factly.

The last time he was down, he was having trouble with his dog, a young terrier, who had not yet encountered a porcupine. Amby thought, quite rightly, that the sooner the pup got that over with and learned better, the happier they'd all be; but there weren't any porcupines on the Island. However, while patrolling his beat down the Lower Richardson, he stopped in at Spirit Island, where a group of boys were camping, and found that they'd

caught a porcupine and had it in a box. It is against
the law to confine a wild animal without official permission, although ordinarily Amby wouldn't have bothered
about a porcupine, because he knows that whenever it got
ready a porcupine could gnaw its way in half an hour out
of any box ever made. This time, however, he needed it
himself, so he confiscated it and took it home in a water
pail.

When he got to the Island he turned it loose and called
his dog. Porcupines are slow and clumsy, but nevertheless
it managed to scramble up a tall pine before the dog
caught up with it, which is probably just as well for the
dog. This was about four o'clock in the afternoon, and the
dog sat at the foot of the tree and howled until half past
three the next morning, ignoring all commands to come
into the house and forget it, and completely shattering
any ideas of sleep that the Hineses might have been entertaining. At half past three the dog called it a day and retired under the porch to rest. As soon as the coast was
clear, the porcupine came down, swam to the mainland,
and vanished. Amby was discouraged when he stopped at
our house. He had to start his porcupine hunt all over
again, and this time he wasn't going to be lucky enough to
find one all crated for him.

A fire warden has to work hard. He has an area to patrol,
and he has to see that no one builds a fire within that area,
except at State-designated camp grounds. You just can't
go into the woods and camp anywhere, for obvious reasons
of safety. Then if there is a lumbering operation going on,
he has to manage to show up in the slashes, unheralded and
ghost-like, often enough to deter the men from smoking
in the woods. This involves a lot of walking in the course

of a week, and lots of patrolling around the lakes in a kicker boat. If a forest fire starts in his territory, he has to organize the fighters, and if it's in someone else's territory, he has to go over there and help. He has to co-operate with the game warden in seeing that the game laws are observed, although naturally this is a reciprocal arrangement, and he can call on the game warden for help whenever he needs it. If someone gets lost, they both have to join the search, along with whatever talent they can scrape up around the countryside. But the really rush period in a fire warden's life comes when the State does what is colloquially known as "slap a band on the woods."

The band is slapped on whenever there is a protracted drought, and the woods are consequently tinder-dry. Actually the Governor proclaims that the woods are closed to hunters, fishermen, campers, and any other unauthorized persons; in other words, it *bans* use of the forest areas, and forbids building of fires or smoking by anyone whatsoever. The fire warden is like a cat on a hot griddle when a "band" is on. He has to be everywhere at once, telling people to leave the woods immediately, and riding herd on legitimate occupants like us, who belong there, and on himself. Neither he nor we want a forest fire—he, because it's his business not to have one, and we because we naturally don't want to burn up. But you'd be surprised how easy it is, if you are an habitual smoker, suddenly to find yourself in the middle of a dangerous area with a half-smoked cigarette in your hand and no recollection at all of having lighted it. We just stop carrying smoking materials when a "band" is on, and so does the warden. If you haven't got them, you can't smoke them. The result is that every now and then he appears at our door with the announcement, "My tongue's hanging out for a smoke. Mind if I bum a cigarette and come inside and smoke it?" It's all right to smoke in the house during a "band."

Our game warden, in spite of the fact that he is a respectable married man with four children—including a pair of twins—looks like the scenario writer's dream of the perfect Northwestern Mountie. He wears his uniform with style—he's got the right build for a uniform, with wide shoulders and slim hips—and he walks with a sort of cat-footed swagger. His face is lean and handsome and dark, and he has a tough and reckless air about him. I guess he is tough, if he wants to be. Fortunately, we keep on excellent terms with him, simply by observing the game laws. I don't want to sound holy and smug about this, but we do make a point of not breaking them, because we believe in them. In fact we believe some of them are not rigid enough. They are necessary laws and if we weren't convinced that this is so, we'd probably be the worst poachers in the county.

We always ask the game warden how business is, and often he has an unusual arrest to tell us about. He tells a story well. A recent adventure happened over on the other side of his territory. He was up on a mountain patrolling a closed brook when he came on a boy fishing with his pockets crammed with short trout, about twenty of them. Naturally, he took the offender into custody and led him down the mountain to where his car was parked by the road. But he saw no reason why he should carry the four or five pounds of illegal fish over the rough trail. Let the guilty party do it. The guilty party had other ideas, however, and managed to put them into effect. By the time they had reached the road, he had surreptitiously got rid of the evidence, dropping the little fish quietly at intervals along the trail. So there was our Mr. Leon Wilson with a prisoner, but with no evidence and no case. He was pretty mad about the whole thing.

But not for long. Presently the boy's father came out of the woods, having apparently been just behind them all the way down, all ignorant of his son's arrest. He didn't notice the bad company his son was keeping. (By most people around here, a game warden is generally considered about the worst company to be found in.) "Hey, Bud," he hailed. "You must have a hole in your pocket. I been picking up your fish along the trail for the last couple of miles!" He had the missing illegal fish in his creel.

Ho-hum! Possession is all that needs to be proved against you, according to the law. It didn't make any difference to Leon whom he pinched. Both of them knew better.

We used to set our guests to work helping pull porcupine quills out of the dogs. This was when we had five dogs, and ideas about a dog team. They didn't work out. In the first place, it cost more to feed five huskies than to feed the whole Rich tribe. In the second place, we were always in hot water with those darn dogs. Either they'd get loose and chase game, or else they'd scare people going along the road—the dogs were perfectly harmless, but some people are timid—or they'd tear the wash off the line and chew it up. And one or the other of them was always coming in full of porcupine quills. They always chose the most inconvenient times for these forays into the sporting life, and you can't postpone a de-quilling operation. The longer you wait, the deeper the quills work in, until you can't get them out at all. This won't necessarily prove fatal, as often they fester and eventually come out by themselves, after a week or so. But if you love your dog—and we loved each and every one of that wolf pack of ours—you can't stand seeing him suffer. So we've delayed dinner three hours on occasion, to pull quills. We've even arisen at one o'clock in the morning and worked until daylight, with me sitting on a dog's head in my nightgown, while Ralph wielded the plyers.

We don't have that trouble any more. Thor we had to shoot, because he tried to swallow a porcupine. Cookie, the dearest and smartest dog that ever lived, was struck by lightning. Metak and Mukluk we finally had to give away. It doesn't take long to write those four lines, but every word of them represents heartbreak. We loved the big bums, even if they did keep us in a continuous turmoil. Now we only have Kyak, the art dog, left. Kyak's stupidity doesn't extend to sticking his own neck out. He ran afoul of a porcupine just once, when he was very young. A great many dogs never learn to leave them alone, but will go through the agonizing experience of quills weekly until the day of their death. Not so Kyak. He'll look, but he's never touched one since that long ago disaster.

I have referred to the dogs and a dog team and I suppose I'd better clear up the matter once and for all. We thought at one time it would be a good idea to have a dog team. In this country the cars go out of use after the deep snows come, there being no possible way of keeping the road open, and that means that every pound of mail and food and material must either be carried on someone's back, or dragged on a hand sled, the two long, hilly miles from Middle Dam to here. And that's no fun. It's really mysterious how a reasonable load of groceries can multiply its weight so enormously in the time it takes to walk it two miles.

The second winter that we lived here, in the middle of February—a very well chosen time, since we were just about fed to the teeth with lugging things on our backs—Stumpy Crocker and Norman Vaughn came in to see us, and they came from below South Arm by dog team. Norman had been a dog driver on Admiral Byrd's first Antarctic Expedition, and he was full of enthusiasm for this particular mode of travel. His team consisted of nine dogs. I had always been led to suppose that huskies were vicious brutes, but these nine weren't. They were sweet. Of course, they periodically fought terribly among themselves, but as far as humans were concerned, they were a bunch of softies. Ralph and I fell in love with every last one of them. Our infatuation blinded us to the fact that for three days' stay, Norman brought in over a hundred pounds of food just for the dogs, and we fell easy victims to the notion that a dog team was just what we needed and wanted most of anything in the world. This notion was clinched after Norman had ridden us up to Middle a couple of times. It was marvellous just to sit and be whisked up Wangan Hill. Besides, we didn't really need nine dogs, Norman assured us. Five would be plenty.

So when, the next spring, Stumpy offered us a husky pup, offspring of one of Norman's team, we accepted with alacrity. That was Cookie. From the same source the Millers acquired another husky, Karlok—he was an albino, and one of the most beautiful dogs I have ever seen—so what could be more natural than a match between them when they grew up? The final result was a litter of four

pups, of which Kyak was one. And there was our dog team
in embryo. Nothing could have been simpler.

The pups grew. Norman had told us that when they
were about half grown was the time to start training them;
so when they were five or six months old, we put them in
harness. He had said nothing, though, about the desira-
bility of having an experienced dog with them to show
them the ropes. So we just hitched them up and told them
to mush. Cookie looked at us in amazement. This was a
new game, and one she wasn't sure she liked. Kyak lay
down on his back and went limp, his legs like boiled
macaroni. Nothing we could do would get him onto his
feet. Every time we stood him up he just collapsed. Metak
and Richard just stood and shivered. Only Mukluk got
the idea, and he very soon became bored with pulling not
only the light sled we had, but all his relations as well. He
finally sat down and looked disgusted, and I didn't blame
him.

We might have given up the idea then if Stumpy hadn't
made a fevered telephone call from Fitchburg, where he
lives. Would we give one of his dogs a home? (He was a
victim of the dog team obsession at the time, too.) We
wanted to know, naturally, what was the matter with the
dog. People don't give valuable dogs away without any
reason. It seemed that nothing was the matter with the
dog except boyish high spirits. He was a wonderful dog—
gentle, obedient, well-trained to harness. The only trouble
was that he was a little too powerful. He'd run away with
Stumpy's young son Weyman, and had frightened some
saddle horses on a back road. Unfortunately the saddle
horses were complete with riders, and, even more unfortunate, one of the riders was Stumpy's boss, who didn't ap-

preciate the situation at all. Hell was about to pop unless something was done about Thor. Now we had no saddle horses up our way, so— We'd really stopped listening at the "well-trained to harness" clause. Here was the answer. Thor could be a sort of tutor to the other dogs. We said, "Yes." It seemed evident that Providence wanted us to have a dog team. No sooner did a problem arise than the solution appeared right behind it.

Thor arrived and we immediately renamed him the Hound of the Baskervilles. He was almost as big as a Shetland pony, and had a head like a basket ball. He didn't have teeth. He had fangs. He looked horrible, and he was the biggest bowl of mush I ever saw. He thought he was a lap dog, and tried to sit in my lap whenever I sat down. I just haven't got enough lap for that, so he finally compromised by sitting beside me by the hour with that huge head on my knees, gazing adoringly into my face. My legs would grow numb under the weight, and consciousness of all my shortcomings would rise to the surface under that worshipful regard. Nobody could be that wonderful, me least of all. It was very embarrassing for me. I could have stood it, though, if Thor had been a good teacher. He wasn't. He was perfectly willing to work, and the others were willing to let him. Our dog team, obviously, was going to consist of Thor and Mukluk. Kyak, instead of being shamed by this example of usefulness, just grew limper and limper. It got so that whenever he saw one of us with a harness in hand, he fainted. The dog team, as such, was getting no place fast.

On top of this, it was costing more to feed the dogs than to feed us, and we were continually deluged with complaints by a lot of damn fools about keeping dangerous animals—definitely untrue. My Monday laundry was periodically ripped from the line and torn up, and the only way to insure keeping a whole pair of shoes in the house was to hang them by the laces from the ceiling beams, where the dogs couldn't reach them. In short, we had nothing but trouble and expense in connection with those darn dogs. We were told by experts that we'd never have a dog team unless we stopped making pets of the dogs. It was all wrong to feed them twice a day and let them have the run of the house. Dogs won't work unless they are half starved and kept tied up outside, away from human association. Working dogs aren't pets; they are slaves and should be treated as such. Well! That doesn't go for us. Neither Ralph nor I could ever treat any dog like that—certainly not our own dear dogs that we loved. So we gave up the dog team idea. But we still had the dogs.

Then one by one, things began to happen to them, and, viewed cosmically, it was probably just as well, much as it hurt at the time. After every disaster I said my little say—"Here we had six dogs, and five of them were swell. We're going to end by being left with the only lemon in the bunch, just you wait and see." And so we were. Oh, well; Kyak isn't much of a dog; but he suits us. He's nice with Rufus, and we love him dearly. And that's all we want.

Lots of things crop up to entertain us and our guests. There was the time for instance that we enlivened my sister Alice's visit with a fox hunt. Don't be thinking of red coats and Irish hunters, because it wasn't like that at all. We wore our night clothes and raincoats and rode in a Model T, our sole weapon was a landing net, and while Alice and I strove to establish the right note by shouting "View halloo" and "Yoicks" at intervals, Ralph rather

The author with two of her boys.

ruined the effect with his insistence upon bellowing in moments of stress, "There goes the little son of a bitch!"

You see, he'd gone up to Middle Dam late to mail an important letter, and he'd got talking. By the time he arrived back home, Alice and I had gone to bed. He came busting into the house with the news that at the foot of Birch Hill he'd seen, gamboling in the glow of his headlights, a whole litter of fox pups, apparently strayed from their den while their mother was away, and quite evidently having a time for themselves. In fact, he'd had to stop the car to keep from running over them, and when he got out to look, they'd just sat down in the road and looked right back.

"They're so tame," he concluded, "that I could have picked them right up, only I remembered in time that they bite like the devil."

This inspired Alice. "Look, why couldn't we take a landing net and a big box to put them in—" She didn't have to finish. We got the idea. Before we quite realized what we were about, we were headed up the road, complete with net, box, and flashlight. Ralph was driving, Alice was standing on one running board with the light, and I was on the other with the net. The plot was that as soon as a fox was sighted—or is "viewed" the right term? —the viewer would shout, the car would stop, and we'd all three pile off for the kill—or capture, in this case.

We saw the foxes all right. They were the cutest little articles that ever ran the woods—round and fluffy, with little pointed masked faces, up-standing ears, and wide grins. But they weren't to be caught. The moment we tried to clap the net over one, he just eased off into the darkness where the beam from our flashlight, which wasn't very good anyhow, couldn't pick him up. We spent hours riding up and down the road, shouting and laughing and jumping on and off the car, until we were exhausted. I've always doubted the English theory that the fox enjoys the hunt as much as the hunters, but I do believe these foxes did. They knew perfectly well that they were in no jeopardy whatsoever, which isn't true of a fox with a pack of hounds after him. They kept coming back into the road for more. When we finally decided that if we didn't go home we'd all get pneumonia, they were still dodging back and forth in front of the car, daring us to try to catch them. But we knew when we were licked. We went home, built up a fire, and spent the rest of the night drinking coffee and Barbados rum. (Courtesy of Alice.)

Ralph and Gerrish are forever needing a third person to lend a hand in furtherance of one of their projects, and I'm invariably elected. A plank has to be held while they saw it, or the combined weight of the two of them is just too little to push a crippled car out of the driveway, and will I please come and lean on it, too? Or they want me to hold a rock drill for them. I don't know whether they don't trust each other, or whether they figure that if someone has to get hit on the head with a sledge hammer, I can best be spared. Whatever it is, I have sat for more hours than I care to count, with a sledge whistling down past my nose as I concentrated on holding the top of the drill steady, while giving it a quarter turn between blows. I have got so I can tell by instinct just when to shout "Mud!"—when the water that has been poured into the hole has just exactly been taken up by the rock dust, and the whole works can be lifted out on the drill, leaving the hole dry and clean. Or they want me to be handy with a cant dog in case a motor they are shifting from one cradle to another starts to tip; or to block up a rock as they raise it; or take down the figures while they scale a pile of pine logs; or read a spirit level while they do the leveling. If it isn't one thing, it's another.

And, after all, I'm supposed to be a writer, so I do have to spend a little time writing. Some of the work of writing can, of course, be done concurrently with other things. You can figure out, while washing the dishes, just how to get around the difficulty of having Her discourage His suit without having Her appear to the reader just silly, and also without forcing Her to reverse Her attitude, along toward the end of the story, so completely as to seem actually feeble-minded. You see, there are certain ill-defined but nonetheless definite rules that have to be followed in the writing of magazine stories. There are some things you simply can't do, and some subjects you simply can't touch upon. Within the frame-work of these rules, you have to try to produce the illusion of some originality. It's not as hard as it sounds, but it does require a little figuring, just as it requires a little figuring to get a grand piano up a stair case with two turns in it. I might add that these rules apply to poor, medium, and good stories. If you have a simply swell story in mind, you can forget the rules. A swell story takes care of itself.

VII

"Don't You Ever Get Bored?"

WE ARE OFTEN ASKED IF WE NEVER GET TERRIBLY BORED here and I'm a little diffident about telling the truth. There is something so smug about people who say, with horror and umbrage at the very suggestion, "Oh, no! I'm never bored!" It sounds a little like, "Who, me? With my rich mine of inner resources? ME? With all my rare memories and rich philosophy?" I hate people like that. They're infuriating, and I think they are liars as well. Everyone is bored sometimes. It's a very painful illness, and completely undeserving of moral censure.

But be that as it may, the answer still is no. We're almost never bored. In winter we work too hard. In the summer we still work hard, and there are always distractions to fill in the chinks between jobs—things like guests, and fishing, and swimming. Nobody could be bored in autumn, when the air is like wine, and the hills are hazy tapestries with the red and gold thread of the frost-touched maple and birch embroidering a breath-taking design on the permanent dark fabric of the evergreens. The lakes then are unbelievably blue. All the things you've meant to do all summer but didn't get around to suddenly start crying to get done, and the days aren't long enough to crowd them all in before the first snow.

The only time left to be bored in is spring, when winter is over but it's still too early to plant the garden or move to the big house, and there's nothing very much to do but wait. Spring, as far as I'm concerned, is a vastly over-rated season, and I'd be bored to death with it, for all its burgeoning buds and returning birds and coy extremes of temperature, were it not for the spring log drive. The log drive was not designed solely for my entertainment; that's what is so remarkable and providential about its falling, as it does, in the slump of the year.

The idea of the drive is simple. All up the lakes, from Umbagog to the Little Kennebago, that tiny lost pond in the mountains fifty miles to the north, the winter's cut of four-foot pulp-wood lies boomed on the thick ice, waiting for the spring break-up. Before the first step of the metamorphosis from so many sticks of wood to so many Sunday Supplements, or high explosives, or evening gowns can begin, it must be got to the mills in Berlin, N. H., on the Androscoggin. The obvious method is to float the wood down. So even before the ice is out, the driving crews start filtering into the woods, to the company wangans along the chain of lakes. There is a lot to be done before the wood can start south.

I should explain "wangan." It is an Indian word, and can mean almost anything, like the Latin *res*. It can mean a camp or building. Pond-in-the-River wangan—or Pondy wangan, as the drivers call it—is a long, low shack a third of a mile above us, where the Rapid River crew lives during the drive. There is a sign in the bunk-house that reads,

"Wangan open an hour after supper." That refers to the store where the cook sells candy, tobacco, snuff, and clothing. (It really is a big box in the kitchen, and the reason it isn't open all the time is that the cook doesn't want to be bothered in the middle of his baking to hand out and charge against wages a nickel's worth of makings.) The cook may say, "I lost my wangan when the work boat swamped," and that means that his dishes are at the bottom of the lake. Or he may complain, "The wangan's runnin' low," meaning this time that he's short of food. Or a man may take his wangan and fly—leave the job with his little bundle of personal belongings. You can tell only by the context what the word means, and it's a very convenient word to know. I use it myself a lot, in non-driving connections.

The first year I was here, I couldn't wait for the drive to begin. I knew all about log drives, having subsisted at one time on a literary diet consisting exclusively of Stewart Edward White and Holman Day. I knew all about the thrill and perils of white-water driving—the big jam, the narrow escapes, the cat-footed agility of the drivers on the huge, plunging logs. I knew just what a river driver would look like. He should be big and bold and dark, with plaid shirt, well-cut riding breeches, caulked boots, and a mouthful of picturesque curses and ribald songs.

There is a stir that goes through the woods just before the drive moves in that is difficult to explain. Actually it consists only of suddenly increased activity on the telephone. The telephone man, Fred Bennett, who has long, blowing white hair, the delicate and transparent fragility of great age, and the toughness and staying-powers of a cross between a Shetland pony and a camel, comes slogging in through the woods and swamps and wet snow between here and the Brown Farm, and adds a half-dozen phones to our line. There is one at Middle Dam wangan, one at Pondy wangan, above us, and one at Hedgehog wangan, below, at the mouth of the river. The rest are hung in tar-paper cubicles on trees, in places where crises demanding immediate aid may arise.

Almost as soon as the phones are in, they begin to ring, strange numbers that have nothing to do with our simple, year-round, one, two, three, and four. They ring all the time, and I, neglecting my housework and throwing overboard all ethical scruples that first year, listened in. (That's all right to do, here. Often when I ask someone where they got a piece of news, they say quite frankly and shamelessly, "Oh, rubbering on the telephone.") Just by standing in the kitchen with the receiver to my ear, I could see the drive get under way all up the length of the lakes.

At first all the calls were to Joe Mooney at the Brown Farm, who acts as a sort of liaison officer. First of all came the reports as to the condition of the ice in the various lakes. "She's pretty rotten here on Umbagog this morning. If a west wind comes up she'll be clear by night. The river's all open and we've got the steamer *Diamond* in."— "She's blackin' up fast toward the Narrows. Give her two or three days of hot sun and she'll be out of the Richardsons." (Why are things like ice that won't melt, or inclement weather, or balky motors always "she" to the men who deal with them?) "They brought a horse 'n' sled down the big lake this morning. She won't go out for a week-ten days."

Then—"She's out of Pondy River, and we're puttin' in the *Alligator* tomorrow."—"The *Rowell's* in at Upper

Dam."—"The *Frost's* just goin' off the ways at Cupsuptic."

Then it speeds up. "This is Henry Mullen at Pondy. The cook claims he wants a barrel of flour, couple of crates of eggs, an' a half dozen hams. We got about thirty to feed tonight."—"Middle Dam talkin'. I got to have some inch an' a quarter line and a bunch of pick poles."—"I need ten more men. Thurston's boom's broke loose in the Arm, 'n' it's scattered all over Hell."—"I gotta have some pitch. This bateau at Middle leaks like a sieve."—"Where's that cookee? The cook's raving."—"I gotta close Pondy dam. I can't string no sluice boom with all this water runnin'." And finally, "When's that first boom comin' down? We're ready any time."

The ice is out; the winch boats are in; the crews have come; the ground work is done. The drive is ready to start.

That first year, when the news came over the telephone that they were going to launch the *Alligator,* we thought we'd go up and watch. We had seen her sitting patiently on her ways on the shore of the Pond all winter long, a big, twin-screw, square-ended craft, with a flat deck and a tall wheel-house perched on top. She was ugly and clumsy, but we felt a sympathy for her. We had watched the red leaves of autumn sift down on her deck and lie in fading, flattening windrows. We had seen the snow drift higher and higher about her, the wind-sculptured curves lending her a false and fleeting beauty. We had seen it shrink in the March sun, leaving her exposed and ugly again. We wanted to see her come to life.

Alligator is both the name of this winch boat in the Pond and the name of her type of amphibian boat. Alligators are built like barges, flat and rectangular, but they have a huge steel cable running from a winch in the bow.

The anchor is dropped, the winch unwinds as the *Alligator* runs backward to the boom, and hooks on; then the winch winds up the *Alligator* to the anchor, trailing behind her the boomful of pulp-wood which it is her business to move from the Head of the Pond to Pondy dam, at the foot. When the cable is wound up the anchor is run ahead again and the process repeated. At the foot of the Pond the boom is opened and the wood turned loose and sluiced into Rapid River, to be corralled three miles below in a catch boom, which the *Diamond* will winch to Errol Dam on the Androscoggin. Meanwhile the *Alligator* has gone back to the Head of the Pond for the boom that the *Rowell* has winched down the Richardsons from Upper Dam to Middle Dam and which has been sluiced down the upper section of Rapid River into the Pond. It sounds complicated, but it's just the old bucket brigade principle.

In Canada, where they hail from, an alligator doesn't stick necessarily to one lake, but goes right down the chain. Between lakes they pull themselves across bare ground by fastening their cable ahead to a stump and winding the boat up to it with its own winch. Many of the old pines along the Carry Road have deep girdling scars from the cable on their trunks, left from when they brought the *Alligator* in here.

As we were walking up the road to my first *Alligator* launching, we heard sounds of activity on the Pond-in-the-River Dam, so we swung off down the side trail that leads to it. I'll admit I was in a dither. The men in my life to date had been distinguished more for their intelligence, good citizenship, and consideration for their mothers than for dashing and romantic attributes. The most athletic

played good tennis. The most daring crossed streets between traffic lights and talked back to cops. I'd never
known any men in the business of danger.

We came out of the woods onto the dam. A tall, sad,
thin man with a long upper lip was drooping on the rail,
staring morosely across to where the sluice-booms were being strung—two long, floating log walkways from the dam
up into the Pond, to guide the pulp-wood down to the
open gate of the dam after the *Alligator* let it go. Presumably the stringers were river drivers, those daring heroes
of song and legend. They looked like—

They looked like any gang of men going about a routine job, except they were a little shabbier, a little more
nondescript, a little less arresting than any bunch of road
menders I ever saw. There wasn't a plaid shirt in the crew.
Some of them had on faded cotton shirts, but most of them
were covered from the waist up with what my grandmother
used to call "nice, sensible, woolen underwear," of the
long-sleeved, knitted variety. Nothing is less glamorous,
especially when south of them is worn a pair of ordinary,
store-bought suit pants, which have seen better days, and
which have been cut off, with a hack saw, apparently, just
below the knee. (I later learned to say "stagged" below the
knee. One stags one's pants, one's shirt sleeves, anything
that needs to be abbreviated quickly, even one's hair.) The
head-gear, too, was strange without managing to be piquant. First, tied like a baby's bonnet under the chin and
tucked into the shirt at the back of the neck, was a ban-
danna handkerchief or, failing that, just an old piece of
cloth, such as a shirt tail or a square of flour sacking. On
top of that was the hat proper, which might be a cheap felt,
a visored cap, or a battered derby.

They didn't even do the job with a dash. They just walked apathetically up and down the logs, boring holes, driving pegs and fastening ropes.

Of course I should have remembered that people who do things well almost always do them without flourish. That's the trouble with expert performances; they look too easy to be exciting, unless you can do them a little yourself. I can't skate much, so to me Sonja Henie's stuff looks pretty simple to have so much fuss made about it. But I can shoot and swim and cast a fly fairly well, so a champion in those fields has me standing on my chair. I'd never tried to walk a floating spruce log, so I would have been a little more impressed had there been some arm-waving and catching of balance. I've tried it since, and I know enough now to be plenty impressed, especially since I now know that very few river-hogs can swim.

(Blow No. 2 to my romantic notions:—river-drivers live in books; in life the term is river-hog. And I might as well deliver Blow No. 3 right now:—in a pulp drive there are no log jams; the wood is too short.)

To get back to the log-walking—I can imagine nothing worse than being out on the sluice boom in the middle of the night, as is sometimes necessary, with the black water snarling three inches from my feet. The current goes by with express train speed when the gates are open, and the wood hurtles past in the dark. The boom, although two or three logs wide lashed together, is wet and slippery and anything but steady. Even if a man could swim, he would have little chance. No one would see him go, except by great luck. No one would hear him call, if he had time to call before being knocked senseless. The first time he would be missed would be when the men came back off the boom. And the water is like ice. It would be a cold and lonely way to die.

I also found later that the peculiarities of costume are not merely a misguided attempt at quaintness. Riding breeches bind the knees, and long pants catch on brush and trip the wearer and get wet around the bottoms. The simple solution is long pants stagged. Black flies and gnats can make life Hell in springtime in the woods, and the best protection against them is to keep covered. Hence the woolen underwear and the bandannas. The hats are added, not as a sop to convention, but to keep the neck covering up and the glare out of the eyes.

The sad man spat dourly into the water and looked at us, so Ralph said, "Nice day."

The man said, "Yeah," as though he were cursing it.

So Ralph said, "I'm Rich. I live down below here."

"Yeah, I know," the man said. "I'm Mullen." He didn't have to add that he was the Pondy boss. We knew that from our illicit listening on the telephone. I'd pictured him as being what they call here a "bull of the woods"— a big swaggering bravo who could lick his weight in wildcats. He didn't look to me as though he could lick Rufus, who was six months old at the time.

Ralph rallied first. "Drop in sometime if you're cold or wet and have a drink. I've got some pretty good liquor."

Mullen shook his head and winced. "Not me. Thanking you all the same." He squinted at his crew out on the booms. "I'm off the stuff," he stated violently, and spat again. "I was down to Berlin last week an' I bought me a quart. Then me an' another joker split another quart. Then a feller give me a pint. It was all good stuff too," he explained defensively. "Cost ninety cents a bottle. Then

I went into a lunch room an' got me a can of beer." His face twisted. "You know that God-damned Jees'ly beer pizened me," he concluded simply. "So I'm just through with all that stuff."

We left him alone with his hangover and continued up to the *Alligator*.

There was a great deal of commotion there. Steam was up, and the winch cable was hitched to a dead-man across the cove. The *Alligator* was creaking and groaning and rumbling and not budging an inch. A head appeared through the afterhatch. The sulphurous blue haze of pro- fanity thinned a little when the owner saw me, out of re- spect to my sex. It simmered down to a few heart-felt "Comical Christs," "God-damned blue-bottomed old tubs," "Desprit Jesuses," and "Christless onery bitches," which in the woods is practically parlor conversation. What he needed, it seemed, was some grease for the ways.

"You ain't got no grease?" he asked Ralph hopefully. "If I had a little grease—"

This didn't seem to be my department, but it wouldn't hurt to ask. "I've got some old doughnut fat, if that would do you any good—"

"How much you got?"

"A kettleful. Ten pounds, about."

He climbed down onto the ground. "Lady, you saved my life. I'll have the cook return it to you, soon's he gets his in."

So the *Alligator*, that first year we were here, slid down cinnamon-scented ways into the Pond, and a few days later the cookee delivered at our door an equal quantity of lard and an invitation from the cook to come to lunch.

"Either first or second lunch. Ten o'clock or two. Don't

matter." On the drive there are four meals a day, breakfast at six, first and second lunch, supper at five, and then,
if the men have to sluice after dark, another lunch before
they go to bed, which may be anywhere from ten P.M. until
two the next morning.

We decided we'd go to second lunch, because Rufus
would be asleep and we could leave him. Before we started
up to the wangan, Ralph said, "Now look. There's a guy
up there named Casey that has My Ideal of a hat. It's a
swell hat and I want to make a deal with him if I can for
it. So I'll point him out to you, and if you could sort of
be nice to him—you know, soften him up—"

I knew, and I knew too without asking, what the Ideal
Hat of Casey would look like. It would be a battered felt,
of no recognizable style, with the crown squashed out of
shape and the brim drooping dejectedly. Ralph had been
working on one of his old city hats for years, trying to
achieve that special abandoned and disreputable look; but
it takes a long time to get it. "All right," I said resignedly.
"What is he, an Irishman?"

Every married woman knows the look he gave me—the
very special look husbands save for their wives when they
say something more than usually stupid; the look combin-
ing in equal proportions disgust, resignation and nausea,
with a dash of dismay at the prospect of living to be a
grandfather with such a half-wit.

"With a name like Casey?" he asked. "What do you
suppose he is, a Frenchman?"

The meals on the drive are buffet affairs, unlike the sit-
ting-down meals in a logging camp. All the food is laid
out on a long trestle table in the kitchen, with the knives
and forks and tin plates and pannikins stacked at the end.

You get your tools first, and then go down the table, filling up your plate with whatever looks good to you. The trouble is everything looks good. There are always two kinds of meat—a hot beef pot-roast, for example, and cold sliced ham—and potatoes and three other vegetables. Then there are always baked beans, and fresh bread, and pickles, and applesauce, and, to top off with, three kinds of pie, cake, cookies, and doughnuts. When you can't get any more onto your plate, you look for a place to sit down and eat it. The cook wanted us, as company, to sit at the table, but I saw a hat that could belong to no one but Casey. So I said I'd rather do as the river-hogs did, if he didn't mind, and went outdoors and sat down beside the man with the hat, under a pine tree.

He looked a little terrified, but he couldn't get away, as there was a man on the other side of him.

"Lovely day," I said cordially, and he grunted. "Good cook you've got," I went on, and he showed the whites of his eyes like a nervous horse. "Been working in the woods long?" I asked with neighborly interest, and he definitely shied.

The man on the other side took pity on us both. "He don't understand no English, lady," he explained kindly. "He's a Frenchman."

I gaped at him. This was absolutely too marvellous to be true. After that look Ralph had given me— "With a name like Casey?" I asked.

"Oh, they just call him Casey. He's got some frog name nobody can pronounce. So when he went to work for the company, they put him down as Casey. Sounds as near like his real name as they could get."

I beamed on Casey, not minding that he didn't beam

back. He was unshaven, and ragged and dirty, but he looked wonderful to me. He'd given me a weapon I could use in domestic crises for years to come. I loved him like a brother.

Apparently he misunderstood my intentions, because he got up in a panic and fled. Incidentally, Ralph never did make the hat deal, because next day Casey asked to be transferred to the Middle Dam wangan. I don't know whether it was I who scared him, or whether it was the predatory way Ralph kept looking at his hat.

The remaining driver said to me comfortingly, "Don't mind him, lady. He's bashful. All us fellers is bashful. Lots of folks think we're tough, but we ain't. Any time you want to come up here or to the dam, you come right ahead. Nobody'll hurt you. An' any time you want some chores done down to your place, like splittin' wood, say, you just call me. Just call the cook on the phone and say you want to get hold of Venus."

Would I not! Not every woman has a chance to confound her husband by saying, "Oh, don't bother, if you're busy. I'll get Venus to do it."

We thanked the cook kindly for his hospitality, and said we had to get home, because the baby would be waking up.

"You got a baby?" His eyes lighted. "Bring him up here. There's nothing I like so much as a baby. Any time you want to go any place, you leave the baby here with me an' the cookee."

He meant it too, and I took him up on it a dozen times. I'd come back from an afternoon off, to find Rufus propped up on the cook's bunk, chewing a piece of dried apple, with a circle of men around him, trying to make him laugh. They were wonderful with him—much better

Above: The *Alligator*.

Below: Pulpwood waiting to be sluiced above Pondy Dam.

than I was. Most of them were homeless and familyless, and a baby was a treat. As a matter of fact the first picture ever taken of Rufus was taken in front of the wangan in the arms of Jonesy, the drive cook.

That cook, Jonesy, and his cookee, Frank, were the first of a long line of woods cooks that I now know, and I hold them in especial esteem. Jonesy and I used to hold long conclaves on the culinary art, and he taught me how to make a tough pot-roast tender by smothering it with raw onions and adding a cup of canned tomatoes, salt, pepper, and a little water. Then you cover it tightly and leave in a slow oven for hours. The acid in the tomatoes, so Jonesy claimed, eats the tough fibre in the meat. Anyhow, it works. Another valuable thing he taught me was how to cut fresh bread into thin slices—a neat trick if you can do it, as everyone who has hacked jagged chunks off a warm loaf can testify. The knife must be reasonably sharp, of course, but the trick is to have it hot. Lay it on top of the stove for a minute, every four or five slices. This also works.

In return I bootlegged vanilla extract for him. Extracts aren't allowed in woods camps, and "you know yourself, Mis' Rich—you're a cook—you know a cake tastes like sawdust without no extract."

I thought this was a senseless regulation, and said so.

Jonesy sighed. "They have to have it that way. Fellers'll drink it up as fast as they can tote it in, an' there's nothing meaner'n a vanilla drunk, 'less it's a canned heat drunk."

"But imitation vanilla has no alcohol. That I just gave—"

"Sure. But lots of the woodsmen can't read. It smells like vanilla and tastes like vanilla, so they drink it and get drunk anyhow."

I was glad to hear this, as it confirmed an opinion of mine that getting drunk is fifty percent wishful thinking.

As a cookee, Frank wasn't too good, but he was entertaining in an unintentional way. He spent most of the time when he should have been peeling potatoes and washing dishes—a cookee's lot in life—strumming on a guitar and singing cowboy songs. His ambition was to get onto the Radio, on a hill-billy program. I've heard worse than he, though that isn't saying much. So he'd drone "When the Work's All Done This Fall" happily through his nose while Jonesy and Ralph and I peeled his potatoes.

We were all thus engaged one day when he discovered that by calling the Brown Farm and asking Joe to switch him onto a Magalloway line he could talk to the Camerons. The Camerons have some very pretty daughters, one of whom Frank had met at a dance. He put his guitar away under the bunk and began to bustle around.

"You got a flat-iron, Mrs. Rich?" he asked. "Can I borrow it? I got to press my pants."

I said, "Yes," and Ralph said, "Aren't you a little ambitious, young feller? It's fourteen miles from here to Camerons', and most of it's uphill. You can't walk that distance and back after supper."

Frank was surprised. "Oh, I wasn't planning on it. I'm just going to call her up. An' I ain't going to talk to no girl on the telephone with my pants looking like I'd slept in 'em."

That remains to this day the yard-stick by which I measure all chivalry.

Frank's, I'm sure, was the only singing I ever heard in a driving camp, in spite of the fictional convention that rivermen and loggers top off a hard, twelve or more hour day by sitting around a camp-fire singing French-Canadian chansons and talking about Paul Bunyan. Our river-hogs come in from work, eat their suppers, and go to bed. On the days that there is no boom to sluice or other work to be done, they wash their clothes and mend them, and play stud poker, and sleep. A few that have licenses go fishing and some pitch horse-shoes in the wangan yard, and a very few, since so many are illiterate, read old magazines that we give the cook. But none sing.

The only stories that are told are woods gossip. Nobody ever heard of Paul Bunyan. The nearest thing to him is Sock Saunders, who is more of a poltergeist than a hero. If a man drops a picaroon into the river he says, "Well, take it, Sock Saunders!" If he slips on a log, but catches himself in time, he says, "Foxed you that time, Sock Saunders." If he cuts his foot, he explains, "Sock Saunders got me." There are no stories about Sock Saunders. He's just the guy who hangs around and makes life complicated.

But nobody sings as they walk the boom in at Middle Dam, an event that should call for a chanty, with the boss lining out the verse and the walkers roaring the chorus. At Middle the *Rowell* can't get in close enough to the dam for the current to take the boom in, so on either side of the inlet above the dam is a headworks—a big log raft with a capstan on it. Hawsers are hitched to the boom, and four or more men man the capstan and walk the boom in. It comes reluctantly, inch by inch, as they walk doggedly round and round. It's hard, monotonous, drugging work. But nobody sings.

Around the camp the cook is the boss, no matter who the boss of the rest of the job is. What he says, goes. One year we had a cook named Scotty Maxwell, a veteran of the Boer War, who was at the relief of Ladysmith. How he landed in the Maine woods I don't know, but he is a good cook and he brought British Army discipline right along with him. He's a holy terror in the kitchen. He always has a meat cleaver handy, but he never has to do more than glance at it. He liked sit-down meals, where he could get people lined up in orderly rows instead of having them sprawled every which way, all over the yard. But nobody could sit down if his face and hands and fingernails couldn't pass Scotty's inspection. Whoever fell below his impossibly high standards went back and washed, ten times, if necessary. I went into the kitchen one day at first lunch and found five terrified Frenchmen sitting in a row on the floor with their plates between their knees. They'd worn their hats to the table, and were being taught gentlemanly conduct the hard way.

The third functionary around the drive is the bull-cook. This title puzzled me, as I never saw the bull-cook, a wizened little man answering to Bones, cooking. Jonesy cleared the matter up. "He's called the bull-cook, but he's really the barroom man."

"*Barroom?* But if you can't even have vanilla—"

"Oh, not that kind of a barroom. It's where the men sleep."

"Bunk-house?"

"Well, city folks might call it that." City folks also call a place to eat a mess-hall. In the woods it's the kitchen.

The barroom man is a combined chore-boy and chambermaid, and his job is no sinecure. He has to keep the barroom clean, keep a fire going in cold weather and a smudge going on nights when the bugs are bad. He also has to keep an outside fire going under an oil drum of water, so the men can bathe and launder. The cook won't have people using his hot water. Then he has to saw wood for his own and sometimes the cook's fires and row the lunches out to the *Alligator* crew when meal-time overtakes them in the middle of a haul.

This last was Bones' cross, because he couldn't row a boat. We used to make book on how long it would take him to get near enough to the *Alligator* to catch a line thrown him by the crew. But his sea-faring career ended one day when the wind came up while he was waiting on the *Alligator* for the crew to finish eating, so he could bring back the dishes. He was afraid to come ashore in the rowboat and spent the rest of the day on the Pond. The barroom fires went out and the boss was raging as was the cook. The *Alligator* crew missed two meals as he sat there and were not pleased. After that Frank rowed the meals out, and Bones helped with the potato peeling.

As May wore on toward June, we became used to waking up in the morning to the hollow *thunk* of the wood as it bumped down the rapids in front of the house. It is a pleasant sound, like distant, slow-beaten drums. We learned to watch the dam from our porch, and to grab our fly-rods and run when a boom came in. In the short interval between the arrival of a boom and the opening of the gates to sluice it, there is often a quarter hour's glorious fishing. The big trout and salmon follow the wood down out of the Pond, feeding on the grubs and insects that drop from the rotting bark. They come up from the green shade below with that powerful and accurate surge that so delights the heart to behold. Standing on the sluice-booms, one sometimes forgets to fish, so lost in awe and admiration does one become for their vicious grace.

After a little the water at our feet begins to stir almost imperceptibly, tugging gently at the wood that is held back by the "trip"—a single long log swung like a gate across the channel. That means the boss has had the gate raised a few inches to warn any fishermen who may be on the river below that they'd better high-tail it for the bank.

We had a boss once named Phil Haley who would not observe this convention. Fishermen got in his hair. They were always underfoot, walking out on the sluice-boom, snagging his men with their backcasts, and asking foolish questions. They disrupted work, because everyone always stopped everything in the hopes of seeing a hundred dollars' worth of Abercrombie & Fitch fall into the river and maybe drown. So when it came time to hoist, Phil hoisted. Let the jokers scramble. Phil it was who once gave Ralph ten dollars to hold for him as safeguard against losing it in a stud game. He said he might need it when he got Outside. He observed that "a ten dollar bill is an awful handy rig to have 'round," which seems to me to cover that both simply and adequately.

Most bosses, though, will warn the fishermen, so when we begin to see the boom stir and the drivers start climbing down onto the sluice-booms with their pick-poles, ready to pole the wood along toward the gate, we reel in our lines and climb up onto the dam to watch them hoist (pronounced heist) the gates.

Pond-in-the-River Dam is an old-fashioned wooden dam with a long, unpainted shed over the center section sheltering the gate-works. The gates are raised by man power, teams of several men each manning the big wheels at the ends of the heavy timber gates. They start turning the wheels over slowly, and the gates creak as they move against the enormous pressure against them. Then, as the tempo increases, the gates come up slowly, dark and dripping, groaning and protesting, and the water begins to flow under them, impatient to be free. The first white spate deepens and greens, and the low whispering rustle changes to a roar. The whole dam vibrates as the gates clear the water, and the boss shouts, "Let go your trip!" The men who have been on the gates come out on the dam, their chests heaving, their faces glistening with sweat, and watch the first wood go through. "She's runnin' good," they will say; and "Ain't that handsome pulp, though? Comes from up back of Metalluc. I was cuttin' on the stump up there last winter."

It's lovely on the dam on a bright spring morning, with the wind blowing down across the boom and filling the air with the sharp smell of resin, so strong and fresh that you can taste it. The planks tremble under your feet, and the roar of the river and the thumping of the wood fills the ears. The river is deep blue and crisping white, and the cut ends of the pulp are like raw gold in the sun. All the senses come alive, even that strange rare sense that tells you, half a dozen times between birth and death—if you are lucky—that right now, right in this spot, you have fallen into the pattern of the universe.

We would like to spit on the last log of the last boom of the drive as it goes through the dam, but we're not sure that this brings luck to any but those who have worked on the drive. So we give the good spitting spots to the river-hogs, who put a lot of store by the ceremony. They spit copiously and accurately, and I hope the charm works I thought I'd discovered a new folk-way when I saw a driver last year throw an almost new pair of work gloves into the sluice after the last log.

"Is that good luck, too?" I asked.

"Nope. I ain't needin' 'em any more, that's all. I'm through."

"Aren't you going on the rear?"

"Nope. I got a date over at the college in West Stewarts-town."

That is the euphemism for the county jail, and so I started to cluck the sympathetic tongue.

But my man threw out his chest. "They can't get along without me over there, when it comes time to plant the gardens," he said with modest pride. "I bossed the plantin' there now five years runnin'. Just happened I got picked up in Berlin every year there for a spell in the middle of May, for drunk an' disorderly. Last year I missed. We didn't get off the Diamond till late, an', Hairy Jesus, what a mess they made of them gardens! So when I got pinched last Christmas they turned me loose—deferred my sentence, the judge called it—till planting time. They weren't takin' no chances this year. Tomorrow mornin' there'll be a boat at Cedar Stump for me, an' I gotta be there."

After the last log has gone through the dam, there are still two or three days of "rearin'" before the drive moves out. Rearing is going down the river and cleaning up all the wood that has been left in the rear, caught on rocks or washed up on the banks. It is pitched back into the river again and finally gathered in the catch boom below. It's the hardest part of the drive. By that time it is hot, and the bugs are bad, the water is still like ice, and the men are wet from morning to night. But it marks the point at which you can begin to think definitely about getting drunk in Berlin, so the crew works with great speed and good humor. Before we know it the flash boards are off the dam, the river is clean as a whistle again, the roar of the rapids is back to normal, instead of rising thunderously one hour and startling us by sinking to a whisper in the next. (Here silence is an uncanny noise.) The men start trekking to Sunday Cove, where the work boat will pick them up and take them out. They call to us as they go by, "My regards to the little feller!" and "See you next year."

The cook does not walk to the Cove. He has his position to think of. He comes in, strange and formal without his white clothes and apron and in a store hat, and asks Ralph to drive him down. "I'll pay you," he says.

That's a pathetic thing about woodsmen. If they ask you a favor, they make it clear at once that they can and will pay for it. It's a telling comment on the treatment they receive on the Outside, where they are considered bums, and are always asked to pay as they enter, as it were. "I'll pay you," they say, protesting their self-respect. They are always so pleased and puzzled when we won't take money, pointing to all the favors they have done us. "Oh, that! That wa'n't nothin'."

So Ralph says to the cook, "Naw, you can't pay me. I'm going down that way anyhow."

The cook climbs into the car, and at the last minute leans out and says to me, "I left a few odds an' ends for you up at the wangan. No sense of throwing good food to the squirrels." I'm used to woods computations now, but the first year I was flabbergasted at the loot. There were a half a dozen pies, a flour barrel almost full of cookies and doughnuts, and ten huge loaves of bread—the cook's idea of a few odds and ends.

The first two or three days after the drive goes out we always feel a little lonely and lost. The wangan looks so forlorn as we go past, with no smoke coming out of the chimneys, no sound of Bones' axe ringing crisply from out back by the wood-pile, no men sitting on the long bench in front, or rinsing their clothes in the brook where it flows under the Carry Road. The windows are shuttered once more, and the benches have been taken inside. By the brook a forgotten pair of socks droops from an alder bush where they were hung up to dry. The trampled grass in the yard is beginning to spring upright again. Down by the Pond, the *Alligator* is high and dry again on her ways.

The drive is over. It wasn't what I had expected it to be. The men weren't romantic, or daring, or glamorous. But they were something much better. They were good neighbors. We're going to miss them.

But not for a week or so. Not until Fred Bennett comes in again and takes the phones out. While they stay we'll be too busy to miss anyone. The fishermen have begun to swarm into the woods. "Sports" the natives call them here; it is a term like the cowboy's "dudes" or the stage farmer's "city slickers." Fishing up and down the river, deep, so they think, in the wilds of Maine, they are amazed and baffled to find telephones hanging on trees.

I know just what they say. They say, "Well, for crying out loud! Look at the telephone! Gee, let's ring it and see if anyone answers."

So they ring it. Naturally they ring one, which is our number, and by the time Fred Bennett gets in we are half insane with trying to explain in a million well-chosen words the whys and wherefores of the situation.

But now, I think we have at last evolved a system. We've got now so we can tell a "sport's" ring from a native's. It has a feeble, wavering quality, quite unlike that of the firm hand accustomed to cranking a battery phone. So when that kind of a ring comes over the line, we take down the receiver, say briskly, "Grand Central Station, Information Booth," and hang up. It almost always stops them.

To be fair to the writers of the romantic school of logging fiction, what they invariably dealt with is the long-log drive, which is quite different from the pulp drive of to-day. They used to drive long logs—and by that I mean whole trees, sometimes as long as sixty feet—here. But those days were a decade or more ago. We would never see their like again, the old river-hogs mourned. And we never would have, if it hadn't been for the hurricane that hit New England in 1938.

The hurricane blew down millions of feet of pine. Pine isn't used for pulp, so there was no chance of its being cleaned up on the next pulp operation. Nobody would gamble on taking it out as the market would be glutted with pine after the hurricane. The prospects were that it would just lie where it had fallen in crazy jack-pots. Inside of a year the worms would be in it, unless a forest fire got there first; and what the worms and fire missed would burn in the slower, surer fire of decay. It's a truly sad thing to see a big tree lying on the ground, even if you know that the bringing low of so much beauty and majesty will serve some useful end. It's heart-breaking when nothing but waste will result.

And then the Government had a good idea—"for the

Gov'ment," as they say up here. They set up a Timber Salvage Administration for the saving of the pine. The lumbering was let out to local contractors who would get the blowdown out of the woods and into Government storage booms in specified ponds and lakes, whence its release onto the market could be controlled. Worms will not attack wood that is in the water, and water won't injure it for years. The Government paid a fixed price, depending on grade, and Government scalers and graders oversaw the work, and presumably prevented the woodsmen, who were paid on a piece-work basis, from cutting any standing pine. It's a lot easier to cut a standing tree than one that is not only down, but also tangled up in a half a dozen others. It's a lot safer, too. You can never tell what a blowdown will do when you get a saw almost through it. It may drop as you plan it's going to. On the other hand the stresses may be such that it will jump with the force of a forty-mule-kick and knock you galley-west. You never can tell, and maybe you won't get a chance to make a second guess.

The nearest Government storage booms were below us in Umbagog, and Jim Barnett contracted to get out the pine lying on the slopes along Rapid River and into the booms before winter set in. He moved his men and wangan into the Pond-in-the-River driving camp in early summer, and by the first of October he was ready to drive the logs, which he had temporarily boomed up in the Pond, down the river to the Government booms. I, personally, was looking forward to this drive with a great deal of interest, because I had long since given up hope of ever seeing a long-log drive. I wasn't glad the trees had blown down, you understand, but since they had, I was glad to be on the spot to see them driven.

And then the Government had another idea. We should have been warned when we read in a two-week-old Boston Sunday paper a feature article on the Romance of Hurricane Timber—that was what they were calling our blowdown Outside—and the Revival of the Old Long-Log Days. We should have been warned, but we were only entertained. We had no inkling of what was in store for us until Jim came in from Outside one day and began telling about meeting the Timber Salvage agent, who, it seemed, had discovered a publicity angle to the pine drive. This long-log drive on Rapid River would probably be the very last of the old time drives ever to be held, and he thought it should be perpetuated for posterity. He was going to bring in a bunch of newspaper reporters and newsreel cameramen to make a living record of this rapidly dying bit of the American scene—his verbiage, not Jim's or mine—and Jim's share in the project was to give them something to take pictures of and write about. It would be interesting to people, he said, and it would be good publicity—for whom he carefully didn't specify. The tax payers were footing the bill for the salvage, after all.

All this seemed fair enough to Jim, and he was perfectly willing to co-operate. The only trouble was that the agent seemed to take for granted deeds of derring-do, heart-stopping crises, and a plethora of almost legendary figures whose prowess had been told in song and story all up and down the rivers of Maine. In the fall of the year there isn't enough water in the lakes to put much of a head on the river, so it was going to be impossible to open the festivities with the expected forty-foot wall of water racing down the channel, the long logs turning end over end along its face like match sticks. And as for legendary figures, Jim was fresh out of them. The men he had had working for him all summer were just natives who knew how to use an axe and a two-man cross-cut, and he'd planned to use the same men on the drive. They were strong and willing, and they could get the pine down the river all right, if allowed to go about it in their own way. But they weren't old-time river-hogs. Most of those boys were either dead or retired to parts unknown. The only legendary figure Jim knew anything about was reposing at the moment at the county jail. However, he was willing to make a stab at putting on a show for the Fourth Estate.

The first requirement seemed to be more water, so Jim had a couple of courses of flash-boards added to those already on Pondy Dam, and stopped driving altogether for two days to give the Pond a chance to fill up. The second requirement seemed to be a prima donna for the occasion. The man over in the jail—whose name I have forgotten but whom I'll call Black John—seemed to be the logical choice. He was presumably available through the simple expedient of paying off his fine; and he had plenty of legends clustered around his name. He was said to have crossed the Androscoggin on floating logs, once when young and drunk, just to give one example. So Roy Bragg, who was bossing the drive and had a drag at the jail, went over to get him.

He came back with Black John all right, but announced that they'd have to return him in good condition as soon as the emergency was over. Black John had been arrested during the preceding month and it was now the last of

September and the court records were closed and couldn't be opened again. They were terribly sorry, over at the jail, and they wanted to oblige; but they didn't make the laws. However, if Roy wanted to *borrow* Black for a couple of days, they'd be glad to lend him, if Roy would be sure to return him in good order. Roy was sure. Why wouldn't he be? There would be no liquor and he had plenty of strong-arm boys to keep their eyes on Black.

Early the next day the work boat brought in the camera-men and reporters. None of the woodsmen had ever been exposed to the gentlemen of the press before, and they were fascinated. So was I. They were exactly what I hoped they'd be, from reading and movie-going. They got every-body in a dither by running around poking their noses into everything and asking questions. The woodsmen were all ready to go out and start driving the logs, and I think they were a little baffled when it developed that first they were to take off their coats and sit around the camp and barroom occupying themselves with their usual Sunday diversions—stud poker, clothes mending, saw filing, read-ing, and sleeping—while they had their pictures taken.

Then the newsmen got a look at Black John, the star of the show. He wasn't much to look at, I'll admit—just a wizened up little old man with a grizzly stubble of beard, a bleary eye, and a slept-in suit of clothes. So the press went to work on him. They combed the camp for a suitable out-fit for him, snatching riding pants—known in the woods as puff-panties—off someone, making someone else kick in with his hat, and assembling every plaid shirt in the outfit until they found one that would not only fit reasonably well, but that would also photograph well. By the time they were through, Black John did look a little legendary, and he'd begun to act legendary, too. I don't think he'd ever in his life had such a fuss made over him. But he rated it. We all realized that, as soon as the gates were hoisted and the river began to roar.

There is a lot of difference between a river full of pulp-wood and a river full of long-logs. Pulp is just thousands of chunks—pronounced "junks" in our country—of wood. There is nothing particularly impressive about it, and it can be a nuisance, collecting in our swimming pool, clogging up the little basin between two rocks where I rinse my Monday washing, and spoiling the fishing. But long-logs—well, they come surging down the current like express trains, shedding green water from their backs, and leaping over boulders. There's something vicious about their bulk and speed—something alive and dangerous. Of pulp you say, "There's a lot of wood." Of a long-log you find yourself thinking, "There was a tree."

Black John climbed down through the dam and clung to the pier, waiting, his feet in their caulked boots a few inches above the racing water. Pretty soon he saw what he wanted plunging down upon him—a big high-riding pine butt. He leaped, and when he landed, light as a cat, his feet were going in a little dance step. The log spun and twisted and water boiled up to his knees, but he kept right side up. He didn't even seem to be paying much attention to what he was doing, and, to give him credit, he wasn't paying attention to the cameras, either. He was just standing there motionless except for his dancing feet. But when his log crashed onto a reef and half its length reared out of water, Black John was in the air a split second before the crash, and as the two wings of water flung out by the settling log collapsed, he was ten feet away on another log, still poker faced, still keeping his feet moving. He was good, all right.

After the cameramen had taken what they considered enough feet of that, they announced to Jim that now they wanted a log jam. So the boss went downriver to find one. With the amount of water running, that should be easy, but just to play it safe, Jim told him to take a crew, and if they couldn't find one ready-made, to make one. In the meantime he suggested that maybe the newsmen would like to see Black John go through the sluice of the dam on a log. Black John balked, however. He'd go for ten dollars, but he wouldn't go for nothing. In the first place this was supposed to be a vacation from jail, and he wasn't going to exert himself too much. He could work back at the clink. In the second place, if he fell into the river, as he was likely to do, it would cost him money. He'd have to reimburse the owners of his borrowed finery, and he'd have to buy himself a bottle of pneumonia preventative. However, he did finally compromise to the extent of agreeing to go down the sluice in a bateau if Jim would get him a crew. By the time the crew was found and had been taken out of their overalls and put into something more suitable, and the sluice had been successfully negotiated, the boss was back with the news that he hadn't been able to find a jam, but he'd managed to start a honey on the rips just above Long Pool. So we all adjourned the half mile down the river.

It was a pretty good jam. The logs were coming around the bend and hurling themselves onto the key log that the men had managed to lodge across the current, hitting with a hollow booming and jumping clear out of water when they struck. The newsreel men set up their cameras and

the reporters got out their pencils, and the entire person-
nel of the camp swarmed out onto the jam to break it up.
Half of the men had never seen a log jam before (pulp-
wood doesn't jam), but by this time they were all infected
with the desire to get into the movies, so it wasn't very
surprising that almost immediately some real action began. Somebody heaved too hard, and somebody else who
was watching the cameras instead of what he was doing
fell down into the crack between two logs. It was no joke.
He went down to his armpits in the icy water, and all that
prevented him from going further was the fact that he
flung his arms around the logs. And the logs kept piling up
from above, and nothing was giving an inch below. It's
not very pleasant to stand on a river bank and watch
a man being crushed within twenty feet of you, especially
when there's not a thing you can do about it except yell.
We all yelled, except the cameramen. They just kept on
turning their cranks. That was their job, and I decided
then that it wasn't a job I'd care for. It requires too much
nerve.

And then Black John ran out onto the jam. He looked
frail and ineffectual beside some of the woodsmen already
there, but he was a river-hog from 'way back. He knew
what to do. It was a very telling demonstration of the
superiority of brains and experience over brawn. One
heave with a cant dog, and the jaws of the nutcracker
opened six inches. Six inches was enough. Out came the
nut, so to speak, and high-tailed it for shore, leaving his
cant dog behind him. Another heave or two, and the whole
jam started downriver.

This I will say for Black John. He didn't let the situation die like that, with a bunch of logs floating off into the

unknown. He threw back his head and howled, "Never mind the man! Grab his cant dog! That cost the company money!" That was the old river-hogs' battle cry. It put the finishing touch on the episode. Black John had a true feeling for style.

That about ended the famous long-log drive—except, of course, for the actual driving of the logs down to Umbagog. Its like will never be seen again. As a matter of fact, I doubt if its like was ever seen before in the annals of lumbering; it was unique. But everybody was satisfied. The newshawks—to quote *Time*—got their stories; the cameramen got their pictures; the salvage agent got his publicity; the woodsmen got their faces in the "moom-pitchers"; and the rest of us got a field day. I'm not sure what Jim Barnett got, except a lot of trouble and expense. If it's any comfort to him, we Riches think he managed the whole affair with graciousness and tact.

P.S. Black John was returned safely and in good condition.

VIII

⌒

"Aren't You Ever Frightened?"

THERE'S NOTHING TO BE AFRAID OF IN THE WOODS—EXCEPT
yourself. Nothing is going to hurt you—except yourself.
This, like all sweeping statements, is subject to a few
amendments; but the basic idea still holds. There is nothing at all to be afraid of in the woods—excepting always
yourself.

When I investigate what lies back of the statement, "I'd
be simply terrified most of the time, living the way you
do," I usually find bears. For some reason the non-woods-
wise expect to be eaten by a bear the minute they get out
of calling distance of a main highway. If it isn't a bear
that's going to attack them, it's a wildcat, and if it isn't a
wildcat, it's probably a rabbit. There may be a little more
danger from a bear than from a rabbit; after all, a bear
is larger. Animals in the woods aren't out looking for
trouble. They don't have to look for it. Their lives are
nothing but one trouble after another. The sentimental
view is that wild animals live an idyll, doing what they
want, browsing on herbs and flowers, wandering happily
along woodland glades, and sleeping where night overtakes

them. Actually the poor devils must live in a constant state of terror. So many things can, and do, happen to them. They can starve or freeze in winter. They are fly-ridden in the summer. Men and larger animals constantly harass them. Their young may be taken from them by any number of means, all violent. They know trouble too well to be interested in making any more. I pity all animals, but especially wild animals, from the bottom of my heart; and it's very hard to be afraid of anything that arouses pity.

I don't want to pose as an expert in animal life. In other words, I want to hedge a little. I don't know anything about lions or rogue elephants or hippopotamuses. People who know about them claim they're something to steer clear of, and I'll take their word for it. I've never happened to get in between a she-bear and her cubs, but I understand that that's not a good thing to do. I'm just talking about the Maine woods and the animals you ordinarily encounter there.

The way to see wild animals to the best advantage is to see without being seen. As a matter of fact, that's about the only possible way to see them. They don't stand around, if they see you first. I always wonder as I walk down the road, how many pairs of eyes have me under surveillance, how many hearts beat with suffocating rapidity until it is certain that I am going straight along the Carry on my own harmless business. I can feel that constant mute and questioning regard from hillside and thicket and roadside tangle of grasses and weeds; deer and bear and coon, and fox, mink and partridge and little white-footed, bat-eared mouse—they all stand and watch.

My favorite animals to watch are the deer and foxes. They are both so quick and pretty and well co-ordinated, and they're both such a lovely red color in the summer. We don't see foxes very often. They do their sleeping by day and their prowling by night. Once I saw one, though, eating blueberries off a bush. Usually we see them trotting their precise and dainty trot along the road. This one looked so informal, with his feet braced and his head out-thrust, pulling the clusters of ripe berries off the bushes, and ducking as the branch snapped back.

We see deer all the time, but we never get tired of them—or almost never. The exception was a deer we named Joe. He started coming into the yard when he was just a young spike-horn, and we took such pains not to frighten him that he soon became very tame. He'd stand around and watch us work. Deer are very curious, and it almost got to the point where before Ralph could drive a nail into a board, he had to shove Joe's nose out of the way. That was all right; what finally fed us up with Joe was his destructive attitude toward our flower gardens.

We'd worked hard on those gardens. One was an old ant hill, which we'd chosen as the site for a bed because it had good exposure and didn't need clearing. All it needed was to have the ants exterminated. Before we got through with that little chore, we wished we'd never been born. Two or three of the beds just had to have the underbrush and roots and rocks cleared away—and, of course, the soil changed over from acid woods mold to good garden earth. But the last of them we made on the vestigial remains of an ancient bridge pier. No one has ever been able to account for that pier. It is just above the house on the river bank and apparently once there was a very sizable bridge there. The pier is made of huge boulders, much too large to have been moved by anything less than an ox team, so the bridge was more than a temporary structure. There must have been a road through there once, but there is no record of there ever having been such a road. Where would it have come from and where would it have gone to? Nobody knows. There is no trace of it now. Someone once advanced the theory that Arnold might have built it on his way to Quebec, but I think his route is pretty well established as having been well to the east and north of here. Whatever the reason for the bridge, it was built a long, long time ago. We had to cut trees with six-inch butts when we cleared off the pier for our flower garden.

But that was only the beginning. When we got the trees cut and the roots and sod cleared away, there was nothing left but bare rock. We had to haul dirt in, from any place we could scrape it up, to fill the pockets in the rocks, and we had to haul in about an even amount of stable dressing to make the earth arable. We'd been all through this with the vegetable garden, but this was worse, because there was no hauling the trailer with the Packard to the scene of the operation and pitching the load off. It all had to be transshipped from the road by wheelbarrow, down narrow planks laid on a steep bank. It was a lot of work, and when we got it done and planted we didn't appreciate having Joe go in there to stamp down all our seedlings and later eat all the blossoms off any plants that survived his first treatment.

It may well be asked why we bother with a flower garden, considering all the sweat involved, especially when we have a whole forest full of wild flowers for the picking. The answer may sound a little silly, especially to those people to whom we have so carefully explained that no, we don't miss seeing other people. We don't miss them at all.

It may sound a little pixyish and whimsical to say that what we do sometimes get lonesome for are civilized flowers, and stretches of lawn and ordered gardens. Our tangles of zinnias and larkspur and violas, slopping over into rather shaggy grass paths, may be a pretty far cry from shell walks and clipped hedges and roses around a sun dial; but we love them and I can have tame flowers to put on my dinner table and around the living-room part of the year.

I hope the foregoing explains why we got bored with Joe. Unfortunately, he didn't get bored with us. He'd go back onto the ridges every fall, and we'd hope for the best. But every spring he'd show up again, bigger and lustier than ever. It didn't make us much happier to learn that a full grown buck makes a dangerous pet. After he has reached maturity, he may, without a moment's warning, turn definitely nasty, lashing out with horns and hoofs for no reason at all. The Durkees in Upton had a tame buck that, after living off their bounty for several years, suddenly chased someone into the lake—it was fall, too, and the water was cold—and wouldn't let him out until someone put a bullet through his head. We didn't want that to happen to us. The situation was solved when we developed that dog team idea. The smell and sound of a pack of huskies was enough to scare Joe into the next county. So some good did come out of that impractical dog-dream after all.

Probably the cutest, sweetest animals in the woods are new born fawns. They aren't red like their mothers, but spotted tan and white, so that when they stand still—as they do, instinctively, in the presence of danger—they look like just another patch of sun-dappled shadow. There is nothing quite so defenseless as a new little fawn, so Nature takes over its protection until it can at least outrun the more deadly of its enemies. Not only does a fawn become practically invisible when it stands still, but it has no scent whatever to betray its presence. A dog that can smell a deer a half a mile away will pass a fawn almost within touching distance, and never turn its head. Oddly enough, the fathers of most of the wilderness young are hell bent on their destruction, so Nature attends to that, too. During the spring and early summer, when the does are dropping their fawns, the bucks are in the velvet. They have shed their antlers during the previous winter, and on their heads are the beginnings of the new horns—two swollen, velvet-covered knobs, which are not only soft, but are also extremely sensitive. The mildest-mannered doe, inspired by mother love, has no trouble at all during the velvet season in bull-dozing the toughest buck that ever breathed. Nobody ever told us that this is the reason for the apparently extravagant antler-dropping, but to us it seems obvious, and I mention it because so many people have remarked to us that they didn't see any point in a buck's growing a fine set of horns only to lose them before the next spring.

Some people who should know better—like some guides and woodsmen—believe that a doe will desert her fawn if she detects the man scent on it, and they warn you not to touch a spotted fawn. I'm happy to be in a position to state authoritatively that this isn't so. This is how I happen to know.

One day in the early summer, Ralph was coming down from Middle Dam in our old Model T, and, as usual, he wasn't sparing the horses. He broke over the crest of

Wangan Hill and around the bend in the road, and there in front of him right in the middle of the road was a doe and a fawn that couldn't have been more than a few hours old. Its spots were bright and it wavered on its slender, impossibly delicate little legs. Ralph slammed on everything and skidded to a halt just as the doe, who stuck until the radiator was almost touching her, jumped clear. She had courage, poor thing. The fawn couldn't jump. It was too little and weak and confused. It went down in the road. Ralph swarmed over the door, heart-broken. He's often hardboiled in his attitude toward his own kind, but when it comes to animals, he's just a bowl of custard. Then he saw that he'd stopped well short of the fawn. It hadn't been touched. It had simply obeyed a command from something that had been born within it—a command to play possum. It lay flat on its belly with its hind legs under its body in a crouch and its front legs stretched straight out, its head between them. The grass between the ruts arched over it, and it lay perfectly supine, even when Ralph bent over it. Only its eyes moved, rolling back to follow his movements. Even when he ran his hand along its spine, to make sure it was all right, the only sign of life it gave was an uncontrollable shrugging of the loose skin on its back. It didn't know what this was all about; after all, it had had only since about dawn to get used to this world; it had nothing to go by except that inner voice; but it was doing its poor little best to follow instructions.

It was obvious that it would go on lying there until snow flew, unless something was done, and Ralph had to get home to dinner. So he picked it up in his arms and started to carry it to the side of the road. Then it came to life. Legs flew in all directions. It was like trying to cuddle an indignant centipede, Ralph informed me later. He put it down off the road in a hollow by a large rock, and leaped into the Ford.

The first thing I knew about the affair was when I heard the car come into the yard, and Ralph's voice shouting for me to come quick and ask no questions. Fortunately, I have long been accustomed to following orders first and finding out afterwards, so I set the pudding I was making back off the fire and ran. On the way back to Wangan Hill, Ralph explained what had happened, so I was all prepared when we left the car at the foot of the hill and walked the last hundred yards to where he had left the fawn. The hollow by the rock was empty.

Then we looked up. There, not twenty feet from us, were the doe and fawn, standing in a little patch of sunlight. It was one of the prettiest sights I ever saw. The little fellow was standing perfectly still while its mother lapped it over from head to tail, to get the obnoxious human smell off it. They both stared at us gravely for a long moment, and then the doe wheeled and trotted away—not frightened, not even nervous—with her child galloping obediently at her heels. If I'd been a mother then—which I wasn't—I'd have known that this was all that would have happened. There have been times since when Rufus didn't smell exactly like a lily, but I've never considered abandoning him for that reason.

The animals we see most, next to deer, are porcupines. I can't seem to find it in my heart to love a porcupine. They're perfectly harmless—they *don't* throw quills, by the way—but they're stupid and ugly, and besides, they do a lot of damage. They fill the dogs full of quills, which is the dogs' fault, I'm willing to grant—and they try to gnaw our houses down around our ears, and they climb trees and sometimes girdle the tops, thereby killing them. The quills stick up all over their backs in an untidy mess, and they have blunt rodent faces with dull, slow eyes. They don't make any noise, except a rattling sound, which I've read is made by clacking their quills, but which I think, myself, they make with their teeth. I can't vouch for this. I don't have much traffic with them. I did catch one once and put it under a water pail in the middle of the garage, so that when Ralph went to back the car in, he'd have to get out and move the pail. I knew what his frame of mind would be toward the blankety blank so-and-so that would leave a pail there, and I thought it would be fun to have him kick it viciously aside, only to unveil a furious porcupine. It didn't work. The porcupine escaped by a sapping operation, and Ralph didn't get home until after dark and never saw the pail. We did have an albino porcupine that lived for a while out back of Gerrish's house, and that, being rather rare, was interesting enough. But porcupines as a tribe are very, very dull. We had a weasel living in the chimney base once, too, but we never could get very matey with him, either. He was too quick for us. We'd see him, brown in summer and white in winter, flowing like quicksilver in and out of the rocks and bristling his whiskers at us. He always gave me the shivers. He was so deadly purposeful, and he had such a vicious eye. I was glad when he moved away.

We've never seen a wildcat, though there are plenty of them around. We see their tracks often enough, and sometimes hear them yowling on the ridges. They aren't dangerous, unless cornered, but they like to make you think they are. One of their tricks is to follow you along the road, just about dusk. They don't stay out in the open, where you can turn around and heave a rock at them. They keep in the bushes at the side. When you stop, they stop. When you hurry, they hurry. After a while it gets on your nerves.

Once in the late fall I was sitting in the living-room of an evening with Ralph and our friend Rush Rogers, knitting. It was a very peaceful scene. For once the room was reasonably tidy, and for once the dogs—we had two then, Kyak and Mukluk—were sensible of their responsibilities, and were lying in picturesque postures in front of the fire, instead of trying to crowd us out of our best chairs. The firelight glanced off the backs of the books on their shelves in a satisfactorily colorful manner, and a little light snow brushed the window panes gently from time to time. The radio was coming in well, and the room was full of music. I should have been purring like a cat, with contentment, but I was uncomfortable, for some reason. I couldn't settle down.

Rush said, "Good Lord, Louise, what ails you? I never saw you twitchy before."

I said, "I don't know. I just feel someone looking at me."

Ralph hooted. "I suppose so. Who, for instance?"

I said stubbornly, "I don't know. I only know someone's looking at me. I can feel it."

I didn't get any sympathy. I just got told that neither of them could stand notional females, and if I was planning to develop a temperament, I'd better go somewhere else and develop it. They both knew a lot of sure-fire cures for temperament.

But I still felt someone looking at me.

Finally I couldn't stand it any longer. I got up, lighted a lantern, and went out on the porch. The dogs raised their heads somnolently, and Ralph and Rush exchanged looks of bored amusement. It was snowing lightly outside and the porch floor on the open end was sugared thinly over—all except for a little spot where a furry rump had been planked, and two smaller ones that were clearly paw marks, directly outside the window at which I was sitting. A scramble in the snow told of a hasty departure when I had opened the door. The evidence was easy to read. A wildcat had been sitting within three feet of me all evening, watching me knit. I learned later that this is not at all uncommon. They love to look in at lighted windows. I can't imagine why. I can't imagine, either, what ailed the dogs that they didn't put up a howl—except that they have a real talent for always doing the wrong thing, even when the wrong thing is nothing.

We see bears only once in a while, although there are plenty of them around here. They are shy animals, not easily caught unaware. We usually come on them in various berry patches, when their attention is concentrated on picking berries and they are off guard. These encounters are carried off with a minimum of excitement. We say, "Oh," and start south, and the bear says, "Oh," and starts north. Not that anybody is afraid of anybody, you understand. We just don't like to intrude on each other's privacy.

We don't believe in confining wild animals. Nothing makes me madder than to see a lion in a cage or some luckless racoon chained up at a gas station. I'm not a reformer by nature, but that's one thing I will crusade about. I think it's all right to kill animals if you have to, or even if you want to, but it's not all right to imprison them. I always feel like declaring a holiday, and Ralph does declare one, when we hear about a service station's confined bear running amok and maiming a few attendants and customers. It serves them darn well right. So, feeling as we do, we never try to make pets of the wild life around us. Just once did we make an exception, and that was none of our seeking. It was more or less wished on us by circumstances.

This is the way it happened. I had asked Coburn's driver to bring me in three lemons, so when Ralph came home with the mail and handed me a little paper bag, I thought I knew what was in it. I tipped it up and dumped the contents out on the kitchen work bench. Then I did a typical female, clutching my pant legs and shrieking, "Eeeee! Take that thing away from here." My lemons had suffered a sea-change into a two- or three-day-old skunk.

When I recovered my composure enough to look the thing over, I had to admit it was cute. It was about three inches long, with an equally long tail and about half inch legs, and it was striped black and white like any other skunk. Ralph had seen it in the road when he went up to get the mail, and when he came back over an hour later, it was still there. By then it had fallen into a deep rut and was unable to get out. He stopped the car to help it, and found that it was almost too weak to stand. We discovered later that, the day before, a mother skunk, accompanied by her new and numerous offspring, had had a skirmish there with one of Coburn's guest's dogs. (The dog lost, incidentally.) In the fracas, this little fellow, whom we named Rollo, got lost.

You can't go off and leave a young thing to die of starvation, naturally, so Ralph picked it up and brought it home. He put it in the lemon bag so he could hold it without hurting it while he drove with one hand. He thought he could probably figure out some way to feed it after he got it home.

Cookie, Kyak's mother and the best dog we ever had, was our dog of the moment. Not to put too strong a point on it, she was the best dog anybody ever had, bar none. Kyak and the other pups were a couple of weeks old, and we were still keeping them in a pen in the corner of the kitchen, where they'd be warm and where Cookie could reach them easily. While we were debating the skunk commissary question, she came in to dispense the evening meal to her family. That seemed to be the answer. We found an unoccupied nipple, told Cookie everything was under control, and added Rollo to the roster. She looked a little startled, but, being the dog she was, took our word for it that the situation was entirely *comme il faut*. That's the kind of a good dog she was.

Cookie was willing, and Rollo had the right idea, but a husky is built on a somewhat grander scale than a skunk, so it wouldn't work. Then we thought of a medicine dropper, and that did work. Poor little Rollo went at it, clutching the dropper frenziedly with both front paws, and never stopped drinking the warmed canned milk and water until his little stomach was as round and hard—and about as large—as a golf ball. By this time Cookie's four pups were gorged and asleep, so we dumped Rollo in with them. Cookie looked at us, smelled of him, and looked at us again, trying to understand what was expected of her. Cookie definitely was a lady, and she always tried to live up to her station in life. She understood that we meant that she was to take care of this odd-looking addition to her family. So she rolled him over with her nose and, despite his struggles, lapped Rollo thoroughly from stem to stern, just as she washed her own children. After that Rollo belonged. Nobody was going to accuse Cookie of favoritism; and from that day on, Rollo was just another husky puppy, as far as she was concerned.

I think he, himself, thought he was a dog. Certainly the other pups treated him like one of themselves. The whole lot of them played together as puppies do, roughhousing and mock-fighting, chewing each other's tails and ears, and attempting mayhem in any form. At first we used to try to rescue Rollo. The pups were almost ten times as big as he was, and I was afraid he'd get killed. But he didn't thank me at all for my solicitude. When I put him down again at a safe distance from the fray, he'd stamp his hind legs in a towering rage—the skunk method of expressing extreme irritation, and the last step before the gas attack—and rush back to fling himself into the battle. I still don't understand why he didn't get completely ruined. I've often seen one dog grab him by the scruff of the neck while another grabbed his tail, pulling him in opposite directions with all their might, growling and shaking him as puppies will do with a piece of rope. It made my stomach ache to watch, but he apparently loved it for when they released him, he'd always rush in for more. It's my opinion that that twenty-four hours of being lost in the wilderness so early in life left a bad scar on his subconscious, so that he valued any attention as preferable to no attention. He'd never let himself be left alone for a moment, if he could help it, and when the pups slept, he was never content to sleep on the edge of the heap. He'd always burrow down into the center, completely out of sight.

He used to follow me around like a shadow as I did my housework. He'd be at full gallop never more than six inches behind my heels, and if I reversed my field, he'd side-step and fall right in again. It was lucky he was so fast on his feet. Half the time I'd never know he was there and, if I'd ever stepped on him, there wouldn't have been even a grease spot left. He was so tiny he could easily curl up in one of my shoes and have plenty of room left. It made him simply furious to have me go upstairs. The risers of the steps were much too high for him to negotiate, and I'd come back down again to find him stamping back and forth in a dudgeon below the first step. That stamping never failed to amuse me. He'd not only be mad—he'd be just damn good and mad! And yet, though he obviously wanted to make a noise like thunder and stamp the house down, the best he could make was a little pattering sound on the floor. If you're ever gone out of a room in a fury and slammed the door behind you with what was supposed to be a shattering crash, only to find it was equipped with a pneumatic check and so eased soundlessly into place, you can appreciate how he probably felt. Still despite his rages, he never in all the time he was with us made the slightest smell in the house. We thought some of having him operated on, but the vet in Rumford said frankly he had never done such an operation, so we let it go. We are glad now that we didn't find someone who could do it. He was cleaner around the house than any cat we ever had and he never, even in his infancy, made a single error.

Only once that we know of did he ever make a smell and we couldn't blame him for that; in fact, Ralph applauded him. We had at that time a cat named Jane, and she and Rollo had always hated each other, for no good reason that we could ever see, for they always left each other strictly alone. One evening I had made a chocolate malted milk for Rollo—that was his favorite food—and set it out. Rollo was just starting in on it when Jane appeared around the corner. Rollo stamped violently but Jane continued to approach and sniffed at the saucer. She wasn't going to touch the contents, I'm sure; she was just curious. But he had warned her and she had paid no attention. Faster than the eye could follow, he turned end for end, arched his tail over his back, and—whisht! smack into Jane's face at a range of less than a foot. She rolled right over backward, scrambled to her feet, and went off like a bullet. She never came back. Presently she took up her abode at the nearest lumber camp.

We had been afraid that after the pups and the skunk reached the age where they could eat solid food, Rollo would starve unless we fed him separately. He could never hold his own, we thought, against that gang of ruffians. We might as well have spared ourselves the worry. He was quite capable of looking out for himself. When the crush around the communal pan of puppy biscuit and milk became too great, he would wade right into the middle of the dish, forcing the pups to eat along the edges while he stuffed himself practically into a coma.

Rollo became a terribly spoiled brat before the summer had advanced very far. We gave him too much attention, and so did the dogs, and so did the sports who kept coming in in increasing numbers as the news of our pet skunk spread. I never thought to have my social career sponsored by a skunk, but that is what it amounted to. I met more new people during that summer than I ever have before or since in the same length of time. Perfect strangers, they'd come drifting into the yard from God knows where, say "Good morning" and then come to the point:—"We heard you've got a pet skunk." The upshot was always the same:—would it be all right for them to have their pictures taken holding Rollo? The folks back home— Rollo became as camera conscious as a child movie star, and as objectionable. He'd look bored and sulky—but he'd never miss the chance to have his picture taken. His complete composure served as an excellent foil, I might add, to the nervous apprehension on the faces of his picture-companions. Nobody ever seemed to quite take our word for it that he was perfectly safe.

Skunks are a horribly maligned animal. Everyone shuns them. Everyone accuses them, and without ascertaining the facts, of various crimes, such as hen-killing and egg sucking. They do no such things. Actually they do no damage at all; on the contrary, they are the natural enemies of vermin of all sorts and among man's best friends in the country. They are naturally gentle and easily tamed. A skunk will never attack until he is sure his person is in danger, or unless he is suddenly startled. I wish more people would bother to be nice to skunks. We were, and it paid. Rollo, in spite of being spoiled, made a perfect house pet while he was with us.

We never made any effort to confine him so it couldn't last forever. He was always free to come and go as he pleased. We even untacked a corner of the screen in the kitchen door so he could get in and out at will. As he grew older, he began to revert to nature, and the skunk nature is nocturnal. He slept more days, and roamed about nights. When we went out to the woodshed in the early, dewy morning to get kindling to start the breakfast fire, we would more and more often meet him, just coming home from a night's ramble. Then for a while he wouldn't come home for two or three days at a time, and finally he didn't come home at all. We'd meet him sometimes a mile or more down the Carry Road, and he'd run up to us and we'd pick him up. He never forgot us, and we never forgot him. We just grew apart, as those whose interests diverge always grow apart. Finally we stopped seeing him altogether. I don't know what eventually did happen to him—whether he wandered away, or whether he met with an accident. Very few wild animals die of old age. One thing we were glad of then—that if he did meet with death in any of the common swift wilderness forms, at least he was able to go down fighting. We hadn't rendered him defenseless.

Actually I've only been frightened once by animals since I came here to live. That was up at Miller's, and was a completely silly performance. It happened a long time ago, when Cookie was only a puppy. She had an enemy—Miller's older cow—who never overlooked an opportunity to chase her. I don't know how the feud started, and I don't know whether the cow would have hurt Cookie if she had caught her. It may have been just her bovine idea of a game. However, that may be, she certainly looked like business as she thundered after that terrified little ball of fur, with her head down, her nostrils flaring, and her tail out stiff behind. I don't blame Cookie for putting her tail between her legs and scuttling.

It was in June, and Alice Miller had a houseful. There were her sister Amy and two small girls, a half dozen men who were working repairing the dam, a woman named Polly Gould who was doing the cooking for them, and her little girl, besides Alice's own family. We went up there one evening to visit with the assembled multitude, and in the course of events, Alice, Amy, Polly and I took the collection of five small children and my small dog up into the back pasture to see if the blueberries were ripe. The two cows and Betty, the horse, were grazing off toward the edge of the woods, but we didn't pay any attention to them. Betty is as cross-grained a piece of horse-flesh as ever drew breath, but usually she minds her own affairs.

Cookie saw her old enemy in the distance, too, and I suppose she thought that now her inning had come. She'd been the chasee all too often. Now she was with me, the all-powerful; it was her turn to be the chaser. I don't suppose it ever entered her addled little head that the creature lived and breathed that would have the temerity even to think of attacking me or Ralph. We were God, as far as she was concerned. If you're walking with God, there's nothing you don't dare. You even dare to run yapping after a dragon and nip at its heels.

Unfortunately, neither the cows nor that limb of Satan, Betty, were True Believers. As one, they threw back their heads in affronted amazement, snorted, and took off after Cookie, who knew only one thing to do. She turned in her tracks and sought sanctuary under the shadow of my wing.

The first I knew about the whole business was when Amy shrieked, seized her youngest by the arm, and started running for the gate. The rest of us looked up. I don't know how two cows and a horse could create the illusion of being a whole herd of Texas longhorns gone loco, but they did. We each grabbed a child, and the whole bunch of us streamed off across the field, women shouting for help, children screaming with terror, and poor little ki-yi-ing Cookie bringing up the rear. None of us up to that time had been famous for her track work, but that evening, in spite of the rough ground, the boulders, and the bushes, we shattered all records for a two-hundred-yard dash. I swear that as we fell over the rail fence, hot breath was fanning the backs of our necks and horns were grazing our posteriors.

That's the only time I've been frightened in a country where bear and wildcats are common, and cows and horses extremely rare; and because I was so scared, and the whole thing so ridiculous, my immediate reaction, once we were safe, was unbounded rage. I was mad at Miller's livestock, at Cookie for bringing them down on us like a wolf on the fold, and at myself for running. But I was maddest of all at Ralph and Renny Miller and the crew of workmen off the dam. When we had got our breaths, and the spots had stopped dancing around in front of our eyes, did we see them running anxiously to our aid? We did not! We saw them all lying helpless on Miller's back stoop, weak with laughter.

Classed with animals as an A Number One Menace, by females from the city, are what they always refer to as "drunken lumberjacks." I am not a psychiatrist, but as a writer whose stock in trade is human nature, I am interested in all its various manifestations. One of the least explicable to me is the phenomenon of the woman who would not allow such a crude and lusty word as "rape" to pass her well-bred lips, but whose every inflection indicates that that is what she is hoping to be told about when she asks obliquely and with bated breath if I am not afraid of drunken lumberjacks. Well, I'm not. In the first place, very few of the lumberjacks I see are drunken. They may have been when they left civilization, but by the time they get in here, they're only sick and sorry, and in no state to menace anything larger than a day-old chick. In the second place, drunk or sober, they're twice as scared of me as I am of them. I hope that settles that question once and for all. I'm just a little bored with women who claim to be afraid of men, or who feel either inferior or superior to men, or who consider men as being anything other than so many more people.

There are, of course, a few things in the woods that anyone with sense is afraid of. So are there in the city, or on a farm, or at the seashore, or anywhere else, except possibly in the grave. A reasonable amount of danger is part of the price of living.

The hurricane of September 21st, 1938, was something to be afraid of—only none of us except Ralph had ever been in a hurricane before, so we didn't know enough to be afraid until it was all over. Then there was so much else to do that there didn't seem to be any time for fear. I'm not going to go into any great detail about the hurricane. Everybody who lives in New England has his own version of that cataclysm; and everybody in the world knows somebody in New England, and has therefore heard all about it, probably *ad nauseam*. Let me just say that after three days of pouring rain, along about dusk of the fourth day the wind started to blow very, very hard. Ralph was at Middle with Fred Tibbott, who was visiting us, and Edith Tibbott and I were at home with Rufus. After we'd waited supper half an hour, they called up from Miller's to say they couldn't get the car started, so they'd have to walk home, and for us not to worry. Up to then we hadn't considered worrying. We'd heard quite a lot of noise outside, but the woods are always noisy when the wind blows.

I decided that this was as good a time as any for me to go to the john, so I threw open the kitchen door, and almost walked into the top of a tree that was lying where the porch had been. The porch was at the bottom of the cellar hole, twelve feet below. That was the big birch at the corner of the house, I made mental note, and Ralph was going to be good and mad when he saw it down. In the meanwhile I still had my errand to perform, and there was still the front door. I turned the knob, the door crashed back against the wall, and I stepped out into the top of a pine that lay across that porch. This was no night, I concluded, to go ramming around in the dark. I shut the door and tried to call up Miller's, to tell Ralph and Fred not to start home. The line was dead. With rare perspicacity I diagnosed it as trees down across the wire. There was nothing to do, so Edith and I ate our supper, brought Rufus downstairs to sleep—a tree had fallen across the roof right over his crib, waking him up and starting a leak that dripped onto his pillow—and sat down to read. This sounds like courage and composure, but it was only ignorance.

After a while Fred and Ralph came in, soaking wet and full of tales about dodging falling trees all the way from Middle Dam. There must be, they said, at least two dozen blowdowns across the road. Ralph was, as I had foreseen, sick about the trees in the yard blowing down, but since there was nothing to be done about it, the two of them ate their supper, we all had a game of Mah-jongg, and went to bed.

In the morning we woke to a ruined world. We couldn't even get across the yard; trees lay criss-crossed in a giant tangle from the back steps to the road. The sky line all around us was unrecognizable. Where had towered tops that I regarded as personal friends and eternal landmarks, now gaped ugly holes. It was heart-breaking. A house you can rebuild; a bridge you can restring; a washed-out road you can fill in. But there is nothing you can do about a tree but mourn, and we had lost twenty-eight of our largest trees right in our front yard. Somehow it made it worse that the sun shone brightly, and that the still, washed air was as soft and warm as down. The day was like a bland and lovely child under whose beauty lay the horror of idiocy.

Fred and Ralph worked all day with axes and a two-man cross-cut, cutting a way through the mess to the road, the woodshed, and other frequently used points. Late in the afternoon, one of the dam crew staying at Miller's managed to get through from above with the news that instead of two dozen trees across the road, there were over two hundred. We needn't let it worry us, he concluded comfortingly. There was no reason for us to go up to Middle anyhow. The Lake Road to the Arm from Andover was plugged, too, and the mail wouldn't be coming through until God knew when. By that time they'd have the Carry Road open, for they had to be able to use it to get back and forth to Pondy Dam which they were repairing.

I thought then, and I still think, that it was a terrible waste no one was murdered on the night of the hurricane. The writers of the whodunits work dreadfully hard thinking up and presenting plausibly the very strict frameworks of their stories. Here we had it all handed to us on a silver platter. We were a very limited group; we were cut off from the police and from all outside help; there was no way of escape for the murderer; the night and storm served not only as suitable atmosphere for crime, but created the confusion necessary for the successful perpetration of that crime. And nobody even got hit by a flying branch.

We don't have hurricanes more than once in a century in New England, so they rate rather as an exciting novelty than a true source of apprehension. We've had our allotment of hurricane. What we have to worry about now are the consequences of it.

The consequences are not all bad, we discover, in spite of our initial myopia to silver linings. The birds, deer, and small animals have increased greatly in numbers around here since the Blow; the condition of the woods has made it difficult for hunters to get around, and the great windrows of blowdown afford marvellous cover. I'm all for anything that will conserve wild life, even if it incidentally jeopardizes my own roof-tree. And actually my own roof-tree will profit, too. Old opportunist Rich immediately saw the possibilities.

After the hurricane, as I have explained before, the Government organized a pine-salvaging project. However the pines that had blown down across the Carry Road couldn't be salvaged by them because they had been butchered into every imaginable odd length when the road was cleared out. The idea then was to open a thoroughfare, so every tree lying across the road was cut twice—where the gutters would be, if we had gutters—and the piece in the middle was rolled off to one side. The result was several hundred good pine logs of no commercial value because they were in crazy, hit-or-miss, non-saleable lengths. We had long

been planning extensive remodelling of the summer house,
building a new shed for the rolling stock, and what not.
We didn't object to unorthodox lengths for the jobs we
had in mind. So Ralph made a deal with the landowners
whereby he acquired them to the benefit of all concerned.
All the next summer he and Gerrish worked like dogs getting these logs into a boom they strung in our boat cove
in the Pond, where they would be safe from worms, fire,
and rot.

That's easy to write, but it wasn't easy for two men to
do. What they lacked in numbers, they had to make up in
ingenuity. They finally worked out a rig that was the marvel of all beholders to take the place of the rest of a four-
man crew. They took the front axle of the deceased Packard, complete with wheels and tires, and equipped it with
a drawbar that could be fastened to the rear of the Big
Green "Mormon." The butt ends of the logs rode on this,
while the top ends dragged. But two men can't lift a three-
foot green butt eighteen inches off the ground and roll a
pair of wheels under it. So they built a portable ramp
which they carried along in the car, studded with spikes
to prevent slipping, and rolled the ends of the logs up onto
this, using a combination of cant dog leverage and roll
hitches. Once the log end lay on top of the ramp, project-
ing sufficiently ahead, the axle was rolled under, the log
was dropped on it and secured with ordinary logging
chains, and off they went, as merry as could be. At the Pond
they had built a log rollway, and it was comparatively
easy to unchain the log, haul the axle out from under it
with a quick jerk of the car, roll it over to the top of the
rollway with cant dogs, and let her go. I used to go up and
watch them unload and roll in for the simple and elemen-

tal pleasure of seeing the big splash. I felt a little sheepish about this at first, and advanced the excuse that I really went because Rufus liked to watch the water fly. Very soon, however, I noticed that many of the crew that worked on the pine drive managed to be around kibitzing when unloading time came, and that, while they were interested in the mechanics of the operation, they always cheered when the great fan of water rose twenty feet into the air. After that I didn't apologize for my simple tastes. After all, where would Niagara's popularity be if people didn't like to see water splash?

This landing the logs in the Pond, however, wasn't even the beginning, since we aren't planning to build a deluxe log cabin. We're planning to rebuild a house, with pine paneling throughout the common rooms. So the logs in the Pond have to be transmuted into boards and timbers, and since that is impractical to do by hand with a broad-axe, we have to build a small sawmill. You see how one thing leads to another, when you can't just call up a dealer. At present the foundation of the mill is partially built, and sooner or later it will be running, powered by the old Packard Twin Six motor. I can already foresee the end. The logs in the Pond will be hauled out and sawed up, and the paneling will be made and put up, and the house will be finished. Then we'll have a sawmill with nothing to saw. This will be a challenge to Ralph, and he'll start thinking up other things to build, so he can use the mill. Then after every available inch of our property is covered with buildings of one sort or another, we'll probably end with an eighty-foot schooner, or something.

The most immediate result of the hurricane is really a legitimate worry—or rather, an increasing of one of our few standard dangers—the danger of forest fire. That's a thing that is never out of our minds, and a thing we have a right to fear, because we have so little control over the starting of a fire. We, ourselves, are almost fanatically careful about matches, and cigarette butts, and lunch fires. Everyone who lives in the woods is. I've known men to get to worrying over whether every ember of a fire they'd made at noon was out, and to back-track eight miles, after dark, just to make sure. But these were woodsmen. People from the Outside aren't conditioned to the fire hazard as we are. They don't mean to be careless, probably. They just don't know any better. If you're used to throwing a cigarette butt down wherever you happen to finish it, it doesn't register whether it lands on an asphalt pavement or in a brush pile. (Just thinking about the latter makes my palms sweat.) And fires aren't always started by humans. There are plenty of instances where they have been started by lightning, or even by a bit of broken bottle, acting as a burning glass. This chance element is what brings our heads up and sends us running for the field glasses to scan the horizon at the suspicion of a whiff of wood smoke.

It was bad enough before the hurricane, but now it is a hundred times worse. Now the woods are full of dried, dead tops that will burn like tinder. If a fire should start over back of a mountain somewhere, it might take a half a day or more for the fire fighters to get in to it through the blowdown, instead of two hours as formerly. With a brisk breeze behind it, and bone-dry brush to feed on, a fire can travel ten or twelve miles an hour, or even faster. You see, it doesn't burn evenly. It may jump a half a mile over the heads of the fighters, leaving them in an extremely unenviable position. That's why, when a pillar of smoke arises somewhere off in the bush, the telephone begins to ring, and we get out a compass and a map to determine, by comparing the sightings of Joe Mooney and Upper Dam, say, just exactly where it is. If no ponds or barrens lie between it and us, and the wind is in our direction, we get ready to start to collect the things we're going to evacuate.

We don't have to discuss what we'll take with us when we leave. That was all decided long ago. We don't have to discuss where we'll go. If the fire is below us we'll go to Middle, where there are boats to get us out onto the lake. If the fire should be above us or cut us off from the lake, we'll go to the Pond-in-the-River and take to our own rowboats and canoe. If it's a big fire it will get pretty hot and smoky out on the Pond, but we can always submerge ourselves. We won't be very comfortable, but the odds will be in favor of our surviving. For just such an emergency Ralph always aims to have at least one car in good running condition, regardless. The first load out of here will consist of all of us, Kyak, Tom (if we can catch him), the typewriters (which are our living), an envelope containing birth certificates, will, deeds, and other documents, and Ralph's cedar box of Scotch flies (which he sets great store by and which are practically irreplaceable). If there is time to come back for more loads, we can get clothes, guns, and fishing tackle. It's very illuminating to have to make a list, which you will very possibly have occasion to use, of the things you'd save in an extremity. It reduces one's material possessions to their proper place.

Since the hurricane, we have had two or three fires within danger-distance of Forest Lodge. One was over by Magalloway, and the fire-fighters got it under control before it burned over very much woodland. These fire-fighters may be volunteers, but they are as likely as not conscripts. The wardens have a right to draft any able-bodied male they may run across and oblige him to fight a forest fire for thirty cents an hour and meals—if the meals can be got to him at his post of duty. Often they can't. Fire wardens are only human, and it's my opinion that nothing delights them more than to force some stray sport, all done up in the expensive outfit that goes with a fifty-thousand-dollar income, to dirty his hands and burn his clothes for a measly thirty cents an hour. I'm a meany, too; I, too, think it's funny.

The other fires were across the river from us between C Pond and Upton. They were started through the care-lessness of the river drivers on the Dead Cambridge. We could see the smoke, travelling fast and low on the wind, about four miles away, and at night the skyline pulsed with light. When you can see that variation of glow caused by a whole tree suddenly exploding into flame, then you know the fire is too close for comfort. If the wind had shifted and come drawing up the river valley, as up a gigantic flue, nothing could have saved Forest Lodge. We sat up late nights, during that time.

Then the wind died down and a slow and drizzling rain started, the sort of rain that people living as we do actually pray for, forgetting the fashionable scepticism with which education has veneered us. It was a steady, quiet, increasing rain, with the promise of a long wet night in it and, come morning, the surety of sodden woods through which no fire could travel. We tipped the porch rockers against the wall to keep the seats dry, and brought the deck chairs up out of the garden. We closed the windows on the

Above: The Carry Road after the hurricane.

Below: The "Mormon" hauling hurricane pine.

southeast side of the house, and placed a pan on the floor under the annoying gable that always leaks a little after a long drought has shrunk the shingles. We dashed out after forgotten clothes on the line, and brought in logs and kindling for the fire-place. It would be safe to have a fire this evening; the roof would be well soaked and inhospitable to sparks. And everything we did, we did with a sense of reprieve, with the realization that doing these homely things was a privilege of which we might have been deprived. We knew then that it is true that the only way to know how much you love a thing is to see it in peril of being lost.

Another legitimate worry in the woods is sickness and unavoidable accidents. Fortunately, woods life is very healthful. We are never sick, literally. Aside from the period directly following Rufus' birth—and I count that as a natural phenomenon, not an illness—I haven't spent a day in bed since I've lived here. Ralph has spent only two, with a bad cold. He doesn't count that against himself, as he didn't cook up his own cold, but caught it from some Outsider who came in here teeming with germs. If ever medical science wants data on the nature of the common cold, we're the persons who can supply it. We do all the things that are supposed to cause colds—things like walking half a day through wet snow with our clothes sopping wet, or not changing our shoes after coming in after a day in the rain, or sitting on cold stones, or lying full length on damp grass—and the only time we have colds is when someone brings them in from the Outside to us. We don't have things like mumps or measles, because people with ailments like that aren't fit to travel in here. What it amounts to is that we are living in a sort of reverse quarantine, with the germs locked out instead of in. It's wonderful—although I can't help feeling that the minute we get Outside among the coccuses and viruses that are rampant there, we'll be bowled over like nine-pins. Any immunity we may have built up in previous years has probably long since atrophied.

Almost every accident that can happen to you in the woods is avoidable, and soon you learn to avoid them. You have to, with a doctor usually no nearer than twenty miles—and twenty pretty tough miles, at that. You learn to hold wood that you are splitting by the edge and not by the top, so you won't take off a thumb. I don't have to remember here to look both ways before crossing the road —but I do have to remember always to keep an axe on the off side of the log when I'm limbing out, to carry it over my shoulder with the blade away from my head, and never, never, to take a full swing with it unless I've made sure first that I've got plenty of room behind and above me. These things I no longer have to remind myself to do; I do them quite automatically; and if this seems like odd habitual behavior for one who was brought up more or less as a lady, I can only say that there's no comfort in being a lady with a few inches of cold blue steel inbedded in your skull.

If you get cut by an axe in the woods, all you can do about it is to try to stop the bleeding, disinfect the wound —with salt, probably, as that is most easily available—and tie it up to get well by itself. If you can't stop the bleeding, you can send for the doctor, if it will make you feel any better in your mind. Almost certainly, however, the bleeding will have stopped by itself, or the patient will have bled to death, before the doctor can get in, unless the accident occurs in the summertime and there happens to be a doctor staying at Coburn's. The three weapons to use against axe cuts then are: (a) sense enough not to get cut, (b) a good working knowledge of how to apply a tourniquet, if the worst occurs, and (c) a philosophical attitude.

Burns are fairly common in the woods, and they're almost always the result of carelessness, too. You can easily get burned pouring kerosene into a stove to boost up a slow fire, or by tripping over the cat while carrying a kettle of scalding raspberry jam, or by unscrewing the cap of a boiling car or tractor radiator, or in any one of a dozen other damn fool ways. The only time I ever heard of anyone getting burned in complete innocence was last winter when a lumberjack was walking by the stove in the barroom, minding his own business, and for no reason at all the stove tipped over at that moment and dumped its blazing contents onto his feet. That was just tough luck, but it didn't make it any the less painful. As usual in an emergency of that sort, we were summoned, and we applied our sole remedy for burns—compresses of strong, cold, freshly made tea. This may sound like witch doctoring, but of course it's really the standard tannic acid treatment. He got well. Our burn patients always get well if they stick with the tea treatment faithfully.

Tea, therefore, besides being a beverage in our house, is a permanent item in our medicine cabinet. So is iodine, for small cuts and bruises. So is a five-pound package of Epsom salts, which we wouldn't dream of administering to our worst enemy internally. We use it solely in hot saturate solution for soaking infections. Because our lives are far from sedentary, and our diet is correct, we never need what are euphemistically known as "little pink pills," but we do keep on hand a bottle of Castoria, in case Rufus needs it, and one other laxative, for the use of visitors. We also have a bottle of fruit salts for alkalizing the system after we have been exposed to someone else's cold. I keep aspirin on hand, and take perhaps three tablets a year. Ralph takes none. Gerrish sometimes suffers from neuritis, and he takes the rest. Add a jar of some soothing salve, some gauze bandage, some adhesive tape and absorbent cotton, and baking soda for insect stings, and you have our complete medical equipment. Ralph also keeps a couple of pound cans of anaesthetic ether on hand in case the doctor if called for broken bones should forget to bring any. Our equipment isn't elaborate, but it's quite adequate.

You can break bones in the woods, by not paying attention to what you are doing or where you are going. You can drown, by the same method, or freeze to death, or smash yourself up in the rapids, or lose yourself in the woods. It always boils down to the same thing, though— you weren't using decent judgment. So I still insist that, aside from forest fire, there's nothing to be afraid of in the woods, except yourself. If you've got sense, you can keep out of trouble. If you haven't got sense, you'll get into trouble, here or anywhere else.

I lost myself just once, and I'm glad I did. It was an experience worth having, since it turned out all right. It was, of course, my own fault, from the very beginning. The reason I made up my mind to go to B Pond three days after the hurricane was because the day before one of Coburn's old guides started out for there, got lost, never even saw B Pond, and after hours and hours of wandering, finally came out on the Dead Cambridge, some four miles beyond his goal. From there he eventually got out to Upton. I decided to show the world that I was a better guide than he was; and that, I submit, is the world's least worthy excuse for taking a chance. I would even have gone without a compass, if Ralph hadn't made me take one. Me get lost just stepping over the ridge to B Pond? Don't be silly. I don't need a compass. But I took it to save argument, pinning it into my shirt pocket with a safety pin, because Ralph said he'd scalp me if I lost it.

Well, I got to B Pond all right. It took a lot of doing. The trees were down across the trail in windrows, some of them twenty feet high. I could see how Coburn's guide got lost. He did what I did—went around the piles instead of over them. I did what he didn't do—always worked back to the trail again before trying to go forward. Therefore I never piled up any considerable drift away from the correct line, as he did. His error eventually added up to several miles. Mine was never over a hundred yards, a fact for which I take no credit. I was only profiting by his mistakes. I got to B Pond. There was a watchman, Fred Davis, staying in the lumber camp over there, so I have his affidavit to prove it.

It was on the way back that I got lost. Fred Davis fed me doughnuts and coffee and advice before I left for home. I think he was a little doubtful of my sanity, because he talked to me as if I were a child. "You've got a compass? All right. If you have to use it, remember it's *right*. A compass is always right. Remember that. You've got matches? All right. If you find yourself hurrying, sit down and smoke a cigarette. Smoke it slowly, right down to the end. Don't get scared, no matter what happens." I listened politely. He meant well, even if I didn't need his advice.

I'd already been over the ridge once, hadn't I? Well, then—

It was that cocky attitude that lost me. I didn't think it was necessary to follow the trail quite as closely as I had coming over. That was primer stuff. I knew roughly where the trail was. I could get back to it any time I wanted to.

Only I couldn't, I found. Suddenly nothing was familiar. I was in the middle of a black-growth swamp that I hadn't even known existed. I had no idea whether I was east or west of the trail. I thought I was on the west side, but I could have crossed the trail unwittingly while crawling through or over one of the tangles of blowdown. There was just one thing to do—get out the compass and go by it. If I went slightly east of north, I'd come out somewhere on the river, and from there I could find my way home.

My first look at the compass shocked me. I was going directly southeast, according to it, and that was obviously crazy. The compass was wrong. I must have broken it coming over. Or else there were mineral deposits around here that no one knew about. Whatever the reason, the compass was obviously wrong. I *knew* I was going in the right direction. Then I remembered what Fred Davis had said. "The compass is always right." Ralph had told me the same thing many times. "*Always* believe the compass." All right, then, I'd give it a try, in spite of my better judgment. I lined up a topless maple about a hundred feet away, pinned the compass back into my pocket, and started across the tangle of spruce and fir blowdown.

That was the most hellish trip I ever took. I was almost never on the ground. Sometimes I was twenty feet in the air, with nothing to step on, with twigs scraping my face, and with the knowledge in my mind that if I slipped here, I could easily break my back and die slowly and horribly, with not a chance in the world of being found. But worse than that was something that wasn't mind or heart or anything else that I've ever felt before, pulling me irresistibly around to the southeast. To go against it, to follow the compass, was almost physical agony. It was something that can't be conveyed to anyone who hasn't experienced it. I would climb laboriously over a tangled jack-pot, and stop and get my breath. All around me, hemming me in, were more towering piles of blown down trees. I would start over a pile of them, and then remember that I was supposed to be following the compass. I would unpin my pocket, take the damn thing out, and look at it. If it was right, my proper route lay almost at right angles to the way I was going. But it *couldn't* be that way! However— I'd pick a landmark by it, put the compass back in my pocket, pin it in and start climbing; and all the time that thing inside me was twisting and turning and pulling me over to the right. Fighting it was harder than fighting the blowdown. I've talked with other people who have been lost, and they all agree with me that the feeling is something that can't be conveyed. It's like being under a spell.

Then at long last I heard the river. It wasn't where it should be at all. It was where the compass said it would be, which was something quite different. I came over one last gigantic windrow, and could see it shining through the branches. I heard an axe. There, only a few rods above me on the other side was home. I could see Ralph chopping away at a tree in the yard, and Edith Tibbott sitting with Rufus on the porch. They looked like people in a mirage, small and clear and unconcerned. I felt as if, should they glance in my direction, they wouldn't see me at all. If I shouted, they wouldn't hear me. They couldn't really be there. I took a long drink of river water, washed my face, wiped it on my shirt tail, and started up the shore toward the dam.

I'm glad I got lost; it was an experience. I hope I never, never get lost again, and I don't think I ever shall. You see, there's nothing in the woods that can hurt you, except yourself. I know better now than to hurt myself that way again.

IX

"Don't You Get Awfully Out of Touch?"

SOME TURNS OF SPEECH ARE USED SO FREQUENTLY THAT THE meaning has worn off them, just as a hero's head wears off an old, much-used coin. They still pass as legal tender between one mind and another, but they are really only blank and worthless tokens for what once were ideas. We use them just as we use a thin dime; we accept them for what they represent, not for what they are; but if we stop to weigh and examine them on the scales of sense and in the light of reason, we see by how much time and rough usage have reduced them.

I know perfectly well what people mean when they say, "I should think you'd get frightfully out of touch!", but it's a silly expression all the same. Out of touch, indeed! I don't see how anybody, actually, can be "out of touch." The demented are in touch with some world of their own. The castaway is in touch with his physical surroundings, his material needs, his thoughts and his memories. The sleeper has his dreams; and the dead—who can say surely what or where the dead touch?

So I ask sourly, "Out of touch with what?"

The answer is always the same, and always delivered a little vaguely, it seems to me, in my annoyed and hyper-critical mood. "Oh, the new books, and plays, and music. You know. Culture and world affairs. Your own sort of people."

There's no answer to that, except, "Oh, nuts!", and ordinarily I don't go around saying "Oh, nuts" to anybody outside the family.

The reasons I feel like saying "Oh, nuts" are manifold. Just as a starter, I have often read more new and old books during the preceding year than my interlocutor, and I might add, read them with considerably more attention and appreciation. I don't have to do my reading, you see, for any other reason than my own enjoyment. We happen to have a great many new books, because we are lucky enough to have a rather tenuous connection, through my librarian sister, with a book shop in Boston, and one of the owners—feeling sorry, no doubt, for "Miss Dickinson's poor sister, stuck way off up there in the woods"—sends us, at intervals, boxes of advance copies which are given her by the publishers. These are occasionally bound galley proofs and sometimes regular copies as they will appear on the book stands, except that they have paper covers. Now this, I know, is childish, but I get an awful kick out of reading books in galley proof, in spite of the fact that they are tough on the eyes. It makes me feel tremendously in the know and *au courant* of literary matters. If I happen to find in the book, as we often do, a little slip of paper announcing the first day of sale to the public, and if that date happens to be, as it sometimes is, some time week after next, then my cup of bliss is full. Not only am I reading a new book, but I'm reading it before my friends in the city, so enviably "in touch," can possibly get it. All right; I admitted it was childish, didn't I?

Then, too, I actually do have time to read those books that I always planned to read, but never got around to, or that I have read once hastily—in the days when I lived in civilization and had to read the books "everybody" was reading, or else suffer looks down the nose because of my ignorance—and always planned to go back to for more intelligent perusal. I have read all of Proust, for example, under this scheme (I didn't think very much of it, either), and "The Education of Henry Adams" (which I think very highly of indeed), and I've reread "The Case of Sergeant Grischa," which I remembered rightly over the years as containing some passages of extremely beautiful and moving prose—notably the description of the march to face the firing squad. I memorize a lot of poetry, too, so I'll have something to be saying to myself on long walks. A poem to repeat, either aloud or silently, will help you over a hill or on a long mile as surely as a neighbor who stops his team and gives you a lift.

I never can get over the power of some combinations of words to stir the heart. They are, after all, just words, and taken separately they don't quicken the pulse at all. But there's something about certain alliances—. Take for example "Fills the shadows and windy places with the lisp of leaves and ripple of rain." Take almost all of "The Garden of Proserpine," which doesn't even make sense, but is so musical and beautiful that it doesn't have to mean anything. It is full of such lines as "Blind buds that snows have shaken" and "Red strays of ruined springs." Bertrand Russell can make my scalp crawl any old day with such examples of his own particular brand of cold and chiseled prose as the last paragraph of "A Free Man's Worship," which begins "Brief and powerless is man's life; on him and all his race the slow, sure doom falls pitiless and dark," and ends "—to sustain alone, a weary but unyielding Atlas, the world that his own ideals have fashioned despite the trampling march of unconscious power."

What wouldn't I give to be able to write like that!

I'm very sorry to say—and I mean this; I am truly sorry, because I know I miss a lot—that I don't appreciate good music. I don't understand it and it doesn't speak to me at all. I wish it did, but about the most complicated compositions I can enjoy are Sibelius' "Finlandia" and something called "Kammenoi-Ostrow" by Rubinstein, and these I can hear on the radio often enough to satisfy me. If I did comprehend and love classical music, I could still hear it on the radio, for I could listen to the Philharmonic, and it would cost me neither money nor effort. I could sit in my pet rocker with my ski-panted legs folded under me and smoke a cigarette and have a fine binge for myself; but that just isn't my kind of binge.

The same applies to plays. I never was a theater fan. When I lived in cities, I missed a great deal of possible pleasure because of this blind spot of mine; but since I have lived here, it has proved to be a blessing. I'd be miserable if I read of the opening of something new and enormously good, and knew that there was no possible way I could get to see it. As it is, my appetite for the dramatic has to be satisfied with the situations that arise in my own life, or the lives of my friends, or in the general world condition. These bits of theater are less artistic and well-shaped than the scenes that appear on the stage, but since

I don't know enough about good theater to be critical, they keep me happy.

If the foregoing is a confession of self-centeredness, lack of imagination, of taste, and of background, I can't help it. It's the truth.

I don't see how people living in cities, instead of off in the woods as we are, can really know so very much more about world affairs than we do. If living in civilization meant that they were in the confidence of Winston Churchill or had daily tête-a-têtes with even a second under-secretary of an under-secretary of the Secretary of the Navy—maybe yes. But as a matter of fact, they know only what they read or hear, and that's exactly what we know. The only difference is that in the city you can get ten conflicting reports a day on any given situation, while we have to wait until *Time* comes in the Friday mail to find out what the whole thing really boils down to. We get our news a little late, but I wouldn't be surprised if in the long run we have a clearer and more sensible idea of what is going on than those who read every special edition and listen to the special spot-news broadcasts on the radio all day long. Frankly, I don't see how they can possibly know where they're at from one moment to the next, and I should think they'd all go raving mad.

We have a radio, too, of course, so if we wanted to, we could hear news broadcasts every half hour or so. But we don't want to. We have too much else to do; and, since ours is, perforce, a battery set, we have to consider before turning the radio on whether what we are about to hear is worth running the battery down that much. It's amazing how much you decide can be eliminated under those circumstances. If it would help humanity or the course of the War by so much as one iota, I would gladly sit all day long and listen to eye-witness accounts of air raids and hour by hour reports on the progress made or not made along the numerous fronts. But it wouldn't help anything, and it would keep me in a constant state of turmoil and indigestion. So we have our fifteen minute dose of everything's-going-to-hell each evening, and the rest of the day we try to forget about it. There's not very much tranquillity left in the world today. It may be that in striving to preserve a little of it we are making the best contributions within our powers. Or it may be that this is pure rationalizing, and we are guilty of the most abysmal selfishness.

In our house, when you turn the radio on, it's because someone wants to listen to something specific. As the batteries get low, we listen to fewer and fewer things, saving the power, until the batteries we have ordered arrive, for what we want most to hear. Elmer Davis, Ezra Stone in "The Aldrich Family," and "Information Please" are the very last things to go. No matter where they stand nationally, they're at the top of the Rich Poll. If we have a little more leeway, we listen to Jack Benny's program, partly because we think it's extremely funny, and partly because we're always in hopes of being able to put our finger on the reason why it's so funny. Then there's a program called "I Love a Mystery," which probably hasn't anything to recommend it at all from an artistic point of view—except the sound-effects—but which we adore. It's full of creeps and horrors and hair-breadth escapes, and the actors are splendid. If there's a prize fight of importance, we listen to that. Ralph and I could once take or leave prize fights, but they are Gerrish's meat, and he's finally managed to get us into the same frame of mind. The idea is that we try to keep our radio in its place. It is our servant, and we try not to let ourselves become its slaves.

I'm not decrying the radio at all. I think it's marvellous —so marvellous that I won't let anyone try to explain to me how it works. We explain too much, in this day and age. Even if I could understand all about wave lengths, which is doubtful, I'd much rather not. I like to feel myself in the presence of a miracle when I turn a switch and the voice of a man in California comes all the way across a continent of snow-covered farms and frozen rivers and mountain ranges and empty plains to fill our living-room with song. Perhaps the miracle would be even greater to me, if I knew just how it's done, but that's a chance I don't dare to take.

In the summer we have a daily paper from Boston, and all the rest of the family read it religiously. I have to admit, though, that aside from reading the headlines and the Household Page, I use it mainly for a game that I play with myself. Like all the rest of my solitary games, it is simple-minded; but, like the rest of them, it entertains me. It consists of scanning the pages carefully and deciding which of the events reported I am gladest I didn't have to attend. Usually there's a wide choice of material, and I'm hard put to it to choose between the Girl Scout Jamboree at Old Orchard Beach (five thousand Scouts between the ages of twelve and sixteen were there, and mustn't that have been a headache for someone!) or the Forty-and-Eight Costume Parade in East Fairview Centre (where three women fainted, and if I know my costume parades, feuds for a generation to come were started over the charges and counter-charges that the judges had been suborned). If this game served no other purpose, it would serve to make me—if such were necessary—satisfied with my lot well off the beaten track.

Another thing that I am happily aware of being "out of touch" with is the world of fashion. I was never very clothes conscious, so my best efforts at chic were never very satisfactory, when I was in circulation. If I looked smart, I felt most uncomfortable and self-conscious; and if I felt at my ease, my appearance was such that my friends would feel called upon to explain to their friends, "You mustn't expect her to look too snappy; but she's awfully good-hearted. When you get to know her, you'll like her."

It's wonderful to sit up here in the woods and look at the pictures in the advertisements of the hats I don't have to wear. (It's my belief that a hat should help your face, not do its best to increase a Simple Simon effect.) My sole attempt at glamor so far has been the purchase and use of a ten cent bottle of red nail enamel, and this was somewhat less than successful in its purpose. I put it on twice, and both times was rewarded by shudders and averted eyes on the parts of Ralph and Gerrish, and wails from Rufus because "Mummy hurt self!" I finally abandoned it and Rufus appropriated it. He painted Kyak's toenails red and slopped some on his fur. The game warden came in, gave the dog one look and said, "I thought you told me your dog wasn't a deer killer." It took some demonstrating to prove to him that Kyak wasn't reeking with the blood of innocent victims, and when that was over I pitched what was left of the enamel into the river.

There has been just one time in my life that I regretted bitterly not being beautiful and glamorous and marvellously apparelled; and that happened, as of course

Above: The big, green "Mormon" at work.

Below: Bateau crew.

Photo by Fred Adams

it would happen, just before the spring break-up. At that moment my wardrobe was at its very lowest ebb as the transition from winter to summer clothes had not yet taken place. It consisted of a pair of worn flannel slacks, a pair of really impossible ski pants, and some faded wool shirts. Moreover, I was about twenty pounds overweight, my hair was as straight as a string, and I couldn't get Outside to have a permanent—not that a permanent would have helped much, but I think it would have given me moral courage in a situation that I think any woman would have found difficult.

This is the way it happened, and I'll have to go back a little to fill in the background. Ralph has a great many qualities which I love and admire, but tact is not among them. He is just about as intuitive and sensitive to nuances of feeling as an iron hitching post. This works as much for me as against me. If he sometimes seems insensitive to my feelings, I by the same token don't have to worry about his being wounded by a chance word or look of mine. The result is a sort of rough-and-ready understanding of each other that I wouldn't exchange for all the romantic twaddle in the world. But it was not always thus. When we were first married, Ralph used to tell me occasionally what a good cook and sempstress and conversationalist and what-not Sally's mother was. I did have sense enough not to burst into tears, in the bride tradition, and accuse him of not loving me. But all the same, I felt inferior.

Then Sally came to live with us, and she sang her mother's praises, too. There was no reason in the world why she shouldn't and every reason why she should. She naturally loves her mother dearly, and moreover, it is greatly to her mother's credit that Sally never showed the slightest resentment of me as her father's second wife. Intellectually I could see that; but emotionally I developed a simply horrible case of jealousy. I'll never underestimate the power of jealousy to drive its victim to any length. It's a dreadful thing to be jealous. It distorts your whole mental outlook. I, who know, say so. Ralph, the insensitive cluck, of course never sensed that I felt that way, for which I now give thanks.

Then Sally went to Europe to join her mother, and I managed to forget about the whole thing, most of the time. I had Ralph, and then Rufus, too, and a life of my own that was proving more and more absorbing. In short I began to get sense. And then—

Then one fine early April day, Alice Miller called me up on the telephone and said with an air that chilled my blood even before I heard the message, "Well, I've got some news for you that you're not going to like! At least, *I* wouldn't like it, if I were in your boots."

My heart sank. "Now what?" I asked.

"Well, we just had a call from Baltimore on our Outside phone. It was really for you, but of course we took the message as they can't get you on that phone." She was deliberately keeping me in suspense. Before break-up is a slow time in the woods. Then she threw her bomb. "It was from Ralph's first wife. She and Sally are coming in to visit you."

I had thought Sally and her mother were in Haiti. I don't remember what I said to Alice. I do remember, to my shame, walking around the kitchen telling Ralph, "I won't have it. You've got to do something. I simply won't have it!" It really wasn't so much that I *wouldn't* have it, as that I *couldn't* have it. I just couldn't cope with the situation. Here I was, plain, everyday Louise, with a shiny, wind-burned nose and chapped hands, expected on practically no notice to compete with a beautiful cosmopolitan, fresh from the salons of Europe. I didn't have any clothes. I didn't have any conversation. I hadn't been anywhere or done anything interesting. She'd been everywhere. She'd have lots of interesting experiences to talk about. She'd have trunks full of gorgeous clothes. She'd be witty and fascinating.

"I won't have it," I repeated. "You've got to do something."

I know Ralph was stunned by this sudden metamorphosis of house cat into tigress. He just looked at me as though he didn't know me. "But what can I—"

The upshot of it was that poor old Ralph walked up to Middle and called practically every hotel in Baltimore until he found the one at which Sally and her mother had been registered. They'd left half an hour before for Boston. And that, as it turned out, was one of the best breaks I ever had.

Even I in my half-maddened condition—and I can see now that I was being impossible, although I think that almost every woman can understand how I felt—couldn't refuse hospitality to a guest who had come all the way from the West Indies. It was really a compliment to me, I suppose, that Terp felt she could come. Whatever Sally had told her mother about me must have been at least reassuring. Now, after it is all over, I can feel pleased about that.

At the time, though, I simply felt defeated and hopeless when Ralph made his report. "What'll I do now?" he asked.

"Nothing," I said. "There's nothing you can do. Don't worry about it. I'll be nice." I gritted my mental teeth. "If it kills me," I added silently.

It didn't come anywhere near killing me, because as soon as I met Terp, I liked her. I'd better make that absolutely clear at once. Naturally, everybody within a radius of about fifty miles knew about the whole situation before forty-eight hours had gone by. The local grape vine smoked, and the taxi driver who brought Terp and Sally up to the Arm from Rumford must have stopped at every village and farm on his way back, as near as I can figure it, to make his report. I could actually feel a wall of suspense and anticipation tightening up all around us.

Everybody knew who had gone in to Rich's, and they were just sitting waiting to see who would come out. Some probably thought it would be Terp, with a black eye and most of her hair pulled out. Some thought it would be me, with my chin elevated righteously above the folds of a cloak of outraged virtue. But none thought it would be possible for us to live two minutes under the same roof. That it was possible is owing chiefly to Terp's tact and absolute honesty of purpose. She was the perfect house guest, and she had no ideas whatsoever of breaking up my home. She wanted to leave Sally with us again, and she wanted, before she did it, to ascertain what manner of woman she was handing her child over to for a longer or shorter period. This is a motive that anyone can respect.

I'm afraid, however, that locally I got most of the credit for preserving the status quo. I know exactly what everyone was saying and thinking all around us. I know all about the interminable analyses of the situation, and the speculation that was rife, and the inevitable final conclusion—"Well, all I can say is that Louise is better natured than I'd ever be. *I* wouldn't put up with it!" I began to feel like a character in a Russian novel. There was the snow and the deep woods and the surrounding waste spaces, and in the middle of it we sat, a man and his two wives and assorted children. Terp even has red hair, and in Russian novels someone is always a beautiful redhead. All that was needed to complete the picture was a troika and a wolf pack.

It's always nice to have made a new friend, but this visit gave me more than that. It gave me freedom. It made me realize that the things we fear are almost always things which needn't be feared at all. They are creatures of our imagination. There was never anybody like the Terp of whom I was so jealous, but I would still believe in her and make myself miserable on her account, but for the fortunate chance that Ralph got that hotel in Baltimore on the telephone half an hour too late.

Not long ago, a friend who was about to marry a widower said to me, "Tell me honestly, weren't you ever insanely jealous of Ralph's first wife?"

The idea was amusing. I started to say, "No, of course not."

Then I remembered, dimly at first and then with increasing vividness. Yes, I had been exactly that—insanely jealous. I hope I never forget it. As long as I can remember that particular needless hell, there isn't much chance of allowing myself to repeat the experience for any fancied provocation.

We're supposed also to be objects of commiseration because we are out of touch with what are referred to as "your sort of people." There are two major weaknesses in this premise. The first is that I haven't been able to find out in thirty-odd years of living exactly what sort of a person I am. I think that this is a fairly common difficulty. It's hard to evaluate oneself, and self-evaluation is usually tiresomely self-conscious and absolutely inaccurate. When I hear someone say, in all honesty, "Now I'm the sort of person who'd give the shirt off my back," I decide immediately never to ask him for the loan of a common pin. If the analysis runs, "I never forget an injury," I know that I can count on immediate and generous forgiveness and forgetfulness for any injuries I may have inflicted. The only clue I have to my own character is a family saying which runs something like this—"That old loafer! Sure, he's a bosom pal of Louise's. The bigger the bum, the surer he is to be one of Louise's friends."

As a matter of fact, I don't know exactly what is meant by "your sort of people." There are plenty of people around here that we would be highly complimented to be classed with. Perhaps they didn't come from Boston, and perhaps they aren't college graduates. So what? They have the qualities—generosity and honesty and humor—that we would be happy to feel we shared.

The other weakness is that we aren't out of touch with anybody that we want to stay in touch with. After all, the U. S. Mail still operates. Because we have more leisure to write letters than we had in civilization, we are actually closer to a great many people than we ever were before. I know all about the great efficiency of the telephone and telegraph, but I still think it's too bad that the old-fashioned habit of long letters has fallen into desuetude. Brevity and speed are all right in business matters, but friendships can't be put on a business basis, even in the matter of communication. I like to know what my friends are thinking and feeling. If too long a time elapses without my checking up on these things, I find that where once was a friend there is now a pleasant stranger. When I lived in the city, I had lunch and went to the theater with these strangers at fairly frequent intervals. Since I took to the woods, I haven't seen them at all, but some of them have become my friends again. We've had to fall back on letter writing, you see.

There is this to be said for writing a letter instead of having lunch downtown: when you are writing a letter, you are thinking only of the person who is going to receive it. Nothing else is bidding for a share of your attention—neither the funny hat on the woman at the next table, nor the quality of the service, nor the nagging worry as to whether that odd sensation around the calf of your leg a moment ago was or was not a run starting in your new stockings. In short, there is no static. In addition to this, I find it very difficult to discuss intimate matters with anyone. It is embarrassing for me. I start talking about the weather as soon as the conversation shows a tendency to get personal. On paper though there's nothing I wouldn't hash over. Any of my correspondents will probably be glad to corroborate this.

Since I have to depend on letters for many of my contacts, especially in the winter, when, perforce, we have very few visitors, I have developed a few loose rules for being a good correspondent. I don't have to point out, I'm sure, that letters received should be answered within a reasonable time—say a month; but there is such a thing as answering too promptly and writing too long a letter. It makes answering a burden to your correspondent, who will feel obliged to do at least as well as you have done, and will soon be heartily sick of the whole thing. I always try, at least, to answer any questions that have been asked me in a letter I am replying to. Nothing makes me madder, myself, than to have people ignore my questions. I wouldn't have bothered to write them if I didn't want to know the answers. I try also, in order to avoid my frequent difficulty of sitting down to write a letter in which I had thought I had plenty to say and suddenly finding that I've forgotten all the gems I was going to pass along, to make notes from time to time on the back of the envelope of the latest letter received from my correspondent. These make odd reading—"Spare ribs, O. K."; "C. V. arrested for stealing bear out of trap"; "Al's report on Jake" —but I know what they mean. This is a little trouble, but not so much trouble as trying to make the brick of a letter without the straw of subject matter. And finally, I don't expect to get any answer to a letter. Then I'm never disappointed or annoyed when nothing comes of it, and I'm delightfully surprised when something does. This same attitude can be adopted with profit toward almost any aspect of life, I have found.

Not only do the mails run, but the boat still runs, and when in winter it has been hauled out, Larry's snowboat runs. So we can and actually do see some of our Outside friends in the flesh, from time to time. Naturally, we feel drawn to anybody who cares enough about seeing us to make the long, hard trip in here, and most of all to our very favorite flock of loons from Massachusetts whom we refer to as "The Crocks." This isn't a reference to their physical condition, but to the fact that a couple of them are named Crocker. Actually they're a rugged crew. They come in here, singly or collectively, at any time of the year, and by every conceivable method, snowboat, snowshoe, dog team (Stumpy once owned a dog team, but like us decided it wasn't worth the trouble), boat, canoe (Stumpy has some aluminum canoes with outboard motors, that are the marvel of all beholders), and, if necessary, on foot through the woods. They haven't arrived by airplane yet, but that will come as Ralph Smart was a pilot in the last war. It doesn't make any difference how or when they come, we're always enchanted to see Stump and Big and Bill and Ralph. It makes it nice that one of them is named Ralph, too, since that is also Gerrish's first name. When the Crocks are here, all I have to do is request, "Ralph, get me a pail of water, will you?" and I get three. I accomplish this by carefully not looking directly at any one of the three Ralphs.

The Crocks presumably come in here for a rest, but they have the strangest notions of resting that I ever heard of. They must endorse the theory that a change is a rest. The minute they get here, they start splitting wood, or going on jaunts to B Pond, or helping with whatever is the current project around the place. Stumpy and I always plan to go to Sunday Pond across country by compass, just to show it can be done, but so far the world has still to be shown, by us, at least. Meanwhile, my Ralph and the others sneer audibly. Bill is the most normal in his choice of amusements. If it's summer, he goes fishing, which is all right. It's even all right to fish as he does, about ten hours a day. Gerrish adores Bill because he's always crazy to fish, and goes too. Big spent all one Sunday morning, when Ralph was cleaning up the hurricane pine along the Carry, understudying the driver of a tractor that Jim Barnett had very kindly let Ralph have the use of that day. I can see how anybody who has never driven a tractor might want to try it once, but Big started at nine o'clock in the morning and, with Ralph, was two hours late for lunch, while Bill and I waited. That's quite a stretch for a man who ordinarily spends his day behind a desk. And it wasn't as if this was his one chance of a lifetime to horse a tractor around. Big's company in Fitchburg, Mass., owns a dozen tractors, and he could go out and run one any old time he chose. But I suppose that would be work.

Besides themselves, which would be amply sufficient, The Crocks always bring us all the new stories that are going the rounds Outside—and they hear them all and tell them well—and a collection of swell food, always including exotic viands, such as caviar, shad roe, artichokes or palm hearts. I know these things aren't really necessary to the sustaining of life, but it certainly does something for you in the middle of winter, when you have been living on pot roast and carrots, to drink a Cuba Libre and then sit down to a really sophisticated meal—the sort of meal that you have always before eaten off snowy linen, under soft lights, and to the accompaniment of muted music. It doesn't, surprisingly perhaps, taste any the worse for being eaten by kerosene lamp light, off a linoleum table top, to the sound of sleet against the window. If anything, it tastes better for this seasoning of incongruity.

The general impression which seems to be shared by most of our city friends is that we live in the middle of a desert and never see anybody. This obviously isn't true, as I think I have made apparent. We see lots of people, ranging in rectitude from the game warden to border jumpers and notorious poachers. (One thing I have noticed that all poachers have in common is a manner that can best be described as piety put through a collander, a sort of purée of noble thoughts and too-good-to-be-true motives.) Our friends and acquaintances range in geographical origin from Alice Miller, who was born in Andover, Maine, to a lumber camp cook named Roland Thibault, who was born in Saskatchewan and arrived here via Alaska and the West Coast.

In addition to the people we see, we also have friends whom I, at least, have never seen. Joe Mooney at the Brown Farm is one of these. I've talked with Joe countless times on the telephone; we have some very spirited encounters, yet I've never laid eyes on him. Joe is quick on the trigger. He can and does come back instantly with a pertinent comment upon any situation; but unfortunately for purposes of illustration it is usually unprintable. Joe is a swell guy. Johnny West was another. I never spoke to him in my life; I wouldn't have known who he was if I'd met him face to face on the Carry Road; I don't imagine he knew any more about me than my name and where I lived, if he knew that. But I always felt comfortable in my mind when I heard Johnny West go over.

Johnny West was a flyer who ran an air service out of Berlin, N. H., up through the lake country, and anywhere else for that matter. It wasn't a very big business and it didn't run on any regular schedules, but if you had to go somewhere in a hurry, either into or out of the woods, you could call up the Brown Farm, who would call Berlin, and get Johnny to come and get you. His plane had pontoons in the summer and skiis in the winter—he could always find a lake to set his crate down on in our country where landing fields don't exist—and it was always painted red. We'd hear an airplane motor and go out and look. There high up through the tree tops we'd see a flash of scarlet.

"There goes Johnny West," we'd say to each other. "Wonder where he's going."

We might well wonder. He did the oddest business, I should imagine, of any pilot in New England. He flew lumberjacks into camps, when they'd missed the tote team on account of too much conviviality. He came into camps in the winter and flew out cases of the horrors or compound fracture. Once he went into Upper Dam, in the middle of the spring break-up when Upper Dam was inaccessible, to get an old man who was very, very ill. This was to be the old man's first time in the air, after almost eighty years of living. He died before Johnny West got there, but he still got his ride. The body had to be taken out somehow.

Johnny West flew fishermen, and he also flew fish. When the State put about eight thousand stock trout into B Pond, he flew them in in milk cans lashed to the pontoons. That was the only practical way they could be brought in alive. The alternative was to pack the cans in on the backs of guides, which would have been too expensive, and trout die if too many are confined in too little water, unless the water is aerated. Even the sloshing around in the cans that the water would get on the B Pond trail, probably wouldn't be enough to keep the air supply replenished. But they could be flown in in five minutes from South Arm, where they arrived in special tanks with aerating blower attachments. It worked out very well.

I'm not awfully sure, though, that I approve of the

whole thing, on general principles. If you fly fish into B Pond, the next step is flying fishermen in to catch them, and that puts B Pond in the class with any little mud hole on the State Highway. I think a few places ought to be left in a hard-to-get-to condition. There should be some reward for willingness to make an effort. I wouldn't climb a mountain for anything I could think of, off-hand. I loathe mountain climbing. But still I don't think motor roads should be built to the tops of the best peaks. I'd be awfully annoyed if, after a ten-hour scramble up the side of a mountain, I arrived breathless and exhausted at my goal just in time to see a fat dowager in printed chiffon drive up in a limousine to park between me and the view. I'm going to be awfully annoyed if some day I stagger out of the woods onto the shore of B Pond, after negotiating that rough trail, just in time to see a plane full of playboys and girls make a landing.

Johnny West was a beautiful flyer. When he set his plane down on a lake, it was like seeing a red maple leaf flutter to the water. He was company for us, and he made us feel secure. We knew that if something perfectly dreadful happened—something beyond our ability to handle, like double pneumonia or a broken back—we could always get Johnny West to fly a doctor in, or fly us out. He saved a woman's life up in Parmachenee by flying a doctor in in the middle of a bitter winter night, about a year before his death.

Johnny West is dead. He died when his plane struck a high tension wire in the course of a forced landing, just as the early winter night was drawing in. I hope it was the way he would have chosen to die, but I don't know. I didn't know Johnny West. He was nothing to me but a flash of red across a lonely sky, and a thin, steady throbbing over the noise of the river. He was nothing to me but a name—and our margin of safety.

Aunt Hat is even further removed from my orbit than Johnny West was; she must have died years before I ever dreamed of coming into Maine. She didn't even live here. Her place of business was in Bangor, when that was still a lumber town. But Aunt Hat nonetheless is a very real person to me. You see, instead of going to the theater, we who have taken to the woods while away some of our long winter evenings sitting around each other's kitchens, drinking coffee, eating doughnuts, and talking. Talk is the backbone of our social life. It was during one of these evenings in the Millers' kitchen, when the wind was swooping down across the back pasture and the loose snow was driving across the lake like an army of gigantic ghosts, that Renny Miller brought Aunt Hat to life for us. We've loved her ever since.

Renny has his own way of telling a story. He starts slowly with no emphasis, filling in all the details as he goes along. That night he was telling us about his boyhood on a farm near Bangor, and how his first job was in a livery stable in town. "That's how I met Aunt Hat," he threw in casually. "Aunt Hat? Why, in them days Aunt Hat was the toniest Madam in the State of Maine. She ran a house up on the Orono car line. There wasn't a more respected businessman in Penobscot County than Aunt Hat, for all she wore skirts. She ran her place right, too. You didn't find no drunken lumberjacks in her house, like you did down the other side of Bangor. She kept the place clean and quiet, and it was furnished elegant—all gold furniture with red plush upholstery. And her girls were ladies, every one of 'em.

"Just to show you how smart she was— One Hallowe'en night a bunch of boys moved one of them little waiting stations the trolley car company had strung all along the line for the customers to take shelter in during bad weather. They lugged it down from a couple of miles up the track and set it up on the edge of Aunt Hat's front lawn. Now a lot of women in Aunt Hat's business would have been sore, figuring they was being guyed. But not Aunt Hat. She was real pleased. She seen right off what a good idea it was, and she made the company leave it there. They had to build themselves a new one, up where that one was robbed from. She was a smart woman."

"Were you one of her customers?" Ralph asked.

Renny grinned. "Aunt Hat and me was just like that." He crossed two fingers. "We set an awful lot of store by each other. Like I told you, I was working for a feller that ran a livery stable in Bangor. I was a pretty good hand with horses, and after he'd sort of tried me out with the old hacks he had in there for two-three weeks, he figured he could trust me, and he put me in charge of his show rig."

Renny sighed and his blue eyes grew dreamy. "Now there was something you don't see no more," he said nostalgically. "That rig was the prettiest sight I ever laid eyes on. Four coal black horses, he had—not a white hair nor a blemish on any one of 'em. Just like peas in a pod, they were. Them horses was curried twice a day till they shone, and the boss kept 'em so full of oats they danced, instead of walking. Them horses was so proud of themselves, by God, they made a man proud to be seen with 'em. He had a set of white harness with silver buckles made special, and it was as much as my job was worth to let a speck of dust get on that rigging. Every time it was used, I had to clean it and do it up in fresh tissue paper. White plumes it had, too, kind of sprouting off them four black foreheads, and he had a big white carry-all, with black cushions and silver trimmings. On either side of the driver's seat was a big silver lamp, and the whip set in a silver whip-socket. The driver had a uniform, sort of, that he had to wear, in keeping with the rest of it—tight, white britches, and a black cut-away coat and white gloves, and a silk hat with a bunch of white ribbons on the side of it. You'd thought I'd have felt like a fool in that outfit, me being about seventeen at the time, and fresh off the farm. But after I got to know them horses, I wouldn't have any more disgraced them by making them appear in a public place with me in my work clothes than I'd have let them go hungry. The boss hired this rig out for swell picnics and such, and I guess the biggest times of my life then was to go spanking down the main street of Bangor on that high seat, with the silver shining and the plumes tossing and them four big horses arching their necks and stepping high, wide, and handsome. Swell cars is all right—but there was a turn-out!"

That was before my time, but I could see it, too, prancing across the kitchen floor.

"Then," Renny continued, "then come September and Fair time and the Boss busted his arm. He called me into the office one day and said, 'Renny, I don't see no way out of it but that you got to drive Aunt Hat and her girls over to the Fair. I always do it myself, but no one-armed man can hold that team of hell-raisers, and there's no one else I'd trust them with. So it looks like you're elected.'

"Well, for all I was young and green, I knowed all about Aunt Hat. Every year she took her girls over to the Fair in this rig. She'd lease space and set up a swell striped tent she had, and she did a rushing business, besides giving the girls an outing.

" 'I won't do it,' I says to him. 'I won't drive them hussies clear out there in broad daylight and on a public road. I won't be made no laughing-stock.' He pled with me, but I wouldn't listen, so finally he says he'd appeal to Father. My father was a God-fearing man, so I thought that'd settle that.

"But Father took me to one side and says to me, 'Renny, your mother and I ain't going to like this any better than you do. It's going to cause a lot of talk. But it would hurt us a sight worse if we thought we had a son that backed out of a job he'd undertook. Jim's hurt and he's depending on you to take his place. He's been good to you, and don't you go back on him.'

"Aunt Hat wanted to get out to the Fair Grounds the day before the Fair opened, so's to get settled and ready for business. I was out to her place at daylight, planning on getting an early start, before there was too many people on the streets. But she thought different.

" 'What?' she says. 'Go sneaking through town like that at this ungodly hour and throw away all that free advertising? Like Hell, young man! You come back here at ten o'clock; and you can put in the time till then on that silver-work. It may shine bright enough for the Methodist Sunday School picnic, but it ain't bright enough for Aunt Hat!'

"We got going about half past ten. There was four seats besides the driver's, and Aunt Hat piled three girls in each seat. They was all dressed alike in black satin, and they had white feather boas around their necks and big black hats with white willow plumes. Sounds kind of plain, but believe me, it wasn't. Must have been the way they wore them outfits, but they looked a sight flashier than any red dress I ever see. Aunt Hat was dressed the same, only she had a big gold chain around her neck and a watch pinned on her bosom. I was wondering where she was going to sit, she not being spare, exactly, when she hollered to me, 'Where's your manners? Get that rump of yours off that seat and give a lady a hand. I'm sitting up in front with you.'

"I'd counted on skirting around the center of town, but I see there was no use even thinking about that. So I hunched my head down into my collar and tried to look inconspicuous, while I let the horses out a little, so's to get it over with quick. Next I knew, Aunt Hat had her elbow in my ribs; and for a woman as well larded as she was, she had a right sharp elbow.

" 'You hold in them horses, or I'll skin you. Hold up your chin and throw out your chest. There ain't a man on this street that wouldn't swap places with you right now, and don't you think different. You'll drive this rig and be proud of it, or, by God, I'll pitch you off this seat and drive it myself.' "

Renny smiled reminiscently. "She'd 'a' done it, too," he assured us. "So I see there was no use. I threw back my shoulders and set up straight and cocked my silk hat a mite to one side, and Aunt Hat threw out her chest until the seams of her dress strained. I had the checks and the martingales both on; the horses bent their necks pretty nigh into bows, and they trotted as though the street was paved with eggs. When we went by the Bangor House, I see our reflection in them big front windows, and we was something to look at. Them twelve girls looked just as proud and well curried as the horses. They looked the passers-by over, not brash, you understand, like you might expect, nor giggling like some of the girls I'd drove on picnics, but sort of dignified like. I tell you folks that before I got out of town, I'm damned if I wasn't proud to be driving them."

We could all understand that, I think. Renny made us feel just as he must have felt on that long ago September day.

"After we left town Aunt Hat turned to me. 'You done fine, Renny,' she says, and after a minute we was chatting together like old friends. She was a real nice woman, once you got to know her. When we got out to the Fair Grounds, the gates was closed as the Fair wasn't officially open yet. I made to hand the reins to Aunt Hat, so's I could get down and open them, but she put her hand in its black kid glove on my arm.

" 'You set still, Renny. I'll tend to this.' And she stood right up and shouted, so's you could hear her all over the grounds, 'Open up these gates, you sons of bitches! Here comes Aunt Hat and all her whores!' "

Renny laughed aloud at the memory. "I like to died," he said. "I tell you, I never hear that there hymn, 'Unfold, Ye Portals Everlasting,' but what it brings to mind them gates. Unfold—that's just what they did do, and we drove through with a flourish. The Grounds was full of folks getting their exhibits ready, and Aunt Hat says, 'Drive around the race track, and drive like you did back in Bangor.' She shoved my hat over one ear, and off we started. The crowd all come running to the rail to see us, and somebody started to cheer. Round we went, and the cheer growing louder all the time, till when we come around again and drove off, it was bedlam let loose. Aunt Hat never batted an eyelash. When we pulled up in front of her tent she ordered the girls down, kind of crisp like, but pleased, too. Then she says to me, 'Thank you, Renny. You come back and get us Saturday night,' as genteel as you could ask.

"She was a great Aunt Hat. After that I took her and the girls out on plenty of airings and picnics. She'd always ask for me when she ordered the rig. The Boss didn't have a look-in, no more."

Ralph said, just to keep the record straight, "Then you weren't a customer of Aunt Hat's, at all?"

Renny looked at him. "Customer, hell. Anybody could be a customer. I was a friend!"

No, poor Riches, we don't have plays and music and contact with sophisticated minds, and a round of social engagements. All we have are sun and wind and rain, and space in which to move and breathe. All we have are the forests, and the calm expanses of the lakes, and time to call our own. All we have are the hunting and fishing and the swimming, and each other.

We don't see pictures in famous galleries. But the other day, after a sleet storm that had coated the world with a sheath of ice, I saw a pine grosbeak in a little poplar tree. The setting sun slanted through a gap in the black wall of the forest, and held bird and tree in a celestial spot-light.

Every twig turned to diamond encrusted-gold, and the red of the bird's breast glowed like a huge ruby as he fluffed his feathers in the wind. I could hardly believe it. I could only stand still and stare.

And then I repeated to myself again something that I once learned in the hope that it would safeguard me from ever becoming hardened to beauty and wonder. I found it long ago, when I had to study Emerson.

"If the stars should appear one night in a thousand years, how men would believe and adore; and preserve for many generations the remembrance of the City of God which has been shown!"

X

"Do You Get Out Very Often?"

THE FIRST WINTER THAT I LIVED HERE, CLIFF WIGGIN-
Wallace used to call me up. He still does, for that matter,
whenever he gets bored with his own society and that of
his several cats. I'd only seen him once, but we'd have a
good gossip every now and then, and about once a month
he'd ask me what day of the week it was. I'd tell him, shaking my head and clucking my tongue to myself. You see,
Cliff hadn't been Outside for three years, and I thought
I recognized the first sign of his going woods queer. Woods
queerness is a real and serious and fairly common thing
here, brought on by solitude and a growing awareness of
the emptiness all around. It starts in little ways, and gets
worse and worse, until finally it may end in raving insanity.
Every now and then, someone along the lakes is taken
out to an asylum. I thought Cliff ought to go out on a
spree. Three years is too long a time to stay in the woods.

Or so I thought then. I didn't know that it would be
over four years before I myself saw the Outside; and if I
had known it, I wouldn't have believed that the time could
pass so quickly and lightly, that season could roll so
smoothly into season, and year into year.

I didn't spend the whole four years sitting in my own back yard, of course, unless you interpret back yard loosely as stretching from here to the border. I covered the territory hereabouts fairly thoroughly.

For example, Gerrish and I make at least one annual trip to B Pond. It's supposed to be a fishing trip, but we've never yet caught any fish. There are some enormous old trout in there, and once in a while someone brings one out. They're pretty cagey—that's why they've lived to be enormous—but we always hope. This hope is one of the reasons why we continue to go. The other is that we like B Pond.

B Pond deserves a better name. It should be called Benediction Pond, or Sanctuary Lake. It might even be called the Pool of Proserpine:

> "Here, where the world is quiet,
> Here, where all trouble seems
> Dead winds' and spent waves' riot
> In doubtful dreams of dreams . . ."

There is that feeling of remoteness and calm and timelessness about it that makes the scramble of ordinary life seem like a half-forgotten and completely pointless dream. It just lies there in a fold in the hills, open to the sky and wind and weather. Ducks and loons breed in its coves, the gulls fly over it in great white arcs, and the great fish go their secret ways in its dim depths. Once in a while human beings, like Gerrish and me, invade its privacy, but we don't make any impression on B Pond. I always have the feeling that the whole valley in which it lies—the hillsides and the deer on the hills, the trees that grow down to the water and the birds that build in them, the pond itself with all its myriad life—simply waits for us to go. I always want to turn back, after we have entered the woods on our homeward trek, to see what enchanting things take place the minute our backs are turned. It's that kind of pond. There must be many like it in Maine, that the map-makers could so callously label it B Pond, simply because it lies in what was once B Township, and pass along to other matters. There must be, but I can't believe it.

I hope that when I'm sixty and Gerrish is eighty, we'll still be going to B Pond every spring. We'll still politely invite Ralph to go too, of course; and he, of course, will still refuse to have any part of the expedition. That's one of the things I can't fathom about the spouse of my bosom—why he won't go to B Pond. He says it's because of the walk over the steep, rough trail, and because you never catch any fish there, and because he doesn't like trolling anyhow, being a fly-fishing addict, and because he just doesn't like B Pond. The last is probably the real reason. Somewhere he has acquired a deep-seated aversion to the place, so there's no point in arguing with him about it, or trying to understand it. He just doesn't like B Pond.

Let me tell you about the best trip we ever made to B Pond. Some days are enchanted, as everybody knows. Every detail of the day, even the most trivial, falls into exquisite juxtaposition with the next. Commonplace things take on significance and beauty. Perhaps it's a matter of timing. Perhaps for once one walks in sympathetic vibration with the earth, disturbing nothing as one treads. However that may be, this was one of those days.

We got up before dawn and ate breakfast by lamp-light. The stove didn't sulk or smoke, and neither the oatmeal nor the bacon burned. The coffee was good—hot, strong, and clear. When I put up our lunch, the bread sliced without crumbling, and the ham curled pink and thin from under the knife. The butter was just right to spread, firm but not hard. I found a box at once that was just the correct size for our sandwiches and bananas, and I didn't forget sugar and canned milk for the coffee we would make at noon over a camp-fire. Gerrish came in from the garden with a canful of the liveliest, juiciest worms a fish could hope to see. The shiners that we had been keeping in a minnow trap down in the river had neither escaped nor died, and we found a tobacco box that was ideal for carrying them. None of our tackle had been mislaid or broken, and Ralph didn't wake up and come down and sneer at us for going to B Pond.

We went up the road and across Pond-in-the-River Dam just as the sunlight struck the tops of the trees on the ridge. The valley was still in shadow, with steam rising white from the churning water and turning to a lovely pearly pink as it reached the sun-shot air above. I knew how fish feel as they swim about in the depths and look up to see the light of day above them. We went into the woods and climbed the ridge, with the sound of the river fading behind and below us. I never can tell exactly when I stop hearing the river. It fades and fades, but still is there. Then suddenly it is there no longer, and the silence is much louder than the roar ever was.

For once I could keep up with Gerrish with no effort. Usually he has to dawdle, which is terrible for him; or I trot, which is terrible for me; or we strike a working compromise whereby each goes his own pace and we have a reunion at our destination. This morning we moved along together swiftly and silently, watching our footing on what passes for a trail, admiring the woods in the early gray light, and not talking. That's one of the good things about Gerrish. I can talk to him or not, and silence is as comfortable for both of us as speech. When we got to the top of the ridge we met the sun. The woods were suddenly pierced with long, green-gold lances of light, and instantly a thousand birds began to sing. They sang us right down to the shore of B Pond. I'm not a bird lover by trade, but that morning I felt like St. Francis. I felt like an angel coming down a heavenly stair, with the air alive and alight around me with music and the rustle of wings.

The boat slid smoothly out of the lean-to where we keep it and into the water, without the usual knuckle-barking struggle. We sat down on the shore to assemble our tackle, and a shelldrake came flying in from the east, not seeing us at all. The sun was behind it, and as it spread its wings and tail to brake for a three point landing almost in our laps, the delicate rib of every feather was silhouetted black and single, and the down along the ribs was gold and translucent. We could see how wonderfully and intricately it was made. Spray flew up like a fountain of jewels as it plowed the water. It was a bird of fire, coming to rest among diamonds and emeralds.

We got into the boat and pulled slowly away from the shore, paying our lines out behind. The rods vibrated as the spoons began to turn beneath the glass-smooth surface. No breath disturbed the water. Each pine and spruce and budding maple on the shore stood upright on its perfect, unbroken reflection. We went around the pond once—about two miles—and then it was my turn to row. The boat seemed to have no weight at all. The slow and steady pull and recovery were like an opiate, and time stopped.

Two loons appeared from somewhere and swam out to look us over.

Loons are my very favorite birds in all the world. This pair circled around us, curious and unafraid, turning their big hammer-heads pertly and halloo-ing back and forth about us. They showed off, diving and staying under water for incredible periods, and bobbing back to the surface in unexpected places. They stood on their tails and stretched their huge wings, and rolled from side to side, smoothing and preening their broad white bosoms. Then they looked at us again. We were really just as funny as they had thought in the first place. They exchanged glances and their weird laughter echoed from the hills. My eye caught Gerrish's, and in a flash there were four of us laughing crazily instead of two.

Nothing could go wrong that day. A breeze came up, but it only crisped the surface of the water, without making rowing a chore. Big, fleece-topped clouds rolled up from the horizon, breaking the smooth blue of the sky into lovely patterns and sending their shadows chasing over the far hillsides; but they never came near the sun. We went by a little point, and I said, "Isn't that a pretty place!" It was. It was covered with grass and a low growth of scarlet-stemmed bushes. A gray ledge cropped out along the water's edge, and a little clump of white birches, budding misty green, leaned over its own image. Just as Gerrish turned his head to look, a red doe stepped out of the black spruce copse behind and stood with her head high, looking at us. That would never happen again in a hundred years, and I'm glad I have a witness that it happened then.

Finally Gerrish said, " 'Bout time we were leaving, ain't

it?" He rowed a few strokes. "Noticed anything missing?"

"The gulls!" I exclaimed. "They haven't come yet."

We turned toward the rock that serves as a landing. And then we heard a faint and faraway crying. Through a high gap in the mountains the gulls came winging from the east, a dozen of them, screaming with excitement. They flew around the pond three times, white against the dark hills. They swooped to the water and soared to dizzy heights, riding the currents of air up and up without moving a wing, their plaintive mewing filling the air. Then they settled down on the rocks which have been their breeding grounds for centuries.

I'm glad that we didn't catch any fish. I'm not sentimental about fish. I'd just as soon kill them as not. But that day we had enough to bring home with us without adding any corpses.

Trips to B Pond aren't always so idyllic. Fairness demands that I should report on the most horrible one we ever took.

We didn't get started until after lunch. It had been threatening rain all morning, so we should have known enough to stay at home. But the ice had been out two or three days, and we had a theory that now was the time when the fish would be rising. After lunch the clouds looked thinner, so we hastily scratched together our tackle and set out.

I don't know how we did it—we'd each been to B Pond a hundred times—but we got lost. There were some new woods-roads criss-crossing the ridge from the winter before's cut, but we knew the country. We shouldn't have become confused. However, we were. We wandered all over the ridge for an hour, trying to find something that led somewhere. We always brought up in a pulp-yard. Finally we went back to the dam and started all over again, and this time we made it.

We came out at the lean-to, hot and disgusted and tired, and Gerrish held out his hand for the key. Of course—oh, so utterly and completely of course! I didn't have the key. It was too good a padlock to break, although by then only its strength, and no ethical consideration, deterred us from breaking it. We were mad. We'd come to B Pond to fish, and we were going to fish, if we had to build a raft and paddle it with our hands.

It didn't quite come to that. We found an abandoned and water-logged old boat drawn up in the bushes, along with a pair of home-made oars. It leaked quite a lot, but by bailing with our bait can—we dumped the worms out into the boat, where they squirmed around our feet—we thought we could keep afloat.

"We ain't got much time," Gerrish said. "You start rowing while I set the tackle up."

There was a nasty, biting little wind blowing, and the water was gray and choppy. The boat handled very badly, and pretty soon a fine, chilling rain set in. I didn't chill much. I was working too hard keeping up steerage-way. Every time I seemed to be getting somewhere, the water started coming in over the tops of my boots and I had to bail, while the wind drifted us back the way we had come. I could feel a blister developing.

Gerrish in the meantime had his gear laid out on the stern seat and was assembling it. He had a gang-hook full of worms on the end, and along the leader a couple of drop hooks, Archer spinners, spoons, and various gadgets. It was a very imposing and lethal array.

"There!" he said finally, with a craftsman's satisfaction, and threw it grandly over the side.

He hadn't tied it to the line. Paralyzed, we watched it sink irrevocably out of sight. Then we looked dumbly at each other.

Gerrish found words first. He had a very sound suggestion to make. "What say we tie some stones around our necks and jump overboard, Louise?"

And that's the other side of the B Pond story.

There are lots of places to go, all in the woods, it's true, but all different. There's Prospect, a logged-off, burned-over point, eight miles up the lakes, near Upper Dam. You go by boat, past unfamiliar coves and promontories. At one place is a walled cellar hole, now under water, which is all that remains to show where Richardson, for whom the lake is named, tried to establish his ill-fated colony. The fields that the score of families who went with him cleared so laboriously have all gone back to the forest. Nobody knows anything about Richardson—what vision inspired his undertaking, or what lay at the root of its failure. All that remains of him is a piece of excellent dry-masonry and a name curving down a map. A man could have worse memorials. "He was strong and patient and honest," the painstakingly laid stones bear silent witness. "He had courage and imagination," say the letters of his name, so strange and incongruous on the map between Mooselookmeguntic and Umbagog.

From the entrance to the Narrows you can look back across the hills and see Mount Washington, a whole state away, and so faint and lofty as to seem more like an idea than a mountain. From nowhere else on the lakes can you see it. And nowhere else are there blueberries like the blueberries of Prospect, which are what you go there for in the first place. They grow as large as your thumb nail, and have a peculiar dull black lustre under the bright surface bloom, as though soot from the old fire still stains and sweetens them. There are acres and acres of them, and no matter how long and fast you pick, working in the ceaseless wind that blows across the barren from the lake, loud with the lovely sound of water lapping on stones, you can no more than scratch the surface of the plenitude. We come home, wind-burned and juice-stained, with forty or fifty quarts; but no one could tell we had ever been there.

At night, after being at Prospect, I lie in bed and see great clusters of berries slide by endlessly against my closed lids. They haunt me. There are so many of them yet unpicked, so many that never will be picked. The birds and bears and foxes will eat a few, but most of them will drop off at the first frost, to return to the sparse soil of Prospect whatever of value they borrowed from it. Nature is strictly moral. There is no attempt to cheat the earth by means of steel vault or bronze coffin. I hope that when I die I too may be permitted to pay at once my oldest outstanding debt, to restore promptly the minerals and salts that have been lent to me for the little while that I have use for blood and bone and flesh.

Then there is Sunday Pond, small and remote, with a cliff on the north shore. You can see right across the Carry from that cliff, from Richardson to Umbagog. There is the Sandbank across the lake, where the best swimming is; and Smooth Ledge, with the river raging around a great out-cropping of rock. The loveliest pool on the river is at the Foot of the Island, and at Long Pool the deer come to drink and a disreputable old bank-beaver lives. There is the Pocket of the Pond, running up through a hellish black cedar swamp to a tiny icy spring. And there is rumored to be a nameless little pond somewhere up on the hog-back between the Carry Road and Sunday Brook. No one knows exactly where it is. No one knows, really, if it exists at all. But some day soon I'm going to find out. If I get lost, perhaps they'll name the pond after me—if there is a pond. That's the surest way to achieve immortality in this country. Who would have heard of Cluley if he hadn't been drowned in the rips?

I spent four years ramming around the woods, and I could have gone on for the rest of my life in the same way, if it hadn't been for Alice Miller.

She called me up one day in April to tell me that she was going out over the break-up to visit her sister in Lewiston. I said, for something to say, "Well, see a couple of movies for me. I haven't seen one for myself for over four years." I was just talking. I can take movies, but I can just as well leave them alone.

"You'd ought to go out, Louise," she said. "First thing you know, you'll be going woods queer."

I laughed, but she didn't.

"I'm not fooling," she said. "You can laugh, but how do you know you ain't queer already? For all you know, come to get you in crowds and traffic, you'll act like one of these farm dogs in a town, running into doorways and shivering and howling. You'd ought to go out."

I continued to think that was pretty funny for about five minutes after she'd hung up, and then I wasn't quite so sure it was so very funny. After all, she'd spoken with conviction. She'd really snatched at an opportunity to make the suggestion. Maybe she'd noticed something about me— Or maybe Renny had. Renny'd been around the woods most of his life. He knew the symptoms. Maybe he'd said

Two Reasons Why We Don't Get Bored

Above: The front yard.
Below: The view from our porch.

Photo by Fred Adams

to her, "If you get a chance, drop a hint to Ralph about Louise. It's time she went Outside. Or if it comes right, say something to her—" How did I know? The clerk at Barnett's Number One camp the winter before had thought he was all right long after even I could see that he wasn't. So had that big Russian up in the Narrows, and it had taken four men to tie him and get him aboard Larry's boat. So had the lumberjack who had tried to hang himself in the horse hovel down by the *Alligator,* and the woman up on Mooselookmeguntic. And so did I.

It's ghastly to wonder seriously about your own sanity. First you start remembering things. I remembered breaking my pet needle the week before, and all the talking I had done about it.

"Haven't you got another one?" Ralph asked.

"Certainly. I've got dozens. But this one was different. It was balanced just right."

"Well, for God's sake! Whoever heard of a balanced needle? You're nuts."

Of course, he often says "You're nuts" to me. But hadn't he looked at me queerly this time? *Was* it odd to think that a needle could have correct balance? I didn't think so—but how could I tell?

I thought of my Columbiana Pump pencil. It was painted cream-color with gold lettering on it, and it was round. I don't like hexagonal pencils. They hurt my fingers. Most round ones, especially free, advertising pencils, have specks of grit in the graphite. Not my Columbiana Pump pencil, though. The lead was soft and smooth. It was the best pencil I had ever taken in hand, so I said it was mine. I hid it in my mending basket, and nobody was supposed even to think about it. And then one day it was gone.

I flew into a froth. You know:—"Considering the very few things I'm fussy about around here, I should certainly think that when I ask to have a measly little pencil left alone, it could be left alone. I'll find out who took my Columbiana Pump pencil, and when I do—" You can imagine.

It didn't seem to me to be an unreasonable attitude, but how could I be sure? Do sane people go into rages about pencils? Do they make horrible threats? I didn't know, and whom could I depend on to tell me honestly? I remembered the clerk from Number One saying pitifully, "I think I'm going crazy. Do you think I am?" I remembered my answer. "Of course not. Crazy people don't wonder if they're crazy. You're all right." I remembered wondering what I'd do if he suddenly went into a violent phase.

There was only one answer. I had to go Outside. If I weren't on the way to woods queerness already, I soon would be if I began to question and scrutinize my every act and thought. I'd begin to see hidden meanings in what people said to me and in the way they looked at me, or in the things they didn't say or look. Merna and Albert Allen, with whom Sally was boarding while going to school in Upton, had invited me repeatedly to come out with Rufus and stay over night. I'd have to see if I couldn't manage somehow to get out there.

The ease with which my going was arranged, once I let it be known that I wanted to go, did nothing to re-establish my peace of mind. Actually, of course, people were just being nice. In spite of all that is said, and more especially written, about the crabbed New Englander, New Englanders, like all ordinary people, are nice. Their manner of proffering a favor is sometimes on the crusty side, but that is much more often diffidence than surliness. I shouldn't have been surprised and suspicious at all at the co-operation I received after Ralph asked one of Barnett's tractor drivers to ask Merna the next time he was out in Upton if it would be convenient to have me some time during the next week. Ordinarily I wouldn't have been. But I couldn't help remembering how hard we'd all worked, the winter before, to get that clerk out on a legitimate pretext before a strait-jacket was necessary.

The tractor driver, Edgar Worster, said that he knew it would be all right. He lives next door to the Allens and he'd seen Merna two days before. She'd told him to bring me out on the tractor the next time he came, and as it happened, he was going the next day. The camps were breaking up, and he had to take out the beds, stoves, some lumber, and the pigs, and there was no reason in the world why he couldn't add Rufus and me to the load. If I'd just be ready to start around noon—

Ordinarily to get to Upton from here is a problem. You can walk seven terrible miles, or you can go down Umbagog in a boat—if you can get a boat and the ice is out—or you can go to the Arm and then drive thirty-odd miles around over East B Hill. To be able to ride out on the tractor was a break. You can't do it just any old time. There is no road at all. It's possible only when there is enough snow to pack into a reasonably smooth surface. There are limits to what even a tractor will do. So I accepted the invitation with alacrity.

Then the question of what to wear reared its ugly head. Rufus was all right. He had a fairly new snow suit. But as for me—

"Don't give me any of that 'I haven't got a thing that's fit to be seen' business," Ralph begged. "That's what women always say."

Maybe it is, but for once it was absolutely and literally true. I *didn't* have a thing that was fit to be seen, even in far from dressy Upton. I almost didn't have a thing, period. I hadn't bought anything but woods clothes for five years. Woods clothes would have been all right, but even Upton has prejudices in favor of reasonable neatness and cleanliness. My old ski pants had holes in the knees and seat, and my newer ones were filthy and I didn't have time to wash them. I thought briefly of the days gone by when I had worried over such esoteric details as the exact shade of my stockings. Now I had one pair of silk stockings, five years old, and when I put them on, they went to pieces, rotten from lying in the drawer. Mice had eaten the shoe-strings out of my one pair of Outside shoes.

Well, that was all right. I didn't have any overshoes, anyhow, so I could wear what was left of the silk stock-ings, for something to fasten my garters to and hold my unaccustomed girdle down, some wool knee socks, for decency and warmth, and my gum-boots. So far, so good. Then I had a twelve-year-old Harris tweed top-coat. God bless a good tweed! It's passable as long as two threads hold together. I didn't have a hat, of course, or gloves, but nobody wears them in Upton anyhow, except to church. I had no notion of going to church. And I had a suit. It was seven years old, completely out of style, and slightly on the snug side. But if I moved the buttons of the jacket over so it would close, took up the hem, and eked out the waist-band of the skirt with a piece of twine, and then was careful not to ever unbutton the jacket, it would do. It would have to do.

It did do, although when I was ready to go, I under-stood fully for the first time the term "a haywire rig." Since haywire is a fairly common commodity in the woods, it is used universally for emergency repairs. Therefore any-thing that is held together with haywire is a haywire rig. Broadening the scope of the term, so is any makeshift ex-pedient whatsoever. If you run out of cornstarch and have to thicken a chocolate pudding with flour, that's a haywire rig. As I walked through the snow down to where the tractors were waiting, I was the haywirest rig north of Boston.

Two tractors were going instead of one, and the driver of the second tractor I had never seen before. Now, I'm shy. I know that's old stuff. I know I'm awfully tired, too, of having just plain snooty people excused to me by their friends on the grounds of a fundamental shyness. But I stick to my story. I am shy. So I said to Ralph, "You'd bet-ter introduce that man to me, if we're going to ride out to-gether." If Ralph knows a person, he is apt to assume that by a sort of social osmosis I know him too.

He said now, "Why, that's Paul Fuller. You know him."

I didn't. I knew he had a wife named Linda, who was one of Jim Barnett's daughters, and that he had four chil-dren, one of whom was Rufus' age almost to the day. I knew these things as I know who isn't speaking to whom in Upton, and why, without ever having seen any of the characters in the drama. But I didn't know Paul Fuller.

It didn't make any difference. "Hi, Louise," he said be-fore Ralph could go into his introduction. "Four years since you been out, isn't it; and Rufus hasn't ever been out at all. Well, he's going to get an eyeful. You can ride on the big sled, next to the pig crates. Keep an eye on them, will you? Don't want to lose the pigs off. Let's see, the last time you was out must have been when you and Ralph—"

I don't know where I ever got the impression that the

grapevine only works one way—that I sit up in the woods, invisible and inaudible, collecting my data. It came as a distinct shock that, while I knew that the youngest Fuller child is allergic to tomatoes, the Fuller family undoubtedly knew all about the loose filling in my second left upper molar.

We crossed the river on a corduroy bridge that bowed and quivered under the weight of the tractors. I sat on a pile of lumber, beds, and horse-blankets, twelve feet above the ground. There was no road and the sled had no springs. Very shortly I felt as if my spine were coming through the top of my head. I looked forward to where Edgar was hunched in the saddle of the tractor, fighting his machine. It would crawl slowly and powerfully up an outcropping of ledge, balance, and come down *zoonk!* on the other side. Every time that happened—and it happened about every sixty seconds—I saw six inches of daylight between Edgar and the seat. I shuddered for him and took a look at the pig crates, which were inching toward the rear of the load. The pigs weren't happy, either. The only one who was happy, as far as I could see, was Rufus. Tractors are his passion and tractor drivers his gods. He was in seventh heaven.

We crossed a high, beech-covered ridge and came down to B Pond, and from then on it was new territory to me. We left the shore of the pond at the outlet and struck out through a long narrow swamp, between dark, crouching ridges. I had never been there, and yet it was familiar. After a while I realized that it was exactly like that terrible and desolate country of "Childe Roland to the Dark Tower Came," which has always been for me one of the most diabolically inspired pieces of horror writing in English.

It was a level, somber place, with stunted cedars growing out of the swamp, and the snow wasting away from about black bog holes. As for the grass, Browning covered that:

". . . it grew as scant as hair
   In leprosy; thin dry blades pricked the mud
   Which underneath looked kneaded up with blood."

There was even the sudden little river, which crossed our path as unexpected and as vicious as an adder. Then came a place where a forest fire had passed. Nothing grew there any more. Black, limbless stubs pointed to the gray sky. It was neither swamp nor forest—"mere earth, desperate and done with." The tractors, lumbering along like prehistoric monsters, were not incongruous. They were like the incarnation of mindless brutality in this mindless, brutal place. The whole thing got me down, which probably proves that too much education doesn't pay. Rufus and Edgar and Paul hadn't read Browning, and were all innocent of literary connotations. They seemed perfectly happy and unimpressed.

It was odd to be Outside. It was odd to see modern cars, looking like a bunch of water-bugs scooting up and down the road, after our collection of angular antiques. It was odd to go into a house that had electric lights, and to have Merna say, "Sally, run up to the store and get two pounds of sugar." I had forgotten that people lived near enough stores to be able to run up to them at a moment's notice. I ran, too, for the novelty of it, and we took Rufus along. He'd never been in a store before, and he couldn't believe his eyes. I bought him his first candy bar, and he didn't quite know what to do with it. It didn't take him long to find out, though. Probably buying it was an example of misguided motherly indulgence.

There were several people in the store, and they all said, "Hi, Louise. How does it seem to be out?" Sally told me their names, which were familiar to me, and now I sorted them out to go with the right faces. They didn't seem like strangers and they didn't treat me like a stranger. I had a fine time. Albert Allen gave me a bag of carrots to take home, and Jim Barnett tried to give Rufus a pair of white rats, but there I drew the line. White rats give me the creeps. Rufus forgot his disappointment in the excitement of viewing the Allens' hens. Horses, cows and pigs he had seen before, but never a hen. He was fascinated. We kept losing him and finding him leaning transfixed against the hen-yard fence. He watched the cows being milked, too, with amazement. Milk heretofore had been something that came out of a can. He saw a new little calf and a lot of things that turned out to be dogs. I suppose it is news to one whose entire dog experience has been Kyak that a Cocker spaniel is a dog, and, surprisingly, so are such divergent types as setters and toy bulls. It must be baffling. But he loved best of all the other children. It was a discovery that he and Junior Miller weren't carrying the whole burden of perpetuating the race.

The things I loved best, next to watching Rufus react, were eating someone else's cooking and meeting so many friendly people. It wasn't until we were half-way home the next morning that I remembered to be relieved that in a traffic jam in front of the store—three cars and an ox-team all at once—I felt no compulsion to scuttle into the doorway and shiver and howl.

Our one legitimate reason for going to Upton is to attend Town Meeting, which all over New England comes

on the first Monday in March. Town Meeting is supposed
to be a political phenomenon, the purest form of self-
government, or something. That sounds a little overwhelm-
ing. It sounds as though the citizens ought to put on their
best clothes and pace solemnly to the Town Hall on Town
Meeting Day, in full consciousness that they are about to
share in the freeman's most priceless privilege and most
sacred responsibility, that of determining their own des-
tiny. It sounds, in short, a little stuffy and dull.

It's nothing of the sort, in Upton. Town Meeting Day
there combines all the better features of Old Home Week,
a session of the Lower House, a barbecue, and an encounter between the Montagues and the Capulets.

When we arrived a half an hour before the meeting
was called to order, everyone in the township who could
stand on his feet was present at the big, bare town hall,
perched on top of Upton Hill. The village half-wit and
the town drunkard stood on the steps, shaking hands with
all comers, a self-constituted welcoming committee. A
wave of noise, as solid as water, met us at the door. School
was out for the day, and the children chased around the
room. Around the red-hot, air-tight stove at one end the
women sat, exchanging gossip, recipes, and symptoms. At
the other end, around the speaker's table, stood the white-
collar class, the minister, the school-teacher, the hotel proprietor, and the storekeeper—postmaster-telephone-opera-
tor. They were white-collar in name only, as, like the rest
of us, they wore flannel shirts, sheep-skins, and corduroys.
Half-way between, a group of farmers exchanged views on
politics, crops, and the price of grain, while over in a
corner the ribald lumberjack element swapped dirty stories
and lent color to the scene with their bright mackinaws
and high boots. The game warden, tough and trim in his

blue uniform, came in and sat down beside our leading poacher. The one had had the other thrown into jail the preceding fall, over a little matter of an untagged deer, but that didn't seem to shadow their social relations. The town's oldest citizen, Silas Peasley, from whom Rufus gets his middle name and in whom every one of us took an affectionate pride, held court down one side of the room. We all went up and spoke to him, and we all got together later and sadly agreed that he had failed considerable. Last year, on his eighty-second birthday, he had been able to leap into the air and click his heels three times. It would be a wonder if he could manage twice this year.

When the meeting was called to order, things simmered down. The children went out-doors, the men tip-toed to seats, and the women lowered their voices. In theory, they have a hand in the town government, but unless a really bitter issue is at stake they sacrifice the franchise for speculation as to whether the town's latest marriage was a shotgun affair or not. The first business on the Warrant was the electing of a moderator, and someone nominated Cedric Judkin, who runs the store, the post-office, and the telephone exchange. (They are all under one roof, along with his living quarters, so this doesn't require the ubiquitousness that would seem to be implied.) This nomination was routine. Cedric has been moderator since the memory of man runeth not to the contrary. This year he dealt precedent a mortal blow.

"Nope, I can't do it," he announced from the stove that he was stoking. 'I'd like to, but my mother-in-law is sick, and my wife has to stay with her, so there's no one to tend store and sort the mail. I got to be back and forth 'twixt here and there all day. You'll be obliged to get someone else."

"But, gosh-a'mighty, no one else knows this here parliamentary procedure!"

"Well, I'll be in and out. If you get sluiced, I'll help out," Cedric promised.

There was a flurry of nominations, all declined. Nobody wanted to stick his neck out. Finally the hotel proprietor allowed himself to be persuaded, because if somebody didn't, the meeting would never get going. He made it clear that nothing that happened was to be held against him, and climbed onto the platform with the well-mixed metaphor, "Don't know how this is going to pan out, but I guess we'll get through somehow."

We got through the electing of the town officers very nicely, since this is largely a matter of re-electing the present incumbents, the most suitable candidate for each office having been determined days ago. Only death can dislodge one. In that event, the office is apt to rotate for a few years until its predestined occupant is discovered, when it again becomes stabilized. The exception is the three selectmen, who, having the most to do, are most liable to censure. But we have a neat system to take care of that. To fill the three positions we have four suitable men. Each year the one in greatest disfavor at the moment is deposed, and the current spare elected to his place. By the following March his crime has been eclipsed by the blacker, newer indiscretions of one of the trio in office, and back he comes. It's a sort of political Musical Chairs. It works out very well.

This year Article 10 of the Warrant was the Fighting Article. We always have a Fighting Article. Once it was whether the constable should receive a salary of three dollars a year, or whether, instead, the town should buy him a star instead of making him furnish his own. One year it

had to do with the licensing of a beer parlor. And once—
oh, lovely year of which fables are still told and Rabelaisian
quips repeated—it was whether or not the town should
appropriate money to hire the services of a bull for the
convenience of the cow-owning citizens. This year the
Article read: To see what sum of money the town will
grant and raise to purchase or repair snow-removal equipment. Snow removal—"breaking out the roads"—is an impressive item on a Maine town's budget. It costs more than
the education of the young.

"Mr. Moderator."

"Mr. Hart."

"Look, I been running that damn plow for seven years,
ever since we bought her, and she was second-hand then.
She ain't going to go through another winter. She's all
tied together with haywire, and every time I take her out,
something new falls off. I'm sick and tired of the whole
rig."

"I don't see where Bill's got any kick coming," a voice
from the rear proclaimed. "He gets paid by the hour,
whether he's plowing or tinkering. Far as that goes, he was
hired with the idea he'd keep her in good shape, and if he
ain't done it, that's skin off his own nose."

"God A'mighty, there's limits to what a man can do
with a bunch of junk. If you or any of the rest of your
shiftless tribe can do any better—"

"Shiftless! At least my woman makes her own bread, instead of traipsin' up to the store for it, like some I know."

"Address the chair!" the moderator shouted.

"We need a new plow!"

"We don't! We can send her back to the factory and
have them undo the damage Bill's done her."

"*I* done her!" There was more to this speech, but no

one heard it, because a perfectly deafening uproar started outside one of the long windows. A lanky farmer looked out and turned to report.

"Hey, Bill, that spotted heifer of yourn's stuck in a drift outside, bellerin' her fool head off and doing her damnedest to break a leg. You'd better see to her."

"How in hell did she get out?" and Bill streaked for the door. The meeting waited until he got back. The battle with his live-stock in thigh-deep wet snow had improved his temper.

"Look, folks," he said reasonably, "why don't we buy a new snow-plow? We'd be money-in-pocket in the end. Patching up this one's just pouring cash down a skunk hole."

"Couldn't we appropriate some money and let the selectmen study into it and decide—" a mild little man suggested.

"No," one of the selectmen said with finality. "That's what was done fifteen years ago when we put in that cement bridge down by Durkee's. I happened to be selectman at the time and we built the best bridge we could for the money. A good sound bridge, too, 'tis. But there's talk about it to this day. So it's up to you folks to decide what to do, and us selectmen will see it's done."

Bill Hart said hastily, "I move we appropriate three thousand dollars and buy a new plow." His sister-in-law's husband seconded the motion and one of the Hart uncles-by-marriage called for a vote before the opposition could collect itself.

The votes were written on slips of paper brought from home—no sense in wasting the tax-payers' money on printed ballots—and a straggling procession started for the ballot-box, over which the moderator and clerk stood to insure an honest vote. The town half-wit cast his ballot with the rest, and as soon as his back was turned the clerk fished it out and pocketed it, a flagrantly illegal act condoned by everyone present on the premise that there warn't no need to hurt his feelings. It was a close matter, but the new plow won.

A weather-beaten man with a rather fine and intelligent face, who had been figuring feverishly on the back of an old envelope, rose to his feet. "Mr. Moderator, we hadn't ought to do this. It's going to raise taxes sixty percent. I got the figures right here. We'd ought to do a little more considering before we act."

There was a stunned silence, and then a roar. The moderator pounded frantically, and then cut loose with a bellow. "There ain't no use losing our tempers now," he pointed out, demonstrating the derivation of his title. "We voted the money, and it's too late to change our minds."

"Why is it, if we want to?" demanded some untamed spirit.

"I don't know. But seems like it's against the rules."

"Where's Cedric at? Get Cedric."

Cedric had gone over to his store, but when the summons went out, he came splashing across in the March mud and slush with his coat-tails flying. His bearing was rather that of a mother whose better judgment had been telling her all along that she shouldn't have left the children alone with the buzz-saw.

"I don't recall anything about that in the rules," he said when the problem had been put to him. "But I don't see why we can't rig it up. How many want to back water?"

The walls bulged.

"All right. If someone will put it in the form of a motion, just so's it'll be legal—"

The haste with which the matter was put through was indecent. Then the conservative sum of two hundred dollars was voted to repair the old plow, and the Fighting Article was history.

The women had withdrawn some time before, and now one spoke to the moderator from the doorway. "Lee, if you've come to a good resting-place, dinner's on upstairs."

Town Meeting dinner is an event in the year. The food is all donated, and the proceeds—the charge is thirty-five cents—go to the Ladies' Aid. Everyone puts her best culinary foot forward. There were ham and chicken, scalloped potatoes, salad, and hot rolls; the pies were cut in quarters, in the generous country style, and the layer cakes were laced with jam and topped with yellow whipped cream. The coffee was hot and clear. It was insulting to the committee not to have second helpings, and thirds and fourths were subtle compliments. At first everyone concentrated on the food, but after a while the talk broke out.

"—ain't layin' now. Guess I'll hire me a dozen Rhode Island Reds to see me through till spring."

"Extravagant! My land, you'd ought to take one look in her garbage pail!"

"—lost his shirt on that cut in the Diamond. Had to haul five miles—"

"Sure I hired out to them. When them crazy Democrats come around and shove money at me, what'm I supposed to do? Sit on my hands? But when it comes to voting for any such tom-fool notion—"

Maybe the effects of the meal were soporific. At any rate, the afternoon session was as calm as a Quaker Meeting. There was a little discussion about the appropriation for the Poor Account, which is our version of Relief. This was during the depression, so perhaps the argument deserves a note, as being unique. The customary amount granted is five hundred dollars, but since it is never wholly expended, the Poor Account was getting top-heavy, having reached a total of about a thousand dollars, which is MONEY in Upton. Someone therefore suggested that it would be a good idea to skip the Poor Account this year, and let it feed off its hump, so to speak.

The first selectman was doubtful. "I dunno. 'Course, we never do spend it all, but still, it's good to have a backlog, case of emergency. We could cut down, say, to two hundred—"

This was the year when Relief money was running out all over the country, and when food riots were common in the big cities, but that's what we did, all the same. And that doesn't prove, either, that New England didn't feel the depression. What it proves is that rural New England, with its starved farms and hand-to-mouth living, is chronically so near depression that a big slump doesn't matter much. It simply means pulling in the belt another notch, wearing the same clothes one or two or three more years, and going without butter. We don't get guns for our butter, either. We get something even more necessary to the safe-guarding of Democracy. We get self-respect and the right to spit in anyone's eye and tell them to go climb a tree.

And that about covers Town Meeting. Ralph goes every year, since he considers it his duty as a citizen. His sense of responsibility doesn't carry him to the point of taking office, though. It was suggested to him one year that he'd be a good Health Officer. He didn't see why, until his one very special qualification was pointed out to him. He lives a long way from the village. "No one wants the job," they said earnestly. "You're in trouble all the time. Folks

Above: Pond-in-the-River Dam.

Below: A use for spare time—Alec Bright and Ralph shortly before they were wrecked.

get mad if you light into them about the way their out-
houses smell, or where they dump their tin cans. Next
thing, you may find the air let out of your tires, or a hole
in your boat. Now living way off up there, you could come
in every so often and raise hell, and then go back to the
woods till it sort of blew over—"

P.S. He didn't take the job.

As a matter of fact, there's really no point in our going
Outside since for three months of the year the Outside
comes in here, in the form of guests at what we call the
Hotel, but which is, as I have said, Captain Coburn's Lakewood Camps at Middle Dam. That's two miles away from
us, and that's a good distance for it to be. We can see the
Outsiders whenever we want to, but they don't cramp our
style. If I want to wear shorts, which is an error no one
over eighteen should commit in public, I can do so. I can
also run my household as badly as I please, and our house
guests can sun-bathe in the altogether without let or
hindrance. It's ideal.

The Outsiders who frequent Coburn's are known, of
course, as sports—even the fat lady who comes here
against her will, because if she doesn't spend two weeks
in summer here with her husband, he won't spend two
weeks in Florida in the winter with her. She's quite a gal.
She's down, but she isn't out. She'd much rather be home
in the suburbs, but since she can't be, she does her best to
bring the suburbs along with her to the woods. She wears
spike heels and flowing lavender chiffon draperies, and
gives bridge parties every afternoon, at which she serves
the nearest a fishing camp chef can come to a dainty
fruit salad. She herself supplies the cut-up marshmallow
and maraschino cherries to top off this dish. She gives cute
prizes. I find her very tiresome at close range, but at a dis-

tance I rather admire her spirit. And to be honest, she's just as much interested in maintaining this distance as I am. She finds me impossible, too.

One thing about living in the backwoods—You Meet Such Interesting People! Or else you meet so few, and have so much more time to talk with them, that they seem interesting. Maybe everybody is interesting, if you get a chance to hash things over with them while they're in their old clothes and have their mental hair down. I met a woman on the dam the other day. She was sitting in the sun, knitting, while her husband fished. If I had met her at a tea, she would have been wearing a rather dowdy beige lace, a harassed expression, and an unbecoming hat, and we would never have got beyond "How do you do?" because I would have been feeling inadequate and lacking in chic, too. As it was, we covered everything, finally getting around to methods of coping with insomnia.

I'm not an expert, being the kind that seldom remembers hitting the bed; but I advanced my formula. Lying awake in the dark, I plan a trip. It's usually to the West Indies. I start at the very beginning and go shopping. I buy everything, from toothpaste to the exclusive little model that's going to knock them dead at the captain's dinner. Then I buy the very smartest luggage and pack. In theory I also conjure up all the people I meet on the boat, and what we do and say to each other. Actually I have yet to stay awake long enough to get myself aboard.

Her method promises even more entertainment. She starts from the present and moves backward in time, remembering every dress she ever owned and the most important thing that happened to her while she was wearing each one. She says a lot of things come back to her that she had completely forgotten.

I can believe it. I gave the idea a trial spin while I was washing dishes. I remembered dresses I wouldn't be found dead in now. That black evening gown of 1930, for instance, with a hemline above my knees in front and down to the floor in back, forming a sort of show-case for my legs, which were modishly clad in very light stockings. (Why some of my friends didn't tell me?!) I broke my ankle while wearing that dress, which probably served me right.

Then there was a dress—about the only one I can still contemplate without writhing—made of men's heavy silk shirting, striped ivory-color. (Ralph says how can a solid color be striped, but that comes under What Every Woman Knows and means alternate dull and shiny stripes.) It was softly tailored and becoming and lucky, as some dresses are lucky. I first brought my golf score down into the eighties while I was wearing it.

When I get more time, I'm going to play this dress game some more. I still don't know the name of the woman who told me about it, but I owe her a vote of thanks. I collect one-handed means of entertainment. They come in handy in the woods.

There are a few things that sports do that make me mad, such as wearing smoked glasses the first time I meet them. I hate to talk to strangers in dark glasses. I can see the quirk of the mouth, but without the corroborative evidence of the eyes, I can't tell whether it's a friendly quirk or a cynical one. I feel like snarling, "Take those damn things off, so I can tell what's going on behind them."

It doesn't make me mad, though, to have them patronize and laugh at us quaint natives. They don't know it, but we're laughing and patronizing right straight back. They think our clothes are just too picturesque and amusing; and we think beach pajamas a hundred miles from a beach, and waders worn for boat fishing, and shorts and halters in black-fly season are amusing. (You can skip the "just too picturesque." We don't talk like that, and besides, I don't think we're supposed to know what picturesque means.) Their delight in our naivete can't exceed our delight in their gullibility. They ask us what makes the lake look streaked. All right, that's a silly question. Any fool should know it's the wind. So all right, it calls for a silly answer, and we have one all ready, because that's a stock question. "Oh, that's where the sled tracks cross the ice in winter," we say, and they usually believe us.

Pete and Ira Brown and I had a lot of fun with a whole porchful of sports one evening. Pete and Ira are two old guides, friends of mine. They were sitting outside the hotel with a dozen fishermen when Ralph and I arrived for the mail.

Pete said, "Hi, Louise. Been to B Pond lately?"

I said, "Yup. Gerrish and I went over Saturday."

"Catch any fish?"

"Nope. I don't think there are any fish over there."

Ira stated flatly, "You don't fish the right place. There are plenty of fish there."

"Well, I fished everywhere, so I must have been in the right place part of the time."

Ira squinted at me through a cloud of cigarette smoke. His eye had a warning gleam. "Bet you didn't fish under the island."

The silence on the porch was electric. Every eye was turned out over the lake, but every ear was cocked in our direction. I had to play this right.

"Why, no," I said uncertainly. "I forgot all about under the island."

Ira looked relieved. "That's where the fish are, this time of year. In them caverns. Last time I was over, I camped overnight on the island. Couldn't hardly get a wink of sleep from the racket they was making, feeding off the roots of the grass. You try there next time."

I couldn't take it any longer. I couldn't stand the bland expressions on the Brown brothers' faces, and the puzzled credulity on the sports'. I said hastily, "Thanks. I will," and went inside.

I love some of the sports. I used to love old Dr. Aldrich, who came up yearly to fish and play poker. He liked to fish, but he also liked his comfort. There's nothing very cozy about sitting on a hard cold rock, surrounded by a cloud of black flies and mosquitoes, so Dr. Aldrich didn't do it. Every evening he'd go down to Harbeck, a good pool just below Middle Dam, weighed down with impedimenta. First he inflated an air cushion, a process which left him purple of face and bulging of eye, arranged it on a rock, and arranged himself on it. Then he tucked a steamer rug carefully around his legs and placed a Flit gun beside him, its handle, like that of Lady Macbeth's dagger, to his hand. Then he was ready to fish. He'd work out fifteen or twenty feet of line and make a dozen casts. Suddenly he'd reel in furiously, lay down his rod, and snatch up the Flit gun. A fog of insecticide all but obscured him, and the black-fly corpses fell like rain. Then down with the gun and up with the rod, until dark. I used to walk clear up to Harbeck of an evening to watch Dr. Aldrich fish. It was worth the effort.

Something else that is worth the effort once—and it is an effort—are the National Championship White Water Races that are held here on the Fourth of July. I'm not awfully sure they are worth tagging along after more than once. After all, one guy getting dumped into the river is much like another guy getting dumped into the river, and this is one sport that is as hard on the spectators as on the entrants. Harder, maybe. All that can happen to a contestant is getting wet, getting bruised on rocks, and getting drowned. All these things can happen to the spectators, and in addition they can get bug-bites, heel blisters, scratched, sun-struck, exhausted, and lost. So I do my race-watching from my own front porch, knitting and dispensing food and drink to those of our friends who drop in in passing. But I am in the minority. People come from all over the country to spend three days chasing up and down the river.

The reason that these races are held on the Rapid River is that the flow of water can be regulated here. A flood or a drought doesn't matter. Renny Miller can just raise or lower a gate in the dam. And the river, while actually not navigable, is so nearly so that there is always the sporting hope that by some combination of luck and skill someone might get through in a canoe. Most of the races are not canoe races, though. They are run in fold-boats, which are exactly what the name suggests—light little collapsible boats built like kyaks. The frames are made of short pieces of wood with metal sockets on the ends and can be fitted together into the skeleton of a boat. Over this is drawn a rubberized canvas cover, which comes up over the bow and stern, leaving a cock-pit for the operator, who sits flat on the bottom, on a couple of slats, and wields a double-bladed paddle. A rubber apron buttons tight about his waist. With this apron it is almost impossible to swamp the boat. It draws so little water that it can slide over submerged ledges, and the construction is so flexible that it bounces off rocks instead of cracking up on them. So it is comparatively easy to run the river in a fold-boat. But only comparatively, you understand. I don't want to try.

What fascinates me is not the races themselves, although they are exciting, what with spills, hair-breadth escapes, and near-drownings. The real interest lies for me in what I will call the White Water Crowd. Travis Hoke, a friend of ours, is always talking about the various crowds—the Wedding Crowd, for example, college classmates who make a life work of attending each other's weddings, and whose conversation is filled with references of how stinko dear old Pinko got at Blinko's bachelor dinner. Or the Doggy Crowd, with their dead-serious discussions of that little bitch of the Squires', Faux Pas, by Social Climber out of Emily Post.

Me, I adore the White Water Crowd. All day long they slide down the river in their little boats, looking grim and desperate, and stagger back to Coburn's, battered and exhausted, to start all over again. They talk about haystacks when they mean swells, and about amazingly clever bow-work, and about Skowhegan Guide's Models, and they talk about nothing else. Tense and distraught, they come into the yard and ask to borrow some inner-tube patches and rubber cement, so they can mend their boats in time for the next race. They're so deadly earnest about the whole thing. I feel like saying, "Take it easy. It's supposed to be sport." But I know that would be considered a wrong attitude. I know the reason I'm no good at games is that I can never forget that they are games. It never seems very important whether I win or not, as long as I'm having fun playing. I spinelessly don't mind if someone else can hit a tennis ball harder and more often than I can. So I don't dare to suggest that maybe river running isn't exactly as important as they think it is.

They don't even slip into something loose and relax in the evening. Oh, my, no! When it gets too dark to risk life and limb any longer on the river, they trail back to Coburn's, take off their foot-ball helmets, life preservers, and sodden shorts and sneakers—regulation river-running costume—paint their wounds with iodine, and assemble in the lobby of the main lodge to look at each other's river-running movies. The movies are very good, actually. I like to look at them, too. But most of all I like to sit in the dark with all these hearty souls sprawled around me on the floor and hear them talk. I am sorry to say that I can never believe that floor-sprawling is anything but a pose; I have tried it, and it is *not* comfortable; but it looks well in the flickering fire-light, and is in good magazine-story tradition.

"That's Pussy on the Housatonic," someone will say of a fast-moving streak on the film. "Remember? That's the first time Pussy was ever in a fold-boat."

"Sure. But Pussy was always a good canoeman."

"Where is old Pussy now?"

"Pussy? Oh, Pussy's out on the Great Snake in Idaho, trying to make a record. Heart-broken not to be here, of course, but when this thing came up—"

"Ooooh, look! Ace, there's you. Look, Ace! I told you you were putting too much beef in your back-water. See what I mean now? See how your bow weaves and— Oh! Hey, can't we have that run over again? I want to show Ace—"

It all adds up to lunacy. And the lovely lunatic pay-off is that they do all this for a little bronze medal with a picture of a man in a fold-boat on the front and the date, place and occasion engraved on the back; and I, who never wet a foot or scraped a knee, I, with my wrong attitude, get one, too. I get one because Ralph was helpful about carrying them and their boats repeatedly from the finish back to the start in his cars. So when the Presentation of Medals came along, and they had one left over, they gave it to him, ceremoniously, to show their appreciation, which was very nice of them. And he came home to where I was sitting and reading and pitched it into my lap, saying, "Here, Mama. Here's something to add to that charm bracelet you've been claiming you're going to collect." Rubies wouldn't have pleased me more. I like a dash of irony in my dish.

So after all, why should we bother to go Outside? There would be only one reason, to see our friends; and our friends come here instead. We have swell friends, as I suppose everyone has, and we'd much rather see them here, undiluted by people we don't like, than Outside. So if they are willing to put up with my off-hand meals for the sake of lounging around in their oldest clothes and being free to do and say what they please; if they are willing to swap their own good beds for our not-so-good ones plus a lot of excellent scenery and fishing; if they want to take the long, involved trip in with nothing much at the end except us and the assurance that they are very much more than welcome, why, that's the way we want it, too. And that's the way we have it.

Once in a while the river gets to sounding like the wake of a steamer, and then I think maybe I'd like to go somewhere on a boat. I've only been on boats a little—one trip to Europe, long ago—and I love boats. But where in the world could I go to-day? Where is there peace and quiet and contentment? Where—except here.

XI

❦

"Is It Worth-while?"

NOBODY EVER ASKS ME, "IS THIS LIFE YOU ARE LIVING worth-while?" That's a question that I ask myself, occasionally.

I ask it when I get up on a twenty-below-zero morning to find the kitchen stove in one of its sullen moods. Smoke oozes from every crack, but the top won't heat enough to melt the ice in the tea kettle. A cup of hot coffee is a long way in the future. I bang the oven door and the stove pipe falls down, raining buckets of soot over everything, including the butter that I have put on the stove shelf to warm to a spreadable consistency. Smoke pours out of the down chimney in clouds, and I have to open the door and all the windows, or suffocate. My eyes smart and run water, and my hands and feet slowly and painfully turn to ice, and the answer is, "No! Nothing is worth this!"

I ask it when, at the end of a long, hot summer, everyone in Middle Dam has used up his entire ice supply, and I want a glass of ice water. I can't have it. Moreover, the meat is going to spoil unless I do something about it at once, and the butter is unattractively liquid, and the lettuce has wilted, and the tomato aspic that I made this morning isn't going to set. I think of tall, frosted glasses, and salads that are crisp and noisy under the fork, and lemon sherbet, and decide I'd swap the whole north woods for one properly refrigerated meal.

I ask it when Rufus, all snowy and rosy, comes in from a day with his lumberjack pals and croons lovingly, "Mummy nice old son of a bitch." I ask it when I've got the lunch dishes done and the kitchen tidy and am all set for an hour's leisurely reading before going swimming, and a whole hungry gang drops in. Anywhere else, we could drive to the nearest hot-dog stand, but here I have to start from scratch and throw together another complete meal. I ask it when I look at the hands of Coburn's women guests and then at my own, with their short nails, calloused palms, and the burns from the oven door across the backs. The answer is always "No. It's not worth it."

You can't very well stop operations to ponder the problem of worth-whileness when you have a big salmon on the end of a light line. When the reel starts screaming and the rod bends into a vibrating bow and you suddenly remember that you meant to change that frayed leader and didn't; you have enough to think about. The fish starts away from the boat, and you burn your thumb braking the line. Then the water explodes fifty feet away, and you see him, a furious arc in the air, shaking his head viciously in an effort to dislodge the fly. He's a whale! He's easily the biggest fish that— He starts for the boat, and you reel in frantically. The sun is in your eyes, and the landing net is just out of reach—not that you'll ever bring him to the net; your arms are numb already—and then, abruptly, there he is, right up under the gunwale, just as tired as you are. You find that you can reach the net after all, and you ease it over the side, taking care not to hit the leader —and he's yours! He doesn't weigh the seven pounds you thought he did when you saw him break water, but the pocket scales say four and a half, and four and a half isn't so bad. You wet your hands carefully before taking him off the hook, and slide him over the side. You don't think to ask yourself then if that was worth-while. It's enough that it was fun.

"Is it worth-while?" is not a question that I think to ask myself when I am out in the middle of B Pond, watching the gulls inscribe their white scrolls against the sky. I don't ask it when I see a deer drinking at Long Pool, or hear a loon laugh, or when I compare Rufus with other children of his age and discover that he is two inches taller and five pounds heavier than most of them, and that he doesn't enter rooms with a piercing shriek of "It's Superman!" I don't ask it when I get a check for a story, or find that my $1.98 mail order bathing suit looks much nicer than the $15.00 model I saw on a woman up at the hotel— or does it only seem that way because I'm browner and thinner and can swim better than that woman? I don't ask it when friends have such a good time with us that they hate to leave as much as we hate to see them go; or when we all sit on the porch in the evening with our feet on the rail, and watch the tide of the dusk rise from the valleys up the hills and across the sky. The stars come out one by one, and the moon swings up above Pondy Dam, changing the river to a road of restless gold. It isn't a moment to be asking yourself questions. It's a moment to enjoy.

It amounts to this. "Is it worth-while to live like this?"

is a question that I never ask myself under fair conditions. I ask it only when exasperation or discomfort or exhaustion pre-determine *No* as an answer. That's about ten times a year. On the other three hundred and fifty-five days of the year, I don't question anything. Happy people aren't given to soul searching, I find. Revolt and reform, whether private or general, are always bred in misery and discontent. So now, sitting here quietly with nothing to annoy me and nothing to exhilarate me—except that I am at long last on the final chapter of this book I undertook so light-heartedly to write—I will once and for all try to find the answer.

Why did we come to live here in the first place? We thought it was because we liked the woods, because we wanted to find a simple, leisurely way of life. Now, looking back, I think that we were unconsciously seeking to find a lost sense of our own identity. Looking back through the telescope of the last six years, I can see myself as I was and realize how living here has changed me. I hope it has changed me for the better. Certainly I am happier than I was then. Certainly I am more at home in this world that we have created than ever I was in that vast and confusing maelstrom that we call civilization.

Here I dare to be myself. I don't see why it should ever again be important to me what I wear, or whether I have read the latest book or seen the latest play, or know the newest catch word. I don't see why I should ever care again what people think of me. It seems silly now, but those things were once important. I don't see why it should ever matter to me again who does or does not invite me to her house, who does or does not speak to me, who does or does not have more money than I have. Those things used to matter, though, because I had no identity of my own. I

had nothing to go by but the standards someone else had
set up. To define freedom, for which men and women and
children are dying all over the world, in terms of indifference to clothes and social contacts and popular attitudes
seems so trivial and irresponsible a thing to do that I am
ashamed of it, as of a gross impertinence; but that is what
living here adds up to, for me. I am free.

It adds up to more than that. All ordinary people like
us, everywhere, are trying to find the same things. It makes
no difference whether they are New Englanders or Texans
or Malayans or Finns. They all want to be left alone to
conduct their own private search for a personal peace, a
reasonable security, a little love, a chance to attain happiness through achievement. It isn't much to want; but I
never came anywhere near to getting most of those things
until we took to the woods.

I have peace here. It may suffer surface disruptions
when I forget to put my bread to rise, or Ralph discovers
that Rufus has drained the radiator of the Big Green
"Mormon" and poured the water into the gas tank; but the
depths of that peace can't be shaken. We have a reasonable security. Sometimes we may have to figure a little
closely to pay the taxes and outfit the kids and put the
groceries in for the winter; but the things that matter—
our feeling of entity, our sense of belonging—are never in
danger here. Neither is the contentment that comes
through accomplishment. What we have achieved isn't
important to the world. No lives will be saved or unborn
generations rise up to call us blessed for our six years'
work here. All we've done is to take a little slice of wild
land and force it to produce; to take some old ramshackle
buildings and make them livable; to take land and build-

ings and two diametrically opposite personalities and make them into a home.

A great many people ask me if Ralph and I don't get on each other's nerves horribly during the long periods when we see only each other. That's a legitimate question. Everyone knows the corroding effect too great familiarity has on even the strongest attachment. It should have an even more devastating effect on me, as I am, I know, not quite normal in my loathing for having anyone crowd in on me, either literally or figuratively. I can't stand being jostled physically, and I can't stand having my actions questioned or commented upon. I could, quite literally, kill anyone who says to me, "A penny for your thoughts." I'm a New Englander, so I can't talk about love. The only way I can explain why I never feel like killing Ralph is open to unflattering misinterpretation; but I'll try to explain, all the same.

Emily Dickinson once said of a little niece who had been shut up in a closet as punishment, and was discovered there hours later, perfectly composed and happy, "But no one could ever punish a Dickinson by shutting her up alone!" That applied to Emily herself, and it applies to this obscure Dickinson. It applies to my ability to be contented here, away from the world, and to the truth underlying Ralph's and my relationship: that being with Ralph is just exactly as good as being alone.

Now that that's written, it looks terrible; and I meant it to be the nicest thing I could say!

And what about Ralph himself? Does he feel as I feel about our life here? I can't answer for him. No one can truly answer for another person's thoughts and feelings. I can only go by what external evidence I have.

Last summer a visitor, Barbara Wing, asked Ralph a purely hypothetical question, during one of those long rambling discussions that kindred souls get into: "If you had a million dollars left you to-morrow, what would be the first thing you'd do?"

Ralph thought for a long time, and I thought right along with him, wondering whether it would be an island in the South Seas—this was before Pearl Harbor—or a ranch in the Argentine. Finally he said slowly, "Well—that's a hard question to answer. I can't make up my mind whether a bathroom or a new roof for the woodshed comes first." He was serious, so we all laughed; but I don't worry any more about whether he really likes it here as much as I do.

I'd spend my million dollars on Forest Lodge, too, except for a fund I'd invest in letting the kids see the world. I'd send them everywhere and let them taste everything, so that at last they'd come to know what we have here to value. Discontent is only the fear of missing something. Content is the knowledge that you aren't missing a thing worth-while.

I know that many people—perhaps most people—couldn't feel that, living here, they held within their grasp all the best of life. So for them it wouldn't be the best. For us, it is.

And that's the final answer.

THE END

Afterword

And did "they come to know what we have here to value" as Louise wrote in her last lines? Did her children stay, leave, leave and return? What happened to Louise and Ralph, to Forest Lodge, and the woods and waters that nurtured them? Devoted readers have made this book a classic. They care about the people and places they have come to appreciate, and at signings/presentations always ask me these questions.

Well, Ralph died suddenly, which changed life dramatically for the family. Louise held on to Forest Lodge as long as possible, brought the children up in her hometown of Bridgewater, Massachusetts, spent years on the Gouldsboro Peninsula in Maine, and was nursed in her final years (as was Alice, her sister) by her daughter, Dinah. Rufus saw some of the world while in the service and driving a truck, and has built a place on the access road to Lower Richardson Lake, as close as he can get to Forest Lodge. Sally has made made several trips to Forest Lodge, staying at Lakewood (sporting) Camps at the head of the Carry Road. Dinah had never returned once the place was sold. She said she was afraid it would have changed too much. After my book, *She Took to the Woods: The Life and Times of Louise*

Dickinson Rich, came out, Dinah paid me a great compliment by saying she was grateful for three things: that she learned a lot more about her father, that I portrayed the family story well, and that the book gave her the impetus to return to Forest Lodge—which she has done several times. Both Dinah and Rufus have tender hearts, an appreciation of nature, and a great love of animals.

As for Forest Lodge, on October 27, 1955, it was sold to Catherine Luce Jacobs, daughter of Ralph Gerrish. If Gerrish was Ralph and Louise's right-hand man, "Katie" was their right-hand woman. She and her son, Vaughn, spent years with the Rich family. Vaughn still visits the area, and it was he who confirmed that Louise wrote up in the little alcove off her bedroom overlooking the Rapid River. Katie sold to Edgar French in 1960. His son, Aldro, has been working hard since 1970 to protect the land and buildings. There is a heritage trust, land easements, and a building program which, with enough backing, will keep Forest Lodge alive for a writer/artist-in-residence project and the continued pilgrimage of school children, fishing/nature groups, and fans. For information on how to help in this effort: *www. rapidriverflyfishing. com.*

Alys Parsons, as of this writing, is still alive and kicking at over ninety. Running Lakewood Camps for years gave her, by her own admission, a pretty clear sense of human nature. She says she never saw two people as deeply content with one another as Louise and Ralph. Upon Louise's death in 1991, Rufus boated across Lower Richardson and walked along the Carry Trail to Forest Lodge. There, near the roaring Rapid River, he spread her ashes where Ralph's had been left decades earlier.

Louise said the happiest years of her life were spent during that special moment in time she lived in a place she loved, with the man she loved, surrounded by friends and family she loved. *We Took to the Woods* is that love story. Louise is home again.

Alice Arlen
Portland, Maine

CPSIA information can be obtained
at www.ICGtesting.com
Printed in the USA
BVHW041658060621
608851BV00001B/1